Boondoggle

Boondoggle

My Unexpected Career as a Military Defense Contractor

Lloyd Sparks

Copyright © 2016 Lloyd Sparks
All rights reserved.

ISBN: 1530627680
ISBN 13: 9781530627684
Library of Congress Control Number: 2016904866
CreateSpace Independent Publishing Platform
North Charleston, South Carolina

In Memory of Derek Rex

Contents

boon·dog·gle (bo͞on͵dägəl,-͵dôgəl)

- Work or activity that is wasteful or pointless but gives the appearance of having value.
- A public project of questionable merit that typically involves political patronage and graft.
- A waste of money or time on unnecessary or questionable projects.

Author's Note

I'm a doctor and a scientist. I work in hospitals and laboratories. I live in the suburbs. I have a family and a mortgage. I don't do war. Yet, I spent an unforgettable eight years of my adult life working in the defense industry as a contractor. It took a toll on my profession and family, but no experience is a total loss if you get a good story out of it and I got more than one or two.

My original intent was to publish a collection of good stories from my time as a contractor and lampoon the industry, but as my writing progressed, I began to realize that there is much more to be told than a few entertaining anecdotes. While checking my recollection of the events, I reached out to my former colleagues. All encouraged me to publish. Through those conversations I began to see just how deeply a large segment of the defense force, the civilian job market, and indeed the country as a whole have been affected by this new phenomenon.

The "at-will" defense contractor is a phenomenon unique to our time and neither the contribution and sacrifice nor the harm and waste associated with the profession have been described in any depth by those who, like me, worked in the field. In reading up on the contractor phenomenon, I came upon a number of excellent works by scholars and journalists, but none by an actual contractor doing the kind of work I did. I hope my contribution will shed new light on this complex industry. I hope it will encourage other contractors to put their stories in print as well.

I am grateful to Raytheon for taking the time to screen the manuscript prior to publication to ensure no proprietary information was unintentionally divulged. Raytheon managers directly involved in these events expressed no objection to the veracity of my report, even those events that present the company in a less-than-favorable light. Raytheon's legal department screened my story as well – including the parts that describe illegal activities – and acquiesced without protest.

The US Army Intelligence Center and School and the Department of the Army also screened the manuscript for tradecraft and classified information. While much of what I describe is, strictly speaking, confidential and for official use only, everything in this book can be found easily through open sources. I divulge no national secrets.

I have hidden the identities of many of my former colleagues with aliases. Some are still actively doing clandestine work or may resume such work in the future. Others do not want to jeopardize their chances for continued employment and asked that I not use their real names. Out of pity, I've changed the names of still others who, but for their contractor jobs, would have little hope of finding gainful employment anywhere. In addition, a few of the characters in this book have such thoroughly bad reputations, are so universally despised, have behaved so reprehensibly, contributed nothing positive while poisoning anything they touched, that it would be pointless to expose them to even more ignominy through using their real names. The miserable lives they have made for themselves is its own punishment.

To make a cogent story, I've chosen what to emphasize and what to omit. I've left out ten times as much material I could have included in the interest of keeping the story coherent and relevant. In the end, this is my story told through my eyes as I experienced it. Others will certainly remember the same events differently and may take issue with some of the things I've written. My answer is to write your own book. I'll even help. The contractor phenomenon is huge, extremely relevant and largely unappreciated by those not directly involved. More contractors should publish what they've seen.

Prologue

"In the councils of government, we must guard against the acquisition of unwarranted influence, whether sought or unsought, by the military industrial complex. The potential for the disastrous rise of misplaced power exists and will persist."

— Dwight D. Eisenhower, in his Farewell Address in 1961

I was nine when President Eisenhower warned of the threat to democracy presented by a war industry entwined with the profession of arms – the military industrial complex. Big words for a nine-year-old. Abstract, too. And complicated. By the time I entered the military industrial complex at age 54, it was far less abstract but vastly larger and more complicated than even Ike could have anticipated. In 2006 the Army already employed more contractors than soldiers. Like most contractors, I was originally trained by the military at taxpayer expense and stayed in the reserves. The Army could have easily put me on orders at minimal expense to do the jobs I did and taken me off orders when the job was done. Instead, the government spent a huge amount of money to pay me a much higher salary than I would have received as a soldier doing the same job and paid the companies for which I worked even more for the privilege of brokering my services.

We live in amazing times. The Iraq invasion of 2003 has been called the "First Contractor War" – the first war America has fought with more contractors than troops. Civilian labor has always supported the military, mostly in logistics, maintenance and transportation, but up until 1990, the US military employed relatively little contract support. In the Balkan conflicts of the mid 1990s, the numbers of contract security employees reached one for every fifty soldiers, an unprecedented number. With the Bush-Cheney administration, the figures exploded. The number of contractors supporting the Iraq and Afghanistan wars not only exceeded the number of soldiers, we served in every field including combat.[1] (Hagedorn, 2014)

The justification for hiring contractors is that we are necessary to perform missions the military cannot perform by itself. We fill a temporary deficit in talent. Historically, nations have often hired mercenaries when faced with insufficient numbers of trained troops, but the contractors with whom I have the most experience are different from traditional mercenaries. Most are US citizens and almost all were themselves members of the US military and many still serve in the reserves or National Guard while working as contractors.

Since eliminating the draft in 1973 we have had an "all-volunteer" military. This doesn't quite mean what it says. Volunteering for military service isn't like volunteering to help the Red Cross or Boy Scouts with a bake sale. It means choosing to work for the military instead of, say, Microsoft. Whether a mercenary, a contractor, or a soldier, we all choose to do what we do – at least in part – for financial reasons. People like Pat Tillman[2] who leave million-dollar careers to serve in the Rangers and die tragically are rare. Most of us – contractors and soldiers alike – serve both because we love our country and because we need the money. That doesn't make a contractor less patriotic than a soldier nor a soldier less

1 From June 2009 to March 2011 contractors outnumbered troops in Iraq and Afghanistan by a staggering ten-to-one. The ratio was much higher for the State Department and USAID. Christopher Shays, the co-chair for the Commission on Wartime Contracting made this comment to the press: "We can't go to war without contractors and we can't go to peace without contractors."

2 Pat Tillman was a professional football player who left his career to enlist in the Army and join the Airborne Rangers after the September 11 attacks. He was killed in Afghanistan by friendly fire in 2004.

mercenary than a contractor. Most of us oscillate between the civilian and military worlds serving the same missions driven by the same motivations.

Even though former service members are hired back by the military to do work it cannot staff, it would be misleading to imply that contractors are more talented or intelligent than the military professionals they left. They often leave the military to enter the contractor force simply because it pays better and they can always go back. Indeed, military service is often the only way to get the training, experience and security clearances needed to qualify for the contract jobs. Many contractors bounce back and forth and so did I.[3]

The military loses much of its best talent to private industry. Not only does private industry usually pay better, accomplishment in the military commonly goes unrewarded. Indeed, it often seems that the military rewards failure and punishes success. This is because almost everything in the military is done by teams. A unit is only as strong as its weakest link or as fast as its slowest member. You rarely gain anything by rewarding your strongest achievers but the whole unit does better when the bottom performers improve. I saw this throughout my career which began in 1973 when I entered Basic Training. Enlistees who had not graduated high school were given time off to study for their GEDs while the rest of us did double duty to cover their absence. If the higher performers wanted to get an advanced degree, they did it on their own time and paid for it themselves. The physically unfit are put on special exercise programs during duty hours to bring them up to the minimum standard while the rest of us pay out of pocket for our gym memberships and get our exercise in after hours.[4]

The military is a place where unremarkable people can thrive and it is also the starting point for most contractors. During the boon times of

---

3 According to Hagedorn, at least one out of every ten returning soldiers goes to work as a contractor.

4 There are some talented people who make the military their careers. In my experience, they tend to be found at the top and at the bottom, but rarely in the middle. I've met brilliant generals and bright junior soldiers. The military tends to chase away talent and those who stay in deserve credit for putting up with a system that fosters mediocrity.

Bush-Cheney there was opportunity for kids who barely – and sometimes never – graduated high school to enlist for a couple of years, get trained in an easy job, take a two-week course on how to be an instructor and then step into a contract instructor position that paid twice what a high school math teacher with a Master's in Education could hope to make. Starting salaries in the $70 to $80k range were usual. Contractors overseas could make up to $1000 a day, often tax-exempt.[5]

Nothing in the Army is very hard.[6] It can't be. The defense of the nation cannot be left to the unpredictable availability of quality people when the need arises. The military is designed to be run by people of average to below average intelligence and ability. Even in fields where talent makes a difference, unremarkable people can usually find a job.

I worked training military intelligence soldiers, a field where talent matters. Most of my fellow contractors were no more talented than the soldiers they supported, yet nevertheless came to consider themselves subject matter experts and thought these salaries appropriate. Despite having no experience in the professions, they considered themselves highly trained professionals. The constant praise of the public ("Thank you for your service.") and life in a system that gave them a sense of self-respect was addicting. As the country evolved into a permanent state of war, the defense contractor evolved from a temporary job into a profession, something one could hope to do for the rest of one's life. For more than ten years, it was a lucrative profession that offered grossly inflated salaries. Even now, the jobs still pay more than do most entry-level positions in the civilian market. The well-paying jobs have now lasted long

---

5 Instruction and training make up a sizeable chunk of military missions performed by contractors. Everything contractors do – security, intelligence, transportation, logistics, etc. – they also teach.

6 There are exceptions, of course. Aviation, Medicine and Special Forces are very hard jobs that not just anybody can do. But most military jobs aren't meant to be done by college graduates. Military Intelligence, the field I worked in as a contractor and soldier for the period covered by this memoir, is one of those fields that anybody can do but few can do well. In Military Intelligence, the difference between the quality soldier and the minimally qualified is striking.

enough for contractors to achieve expertise that exceeds the soldiers they support.

When the money began to dry up and contractor jobs with it, the marketplace became more competitive. As contracts were rebid, we often found ourselves with the option of taking a substantial cut in pay to work the same job for a new contracting company or moving on. The more talented contractors left for other better-paying work. By 2012 only the least qualified and cheapest labor was being sought. Minimal certifications for the lowest price became the dominant policy. Salaries fell below $60k for CONUS work – work within the continental United States – and slots for overseas work in combat zones began to offer less than $100k. At a time when value – bang for buck – mattered most, our military turned its back on the best people. The drop in quality of intelligence collection and analysis hastened the collapse of our missions in Iraq and Afghanistan and left us once again blind to the looming threat of ISIS.

Rather than save money, scrimping on quality only increased the waste. At the Military Intelligence school at Ft. Devens, Massachusetts, graduation rates plummeted from 95% in 2011 to 50% in August of 2012. In the fall they dropped to single digits and by winter there were no students at all. At the end of 2012, the entire staff of military and contract instructors with all the overhead of a school sat idle with nothing to do but soak up tax dollars.

The scarcity of effective Human Intelligence collectors in Afghanistan and Iraq led to fewer and poorer quality intelligence reports, which in turn led to mission failure. In the fall of 2012 I took a job as Senior Counterintelligence Analyst in support of operations in Afghanistan and witnessed firsthand the devastating consequences of eliminating quality people for the sake of cutting budgets.

We live in absurd times. We are a "nation at war" yet only about one citizen in a thousand wears the uniform. The reserves and National Guard make up two thirds of our deployed forces. Many reservists have seen more combat than any soldier did in WWII. Private companies protect our Diplomatic Corps using elite soldiers trained by the military because the military doesn't have enough soldiers. Blackwater security guards protected Paul Bremer, the US official tasked with transitioning Iraq to self-government, himself a contractor.

Erik Prince, the founder of Blackwater, optimistically makes the case that the military cannot and never has been able to function without the help of private industry. (Prince, 2014) I don't deny this. Even fully staffed and funded, the Army is well capable of failing at every turn. How is it that private industry can accomplish missions the military cannot by using the very personnel the military trained and can still access?

One reason is the profit motive. The military cannot or will not offer soldiers the financial incentives for success that private industry can. Neither will the government reinstitute the draft nor expand the already prodigious budget of the Defense Department, which is greater than all the militaries of the next 19 countries in the world combined. The huge contractor paychecks attract talent away from the military, exacerbating the shortage and deepening the military's dependence on contract help.

But another reason is management. Military officers and NCOs (Non-Commissioned Officers) are not trained to manage the way corporate managers are and they are not rewarded for good management. Success in the military isn't measured by profit. There are no medals for saving money or improving the bottom line. In the military, success and failure are often indistinguishable.[7]

In my opinion, the weakness in Prince's argument is that even when efficient and effective contracting corporations are enlisted to serve the mission, even when they hire the best people, they are still ultimately led by military managers. Even when the contractors fulfill 100% of the requirements of the contract, the mission can still fail and often does. No

7 Much of what occupies the time of the professional soldier is some form of an on-going mission which has no objective criteria for success. For instance, our mission at Ft. Devens was to train soldiers, not to graduate 100 fully trained soldiers by a specific date. The vague, unmeasurable on-going work most full-timers did was, in my opinion, responsible for the usual reply "we're working on it" whenever a unit leader might look into why things were not getting done. Under these conditions, it is very difficult to fire somebody for not producing results when the expected results are neither measurable nor have time limits.

matter how much better civilian organizations perform than military units, they are still subservient to a military organization prone to mismanaging its expensive talent.

So the government continues to hire defense contractors it has trained at taxpayer expense and has access to from companies charging a price several times the cost of just putting them back in uniform. If the absurdity of the taxpayer being gouged to buy back resources the Army already owns weren't enough, consider the situation I found myself in at Ft. Devens. From 2009 through 2010 I was the Raytheon Site Lead managing up to 40 contractors. They worked for me but many were reservists who had to be accommodated when they went on orders. I myself was the Sergeant Major of the local reserve Military Intelligence (MI) battalion whose mission was exactly the same as my civilian job – to train reserve MI students at Ft. Devens. My Raytheon team answered to the Course Manager, a mid-level NCO in my own unit. I worked for him but he worked for me.

Even more fun was trying to figure out a precise chain of command. The Course Manager answered to the 1st Brigade as did I indirectly as Battalion Sergeant Major. But his evaluator was the Ft. Devens Team Chief, who answered to the 80th TTC (TASS Training Command). The 1st Brigade answered to the 100th Division which was also under the 80th TTC. One would think that the commanding general of the 80th TTC would be completely responsible for the facilities as well as the school – TASS stands for Total Army School System – but both the facilities and school were located on Ft. Devens, which answered to the 99th Regional Support Command (RSC). Content of the course was governed by the US Army Intelligence Center and School (USAICS) at Ft. Huachuca, Arizona, under the command of yet a third two-star general.

Dizzy yet? The school was located in Massachusetts, the 1st Brigade in Rhode Island, the 100th Division in Kentucky, the 80th TTC in Virginia, the 99th RSC in New Jersey, and USAICS in Arizona. My Raytheon project in Massachusetts was supervised by an office in Arizona which answered to an office in Florida which was part of Raytheon's Technical Services

Company in Virginia, which was part of Raytheon, headquartered in Waltham, Massachusetts. Waltham is just 30 minutes down the road from Ft. Devens, but might as well be in another galaxy.

Raytheon is an aerospace company and supplying contract instructors for the Military Intelligence schools is not one of its core competencies. Raytheon subcontracted out to a number of smaller contracting companies. Nobody keeps track of the subs which continuously pop up and vanish like champagne bubbles. Although almost all of the government contract work goes to a few big companies, they sub to thousands of smaller, transient companies. In Florida alone there were more than a thousand in 2013. (Hagedorn, 2014)

Nobody knows how many contractors there are, how much money is being spent on contractors or how many contractors are killed, maimed or otherwise have their lives ruined.[8] (Singer, 2008) Because the contracts are regularly rebid, the owners of the contract would change yearly as a rule, sometimes even more often. When that happened, all of us working on the mission would change companies. It was not unusual to work at a single job for half a dozen companies. Between 2006 and 2014 I worked for Anteon, General Dynamics, Oberon, Raytheon, Intecon, L-3 Stratis, and Mission Essential Personnel, all in the same job I could have done as a soldier. And in fact, I did two deployments as a soldier and several short periods on orders during that time as well.

The estimates of the total number of contractors vary widely, but they exceed the total number of military personnel by a wide margin. The Department of Defense census of the industry in 2007 put the number at 180,000. Even that estimate is low because it did not include several of the biggest companies nor those that contracted with the Department of State and other agencies. The Senate Armed Services Committee found the amount of money spent on contractors in 2006

8 The final report of the Commission on Wartime Contracting included an estimate of "between $31 and $60 billion" lost to waste and fraud. Getting any sense of how much money is spent on contracting and for what is hampered by both the dysfunctional databases the Pentagon relies on and the inherent opacity of the contracting industry.

was $151 billion. Even the amount paid to Halliburton-KBR alone for that period was three times the money the US government spent to fight the entire 1991 Persian Gulf War.

The bewildering complexity of the whole system provides ways for the government to get a mission done that might be illegal if performed by the military. All departments have their limitations and hiring civilian corporations to accomplish missions vital to the nation's security is one way to get around those limitations. The whole phenomenon of employing contractors as instruments of national power is so new the laws haven't even caught up, which results in contractors doing things that should be illegal, but aren't yet.[9] The use of civilian interrogators hired by the CIA resulted in some of the more infamous examples and when I entered the contractor world, the military was in the middle of revising its rules and manuals on interrogation.[10]

The complexity of the contractor system makes it easy for bad people to do bad things and continue even after discovery.[11] When a contractor

---

9 This isn't to imply that the government is turning a blind eye to illegal activity. A Google search of any major defense contracting company plus "investigation" returns hundreds of thousands of hits. Investigations of the main defense contractors has so overwhelmed the government that they have resorted to using (you guessed it) contractors to investigate the contractors.

10 Peter Singer, a military scholar at Brookings Institution, points out in *Corporate Warriors* that, although the military has been able to bring charges against the soldiers who committed the misdeeds at Abu Gharaib, it does not feel it has jurisdiction over civilian contractors. Indeed, over the entire course of the war with over 100,000 contractors in country, not one has yet been charged, prosecuted or punished for any battlefield crime. This is in stark contrast to many crimes, great and small, for which US troops have been punished over the same period.

11 The involvement of contractors in both security breaches and managing security breaches could not be better illustrated than the recent Office of Personnel Management (OPM) data breach of April, 2015. First reported in June of 2015 and believed to be carried out by the Chinese, the breach involves the greatest theft of sensitive personnel data in history. The scale of the OPM breach involves the records of some 22 million current, former and prospective federal employees. Stolen data goes back to 1985. The same hackers who accessed OPM's data are believed to have last year breached an OPM contractor, KeyPoint Government Solutions. When the OPM breach was discovered in April, investigators found that KeyPoint security credentials were used to breach the OPM system. To mitigate the attack, OPM appears to be allowing the clearance data of affected individuals to be exposed to unknown

is fired, he can immediately present himself for employment through another company with a newly written résumé, fairly confident that no one will check his history of employment. The law requires that résumés be presented with the names hidden in order to protect people from discrimination. This law protects both the bad along with the good.

The title of this book notwithstanding, technically I wasn't a contractor. I did not have a contract with the US military; I *worked for* a company that had such a contract. This is a very important distinction. Although we are called "contractors," we were actually *employees* of contractors. We didn't work for the Army. We worked for Raytheon and other companies which had contracts with the Army. So our military supervisor could not directly tell us what to do. He or she had to tell Raytheon what to do and the Raytheon Site Lead would do the actual directing. It is illegal for a military officer or NCO to personally direct contractors as individuals. Jail-time illegal.[12]

The Course Managers I worked with, who were usually mid-level NCOs with little education or experience beyond leading squad-sized units, rarely understood this concept and it led to serious friction, especially when the contractor was also a reservist. The rules change dramatically when a contractor puts on a uniform and comes to work on drill[13] weekend as a reservist to do the same job.

---

contractors. But since contractors were at the heart of the initial attack, there is no way of knowing what contractors now may have access to the clearance data based on an arbitrary "need to know" criterion. https://www.lawfareblog.com/why-opm-hack-far-worse-you-imagine, http://edition.cnn.com/2015/06/22/politics/opm-hack-18-milliion/index.html

12 Joint Publication 4-10, Operational Contract Support (Washington, DC: GPO, 2008), xiii-xiv governs the relationship between the military and contract support. Command authority does not extend to contract employees.

13 Weekend drills are now called "Battle Assemblies," a term I could never get used to. Since Vietnam, the military has been trying hard to rebuild its self-respect. Sometimes these efforts take on a comical shine. We changed headgear to the black beret – at that time the distinctive cover of the Airborne Rangers – to make everyone feel elite. It had the opposite effect. All soldiers now are referred to as "warriors" whether or not they have actually fought. It took 30 days in combat operations as an infantryman to earn the coveted Combat Infantryman's Badge, or CIB, when I joined

It is also quite illegal for a military officer to tell a civilian company what to do with its civilian employees. A military officer cannot legally punish or promote a contractor. He cannot legally tell the company who to hire or fire or to demand discipline or block an individual from being hired. Yet this is a common occurrence in the contractor world, especially when the representative of the civilian company also serves in the contracting officer's reserve unit. My civilian bosses walked a thin line balancing obedience to the law with keeping a military customer happy who was dead set on breaking it.

Consider as well that the contract force which was intended to be a temporary solution now represents the most robust pool of expertise available. Active duty is for most soldiers just a temporary experience. Most military jobs are temporary, with soldiers being constantly rotated through and taking their expertise with them. Contractors, by contrast, can stay in the same job for ten years or more, filling the chronic deficit their existence helps to ensure. After a year on the job at Devens, I could confidently demonstrate that my contractors could do everything better than the military staff could. All my "temporary" people had been on the job longer than the "permanent" military staff we worked for.[14]

Even calling ourselves "employees" is a bit misleading. In contrast to normal employment, we were "at will" employees. Most regular employees enjoy rights and protection under American labor laws we as "at will" employees did not. Regular employees are protected from discrimination

---

in 1973. Now it takes only one day in a combat zone. There is even a Combat Action Badge (CAB) for those who have been exposed to fire but are not infantrymen.

Although there are important differences between the National Guard and the Reserves, I will often use them interchangeably when the difference doesn't affect the meaning. Similarly, when I refer to the Army or to soldiers, the principle often applies to all services and service members. I hope I will be forgiven for neglecting the Navy, Coast Guard, Air Force and Marines for the sake of readability. Also, I feel I have earned the right to criticize and even ridicule the Army, but not the other services.

14 A case in point was the vetting of this book. It took Raytheon a few weeks to thoroughly screen the manuscript for classified and proprietary material. The military, by contrast, worked on it for over six months with progress halted by screeners leaving their jobs and being replaced by new people who needed to start all over.

and from unreasonable hiring and firing practices. They have access to benefits provided through the company that we did not enjoy. We didn't get paid extra for overtime and didn't get the normal weekends and holidays off. Regular employees can look forward to bonuses and promotions for excellent performance; "at will" employees, being hired for a single contract, cannot. Since we rarely stayed with the same company for more than a year, we often failed to qualify for the benefits regular employees received. Some benefits like paid medical leave and education funding often do not come into effect until an employee has been with the company more than a year. Even the referral bonuses were usually contingent upon the referral staying with the company for more than twelve months.[15]

In short, "at will" contractors are commodities rather than employees and that left us vulnerable to all sorts of abuse. For example, if the customer – a military commander controlling the contract – did not feel there should be a place for single mothers or lesbians in the military effort, he could fire that person with impunity without stating his reason. This sort of thing happens a lot.[16]

---

15 An unexpected consequence of being an "at will" employee is that, because we work where ever the job takes us, sometimes even deploying with the supported unit abroad, we often do not live in the state of our official residence. When the unit I supported was in Arizona, I was technically an Arizona resident; when it was Massachusetts, I became a Massachusetts resident. Since I couldn't take my kids with me to a combat zone, I left them with family in California while I was gone. Although my youngest lived there for years, graduated from a California high school, had a California driver's license and was a registered voter, the University of California considered her to be an out-of-state resident and charged her out-of-state tuition because I didn't live in California. Federal law mandates that children of soldiers deployed on active duty pay only in-state tuition regardless of their parent's official state of residence. That law does not apply to the children of contractors serving with deployed units.

16 In fact-checking this book, I attempted to contact as many of the people in it as possible to ensure that I remember the events accurately. Several of my colleagues asked that I not use their real names out of fear of possible retaliation both from the military and the companies they work for. None asked that I mask their identities and the work they do for security reasons. It gave me pause that those who are still working on classified projects as Counterintelligence agents and Human Intelligence

Contractors are often treated with spite and slandered as being less than patriotic because we get paid large amounts of money to do the same job uniformed soldiers do for less. Some call us mercenaries. Contractors work for the money, but we often do truly add value – bang for buck – to the military, and when we don't, we are easy to fire. We love our country. I never met a contractor whose primary loyalty was to his company over his country. And contractors suffer even more casualties than the military but are not included in the casualty figures. All of the soldiers I personally knew who died in the Iraq and Afghanistan conflicts died working as contractors.

The US military resorts to employing reservists and guardsmen for the same reason it employs contract support. Standing armies (i.e. Active Duty) are expensive and reserve units are cheap. Reservists perform the same duties as Active Duty but without the need to be paid for the time they are not fighting.[17] This trinity of Active Duty military, reservists and contractors created the vertiginously complex system into which I was sucked in 2006.

The Raytheon Site Lead position was, in all sincerity, the best job I ever had. I looked forward to going to work every day. It wasn't just the pay and benefits. It wasn't the pleasant conditions or limited hours. It wasn't the people I worked with, although there were some gems. It certainly wasn't the prestige. It wasn't the feeling of accomplishment when a project came together and succeeded, though that was important. It wasn't even the teaching, which I love, along with the chance to positively influence young men and women. What I liked best about the job was working with the difficult people.

---

collectors are less concerned about their identities being revealed to the enemy than to their employers.

17 One of the more egregious practices of cheating reservists I witnessed was the habit of the Washington Army National Guard of putting soldiers on orders for four days a week repeatedly. By working four ten-hour days, they could get a full 40-hour week out of a soldier for only four days' pay rather than seven. The brief nature of the orders also excluded the soldier from medical, dental and other benefits enjoyed by full-time soldiers.

Nothing about the project I oversaw was hard. You had to really apply effort to make something not work. But this field is flush with people who are more than up to the task of fouling things up. Even with success virtually guaranteed as long as nobody did anything stupid, every morning held the promise of personal problems to be worked out, petty squabbles to be mediated, covert agendas to be exposed, and good ideas to be held up to the light.

Virtually all the seemingly intractable problems I faced everyday were people problems. They were almost never problems of substance – problems due to lack of money, space, equipment or personnel. They were, by and large, problems that people made for themselves and each other based on nothing more than spite and personal animosity. Realizing this, the solutions were quite simple if one could just identify and address the underlying motivation. It had all the excitement and challenge of inpatient psychiatry except that I couldn't prescribe drugs.

This is the story of my detour into this world. It is a story rich in irony, drama and humor. I originally considered titling it *Catch-23* in allusion to Joseph Heller's fictional lampoon of the WWII military in *Catch-22*. But I am neither a Heller nor a historian. I entertain no delusion that things will change, much less improve by writing about them.[18] I intend only to relate what I saw before I pass on and hopefully in a manner that will afford my readers some entertainment.

And much entertainment is to be had.

18 I have sought avenues of redress, both governmental and military, for some of the activities I felt obligated to report. None bore fruit and neither the companies I worked for nor the Department of Defense have shown the slightest inclination to correct illegal or unethical practices.

CHAPTER 1

Active Duty 1973 through 1976

"The Bible legend tells us that the absence of labor—idleness— was a condition of the first man's blessedness before the Fall. Fallen man has retained a love of idleness, but the curse weighs on the race not only because we have to seek our bread in the sweat of our brows, but because our moral nature is such that we cannot be both idle and at ease. An inner voice tells us we are in the wrong if we are idle. If man could find a state in which he felt that though idle he was fulfilling his duty, he would have found one of the conditions of man's primitive blessedness. And such a state of obligatory and irreproachable idleness is the lot of a whole class – the military."

— Leo Tolstoy, *War and Peace, Book 7, Chapter 1*

"The Navy is a master plan designed by geniuses for execution by idiots. If you are not an idiot, but find yourself in the Navy, you can only operate well by pretending to be one. All the shortcuts and economies and common-sense changes that your native intelligence suggests to you are mistakes. Learn to quash them. Constantly ask yourself,

"How would I do this if I were a fool?" Throttle down your mind to a crawl. Then you will never go wrong."

— Herman Wouk, *The Caine Mutiny*

Watching Fort Huachuca fade in my rear view mirror in March of 1975 after nine of the most exasperating weeks of my life, was one of the most ecstatic experiences of my life. I had just barely graduated second from the bottom of the class, having failed and retested all but one examination in the course that trained prisoner of war (PW or POW) interrogators for the Army. I didn't want to be an interrogator. I didn't volunteer for it. In fact, I had a guaranteed enlistment contract for another job. I was supposed to be a linguist with the Army Security Agency (ASA).[19]

I joined the Army in 1973 with a contract guaranteeing language school and an assignment with the ASA, an assignment which required a Top Secret (TS) security clearance. I didn't aspire to a career in the ASA either, but believed it could be a springboard to something exciting with the FBI, CIA or State Department. Neither was I set on one particular language. I would have preferred Russian, but any major language like Chinese or Arabic would do. Even becoming a specialist in an unusual language like Uzbek or Tamil would have been acceptable. I was eagerly anticipating the experience, no matter which language I would get.

I had clear goals when I enlisted. I intended to finish my bachelor's degree, master a foreign language, get a pilot's license, get certified in scuba and earn a black belt in a martial art. The GI Bill would also pay for any further schooling I might choose later and help me buy a house when the time came.

But my strongest motivation was to do my patriotic service as a soldier, just as my dad had done. For me, it was a rite of passage and 1973 was the right time. I wanted to join the Army and especially to be a

19 The United States Army Security Agency (ASA) was the Army's signal intelligence branch up until 1977, when it merged with the Army's Military Intelligence component to create the United States Army Intelligence and Security Command (INSCOM).

paratrooper. I was adult enough to realize that playing soldier is a stupid reason for joining and even my dad had advised me to go into a field that would produce a skill I could use as a civilian. Paratrooper wasn't it, but Military Intelligence led in a lot of interesting directions. The recruiter settled any qualms I may have had by assuring me I could get a guaranteed assignment to the ASA with language school and volunteer for airborne training any time after I got my assignment.

One can imagine how parents would feel about their child enlisting while the Vietnam War was still raging and in a tailspin toward calamity. My opinion was pretty much the same as everyone else in 1973, liberal or conservative, that Vietnam was a tragedy and a disaster. Everyone knew people who had been killed in Vietnam. I wasn't mature enough to worry about being killed in combat; that kind of thing only happened to others. I intellectually justified taking this path in order to fund my education and launch my career in a new direction, but in truth, I was really excited about enlisting.

I had a contract with the Army, a legal document that the Army was obligated to fulfill, my recruiter assured me. If, by some mishap, I found myself in any assignment but the one I was guaranteed, I was to take the contract to my commander and he would set things right. My father cautioned me, however, that the government doesn't have to obey the same laws the rest of us do. The Army can break or ignore a contract anytime they want under the catch-all justification "needs of the Army."

And, of course, that is exactly what happened.

That contract was the first in an unbroken series of broken promises. In a career that spanned five decades, I never had a contract honored. Until 2000, I'd never even met a soldier that had a contract honored. I thought it was just the way things are. Near the end of Basic Training at Fort Ord, I was called in by the First Sergeant to be informed that I would not be going to language school or to the ASA. The reason, I was told, was that I had failed the Background Investigation (BI) and did not qualify for the requisite TS. I had been a good trainee and distinguished myself by maxing the physical fitness test, shooting expert on the range, and being nominated for the American Spirit award. I had the sympathy of my commander, Captain O'Malley.

He called the language school to find out if there were any slots still open for the next class after I graduated Basic Training. There were: Amharic and Bulgarian. I had no idea what Amharic was, but Bulgarian was close to Russian and it was offered at the Defense Language Institute (DLI) at Monterey. If I wanted Amharic, I would have to go to the East Coast.

The next problem would be finding me a linguist job that didn't require a TS. This job, as it turned out, was 96C POW Interrogator.[20] I had no inclination to be an interrogator, but since we didn't have any POWs anyway, I figured I'd probably work as a translator or interpreter, thus fulfilling one of my five goals of enlistment.

I went to language school at DLI in 1974 where I spent the happiest year of my life up to that point. I loved language school and loved Monterey. I did well. The Bulgarian department was small and cozy with more instructors than students. (My class started with seven and graduated five.) I was even allowed to spend afternoons at the Serbo-Croatian department and left DLI qualified in two languages. In addition, I got my PADI scuba certification, managed to solo in a Cessna 150, and made some progress in karate, aikido and kung fu.

I arrived at Ft. Huachuca in January of 1975 and the contrast between Monterey and Sierra Vista, the town outside the front gate, could not have been greater. After DLI, Ft. Huachuca seemed like the end of the world. Isolated in the high Arizona desert, it is an old cavalry post and the newest buildings dated to the 1940s. Fry Boulevard, the main street of Sierra Vista just outside the front gate, was only paved for a few blocks.

20 Every Army job is called a Military Occupational Specialty (MOS) and has a three-digit code. Prisoner of War Interrogator was coded as MOS 96C in 1975. The Army has at times had linguist positions. My original contract read MOS 04D, which was Linguist, but the Army eliminated them in favor of putting all linguists into language-dependent jobs. Had I gone into the ASA, I would have probably been a 98G Voice Intercept Operator and spent my career wearing headphones listening to enemy radio transmissions.

It was a small, run-down, economically deprived town whose main industries served the mostly male population of the fort.

DLI was like college; Huachuca was Army. And not just the Army I had been introduced to in Basic Training at Ft. Ord. It was Old Army, with WWII era buildings that served both as barracks and classrooms. All of the Army customs we had been spared at DLI reappeared, including daily formations and inspections. Meaningless make-work details were assigned to those of us waiting for our class to start. I was fortunate enough to work for the post recruiter who had nothing for me to do and gladly gave me permission to go to the language lab and take tests in other languages.

It was here I realized what we had only suspected at DLI: all the language tests were practically identical. The Defense Language Proficiency Test, or DLPT, was designed to be a fair assessment of the linguist's ability to read and understand the spoken language. There was no speaking test. The DLPT1 was constructed in the 1960s from the same bank of questions used for all languages. It consisted of sixty questions in each section, listening and reading. The answers were multiple choice. Theoretically, the questions started out simple and increased in difficulty so that the first had simple, one word answers and the more difficult ones required some thought and interpretation. The linguist would receive a score based on the percentage of questions answered correctly and be assessed as 0 (failure), 1 (basic), 2 (intermediate) or 3 (advanced).

The faults in this system are fairly obvious. First, it does not even remotely resemble how language is used. No one is ever faced with a multiple choice answer to questions posed by a foreigner. Second, there is no consideration for which questions are answered right or wrong. It presumes one tends to miss the hard ones and get the easy ones, but often the more complex questions are easier to answer by guessing than questions about an isolated word or grammar point. Third, it is obvious that the questions were written by grammarians trying to test knowledge of specific points of grammar. The trickiest answer is usually the right one.

Fourth, in trying to be fair by posing the same questions in all languages, it presented questions that may be relevant to one language but not to any other.

The most glaring shortcoming is that, since the tests are all basically the same, if a person knows one language well, it is easy to test high on languages one doesn't. I knew native Spanish speakers who would take the test in Spanish one day and then test in their primary language the next, remembering the questions and correct answers from the day before. In language school, we were taught to the test. Every question on the DLPT came from a lesson we had somewhere and were reminded in class to take care not to forget it. I could remember the exact lesson in which the instructors taught us the questions that later appeared on the test. Indeed, my instructors were the very people who recorded the DLPT1 for Bulgarian.

In my down time at Huachuca, I tested in eight languages, scoring 3/3 in each.[21]

All of the career linguists were aware of this problem, that because the answers to all the tests were available, the tests were meaningless. The Army eventually introduced new and improved tests – DLPT2, 3, 4 and eventually 5, each one solving problems from the previous and creating new ones. It was only with the advent of DLPT4 in the 1980s that the Army began to address the problem the tests being compromised. New versions of the DLPT4 surfaced regularly, labeled A, B, C, etc. The problem was so widespread that the military could only focus on a few major languages like Russian and still not keep up with the problem. No sooner were the new tests published than the answers became widely known, rendering them worthless. They ignored minor languages like Bulgarian and Norwegian, leaving the DLPT1 as the only available test. I took the Bulgarian DLPT1 every year right up to 2012. Over my career, I took the DLPT in its many variations in as many languages as I could and scored

21 Bulgarian, Serbo-Croatian, German, Mandarin, Hebrew, Norwegian, Yiddish and Greek. At first I only attempted to test in languages I felt confident I could use if required. Later I threw caution to the wind and tested out in languages I didn't speak at all like Albanian and Lithuanian.

2/2 or above in twenty languages. I believe I hold the Army record, but as you can see, it is really not as impressive as it sounds.[22]

If I were king of the Army, I would revise the whole system, but that is getting a little far afield from the focus of this narrative.[23] Language ability is essential to collecting intelligence information and was a requirement for the language-dependent MOSs like 96C. The Army eventually waived the language requirement, making us the only intelligence service in the developed world that does not require its intelligence collectors to know any languages, let alone the one they work in. This makes us dependent

22 False modesty aside, I'm pretty good. I collect languages like some people collect stamps. I'm fluent in several languages, some at a high level. But the record of my DLPTs doesn't accurately reflect my skill levels, or anyone else's for that matter.

23 The purpose of language is to communicate. Vocabulary, grammar and syntax are probably the least important elements of communication. Facial expressions, tone of voice, body language and culturally-based behaviors convey most of what we send and receive. Although one can learn *about* languages from a book, there is no substitute for putting oneself in the culture and interacting with the natives. It's nice to have someone to explain things, but you really have to talk to people who do not know your language to develop any skill as a linguist. You can't do this living in Monterey. Moreover, language instruction is generally done completely wrong with grammar books that explain the target language to the student in English, ensuring that the student will never think in the language nor develop a native accent.

To learn a language properly, the brain has to get used to the sounds first before advancing to words and sentences. One should be exposed to the most common phrases first. Most communication involves only a few hundred words. Sending the students to intensive emersion courses held at universities all over the world would be a much more effective method than a year at DLI. With distance learning technology, more effective classes can now be conducted in remote areas, even combat zones with greater flexibility than is possible the old way.

In Hungary where I studied and taught medicine for many years, foreign students entered the university every year not knowing a word of Hungarian. They studied the language for half a day while studying other subjects the rest of the time. By the end of the first year, they were comfortable with the language. During their second year they took no more than a couple of hours of language instruction per week in addition to their other studies. By the end of the second year, they were fluent and by the end of the third, you couldn't tell many of them from native speakers.

The military should send their linguists to intensive language immersion programs for the first year if available or attach them to units in the jobs they will eventually do. From the second year on, they should continue to work in their jobs while reserving time every week for language study.

upon translators which the enemy is only too happy to provide, usually through contracting companies.[24]

It also means that it takes at least two people to do one man's job. The utter failure of the military to manage language proficiency, as you will see, became a major point of contention when decades later I ascended to the position of Sergeant Major in a unit full of linguists and became Director of Instruction at the MI school with the mission of training intelligence collectors.

I should have raised my hand immediately when Chief Warrant Officer Waer, the Course Manager for the 96C class, asked us on the first day whether there was anyone present who objected to telling a lie. I had moral objections to lying, of course, but was so curious about where he was going with this I decided to wait and see. I lied about objecting to telling a lie and stayed. The few soldiers who lifted their hands were immediately escorted out. We never saw them again.

So that left us with a room full of admitted liars, a prerequisite for becoming an interrogator. To be an interrogator, you have to be comfortable with deceit. You also cannot be a medical professional. It's forbidden by regulation and by the standards of the medical profession for a medical professional to work as an interrogator. In principle it violates the Hippocratic Oath to not do anything against the mental and physical well-being of the prisoner.

So imagine my amazement at finding myself as a licensed medical doctor back at Ft. Huachuca in July of 2006 teaching interrogation. Even more astonishing, I had none of the certifications required and

24 On September 11, 2001, I was the Command Language Program Manager for a National Guard Special Forces company. On September 12, I contacted my counterpart at 5th Special Forces, knowing they would have the lead in special operations, to let him know I had six fully deployable soldiers that spoke languages used in Afghanistan. The Army never showed any interest in them, but we were all contacted within the week by representatives of contracting agencies offering high-paying jobs as linguists. Ironically, I would finish out my career as a contractor working for Mission Essential Personnel, a company that specializes in contract linguists, but as a counterintelligence analyst.

none of the experience. In my entire life I have never interrogated a single prisoner. I have never deployed with a military intelligence unit. I was not even a certified instructor. But we'll get to that soon enough. Back to 1975...

I wasn't anticipating a good time at the interrogator course. I had heard nothing but bad things about it and I wasn't disappointed. Everything revolved around psychologically stressing the prisoner and, by extension, the students. The actual subject matter wasn't that hard. We had to learn Order of Battle – how military units are organized – and how to question properly and systematically. But the real core was the approach – how to engage a prisoner in such a way as to motivate him to cooperate and give up information.

Some of the approaches were simple and logical. For example, the Love of Family approach is based on convincing the prisoner his best chance of seeing his family again is to cooperate. The Fear Up approach scares the prisoner into talking. The Incentive approach offers a reward for cooperating. Other approaches are a little more complex. The We Know All approach is designed to convince the prisoner we already have the information we need so there is no point in resisting. With the False Flag approach, the interrogator pretends to be someone other than an American soldier, such as a representative of a neutral country and visiting to make sure the prisoners are not being mistreated.

There were some very effective approaches we never did simply because they weren't practical at school. With the Silent approach, for example, the interrogator simply sits expectantly and waits for the prisoner to start talking. The Good Cop Bad Cop, also known as the Mutt and Jeff, requires two interrogators and the program of instruction at the basic level did not allow for collaborative efforts.

I was especially curious as to whether we used torture despite the firm denials. This was 1975, not long after congressional hearings revealed that the CIA and some units of the military were indeed teaching torture and perhaps even using it. Did our instructors know anything about this? Were any of them personally involved?

The closest I got to finding out was in the lecture on Fear Up/Fear Down when the instructor pointed out that it isn't the pain that makes a prisoner talk, it's the *fear* of the pain. You can say whatever you want to scare the hell out of the prisoner, you just can't actually do anything to harm him.

The subjects were presented in lecture with no demonstrations of the techniques we were to master before we attempted to use them. We saw no examples or films of real or simulated interrogations. We had no idea what real interrogations looked like. None of the instructors talked about their personal experience, leading me to wonder whether that was because they didn't have any or because they needed to hide what they had done.

The subject would be presented in lecture one time. Then the instructors would take us into a booth and play the role of a captured enemy soldier. We would have to interrogate them, all the while being graded by the instructor who gave us little or no feedback beyond criticizing our mistakes. If the instructor had to interrupt the iteration and step out of role to correct a student, that was about the worst thing that could happen. At the end we were graded and advised on how to do better next time. If we failed, we got one chance to retest. I failed and retested every unit but one, graduating next to last in my class.

I didn't know what it took to be an intelligence collector; I just knew I didn't have it. I also found nothing in the instructors I cared to emulate. None shared any personal experiences or insight about what really worked and what didn't. They seemed to put a premium on harassing us rather than teaching. Half of the class failed and I couldn't see any correlation between ability and passing. The only student to graduate with a lower score than me was the one clearly outstanding student, Patrick "Pappy" Papaiani. He had been a clinical psychologist and actually enlisted to be an interrogator because he wanted to, in his words, work on the "dark side" of psychology. He was so good the instructors feared him. They tried hard to flunk Pappy out but eventually just settled on graduating him and getting him the hell away from there. I've seen students fluster the instructors so badly the instructor lost control, but Pappy is the only student I've ever seen actually bring an instructor to tears. Training Pappy was like dealing with Hannibal Lector.

The instructors all seemed to be harboring some kind of grudge. They were not only in our faces at every opportunity, they weren't even polite to each other. It seemed to go with the profession. Stan Kluth, who had been something of a mentor to me at DLI and was a trained interrogator, explained to me that this profession requires the ability to get under people's skin. Interrogators are not nice people. They have to be comfortable with inflicting distress.

There seemed to be an ethic of applying pressure to the students to see what we could bear. If a student can't stand the psychological pressure of the school, he or she would never do well in the field. The fallacy of this lies with the power dynamics that change once one becomes the interrogator and has complete control over the prisoner. As a student, it is impossible to forget that you are not really in charge and the "prisoner" is actually your instructor and evaluating your every move.

I found the lectures fascinating. I understood how building rapport, discovering the prisoner's motivations and using them were essential to success in getting information.[25] But when I tried to put them into practice, nothing seemed to work. The instructors didn't respond to the approaches I chose and I didn't know why. I didn't know how I was doing, what was working or why what wasn't working didn't. My critiques from the instructors were not very helpful. Knowing what you did wrong isn't very useful unless they show you how to do it right.

In 1975 the instructors were not very good teachers, but then the Army's training method amounted to little more than presenting the material and threatening the students with dire consequences if they didn't learn it. Looking back, it is now clear that most, perhaps all, of the instructors had never actually done the job they were teaching. There were no stories from their own experience to illustrate the craft. None made

25 An interesting and enlightening book on this subject is *How to Break a Terrorist* by my friend Matthew Alexander.

any mention of time in Vietnam, which had been going on for ten years by then and was really the only opportunity to actually interrogate real prisoners.

Instructors should be drawn from the best of the profession, but in the Army I joined in 1973, being an instructor was mostly for those who could not do the actual job. Indeed, as I would discover later, an assignment at a training center as an instructor was often punishment for screwing up. These instructors who introduced us to the profession of intelligence collection represented the worst we had.

But at this point in my career, I didn't know any better. I felt I really understood the craft but just wasn't cut out to be an interrogator. I wasn't a good liar. I wasn't cruel. I didn't even see the need for cruelty to gather information.

The broken contract and my experience at Huachuca left me less inclined to pursue a career in the Army. But at least I got my MOS and my next assignment was with the 519th MI Battalion at Ft. Bragg, North Carolina.

Ft. Bragg was home to two Special Forces groups, the 82nd Airborne, and the XVIII Airborne Corps. The 519th wasn't subordinate to any of those units in 1975 and had no jump slots even though we participated in all their training exercises. Being a "leg" – paratrooper slang for a non-jumper – at a post like Ft. Bragg is humiliating. I tried to transfer into an airborne unit, but the commander wouldn't let me go. He was critically short of interrogators and needed every single one of us to support the airborne units who were critically short of interrogators.

Not only was the inability to get jump school a major disappointment, the other combat skill schools like ranger, air assault, jungle survival, and SERE (survival, escape, resistance and evasion) were not authorized for us either. Even language refresher and NCO Academy were not available.

We had no prisoners to interrogate. We couldn't get any training that would advance our military careers. We couldn't maintain our language skills. We had nothing to do but look like we were doing something meaningful. In the Army, appearances are everything. Career sergeants are instinctively suspicious of soldiers doing anything they enjoy. If soldiers like their jobs, they must be doing something wrong. We all enlisted because we loved languages, so language study was strictly forbidden. There we sat in a leg unit on an airborne post full of linguists forbidden to maintain our languages and denied airborne training. Not surprisingly, there was not a single reenlistment among the first-timers the whole year I was there.

Most of us had joined the Army for the same reason – to use it as a springboard to other things. Most of my comrades had suffered the same fate I had, which was broken contracts. All of us loved languages. Most of us had some college. None of us saw the sense in the military investing a couple hundred thousand dollars in training a linguist and then preventing the linguist from even maintaining his skill.

The experience was not entirely bleak, however. At Ft. Bragg I discovered the Freedom of Information Act. The FOIA guarantees the citizen the right to access any file the government has on him. I requested the file containing the information on which my denial of a security clearance was based. As it turned out, it contained no negative information. Whoever had been tasked with the investigation had simply not followed through with the paperwork. The Army owed me completion of my BI and the assignment which I had been guaranteed. I tried to negotiate a solution with the post recruiter, who was surprisingly hostile.

I didn't understand the hostility. I wanted to re-enlist. He would get credit for a re-enlistment. Everyone wins. But he saw nothing wrong with the Army not meeting the terms of my contract. I was getting paid, wasn't I? I had no grounds for expecting what in his mind was special treatment.

This left me no recourse but legal action. I sued the Army for breach of contract.[26]

---

26 In an eerie intersection of fate, I was helped pro bono by a local attorney, Elmo Zumwalt III, son of Admiral Elmo Zumwalt, Jr. The younger Zumwalt had been a swift boat commander in Vietnam, patrolling the inland rivers of South Vietnam at a time when a crewman on such a boat stood a three out of four chance of being killed or wounded in a one-year tour. The elder Zumwalt, who was the commander

I won. Sort of.

The court found in my favor stating I should never have been recruited under these circumstances. But rather than going ahead with my security clearance and my guaranteed assignment, they discharged me from the Army. I was inclined to stay in if I could go airborne and after my first enlistment, which was nearing the end, and apply to Special Forces. (In those days, a soldier had to have at least one enlistment and be at least a sergeant to apply for Special Forces.) The Army owed me the assignment they had guaranteed me for which I had already served my time. I was willing to reenlist for an airborne unit. I appealed to the post commander, Lieutenant General Henry "The Gunfighter" Emerson,[27] who sent me to his adjutant.

The post Adjutant, Major General Marx, made a call to the Pentagon and set it up. It was a Monday and on Thursday, I would be starting my new career in the 7th Special Forces Group! I would start out in MI support but would go to airborne school. After a few months when my first enlistment was complete, I could apply for Special Forces selection.

My elation was short-lived. On Tuesday morning the post recruiter informed me I was out of the Army, handed me a folder of out-processing

of all US naval forces in Vietnam, approved the use of Agent Orange to clear the shores of the rivers of the dense vegetation that made such perfect ambush sites. River boat casualties dropped to one in ten after that but exposed these men to a then-unrecognized carcinogen. The younger Zumwalt died in 1988 at the age of 42 of cancer, a disease I would also fight. I swam the Mekong more than once in 1976 in a fruitless effort to locate American MIAs after the war's end.

27 Lieutenant General Henry "Hank" Emerson, who commanded the XVIII Airborne Corps and Ft. Bragg when I was there, was something of an eccentric. In addition to wearing a gunfighter's revolver on his daily uniform, he was also known for employing some highly unusual activities designed to enhance unit cohesion. He sponsored "combat football," a game which only distantly resembles football, has almost no rules and involved teams of forty soldiers. Injuries were common. He was a fan of reverse-cycle training in which troops train at night and try to sleep during the day. He maintained a post-wide standard of "Four in Thirty-two" – everyone on the post was expected to regularly run four miles in under thirty-two minutes. He also mandated that every one of us watch "Brian's Song" to promote racial harmony, which was a serious issue at the time.

paperwork (which usually takes at least a week) with my signature forged on every piece. My personnel file was "lost."

I honestly didn't know what to do. Should I take it back to General Marx and report the recruiter along with his sergeant major and commander? That ran a serious risk of dragging a reputation as a troublemaker into my next assignment with me. Or I could just accept the unlawful discharge, take a little time off and re-enlist for something better, if I felt like it. There seemed to be no advantage to fighting and every benefit to taking the early discharge.

With my exit came the heartfelt congratulations from my comrades in arms from my company commander and first sergeant to the other envious first-termers. All wished me well. The only soldiers who encouraged me to stay were the senior sergeants of Eastern European origin: Horvath, Galzinski and Atanasov. They praised the Army and all the benefits they had received.

I decided to leave quietly and think about my options. I had all my issued equipment, a valid ID card, a valid post sticker on my car, and the Army kept paying me for the next seven months. I took a few months to carefully consider what I should do.

CHAPTER 2

Army Reserve 1976 to 2006

THINGS LOOKED DIFFERENT for me in 1976. I had finished my bachelor's degree while on active duty, which opened a lot of possibilities. I could enlist for officer programs, perhaps become a pilot. I could apply to the FBI or CIA. With the GI Bill, I could afford to go to law school or medical school. I opted for medical school.

Soon after leaving Ft. Bragg, I joined the reserves, first in a transportation unit as a mechanic. Incredibly, I continued to get an active duty paycheck even after I started getting one from the reserves, despite having only one Social Security number. I had both a valid green Active Army ID card and a pink Army Reserve ID card. I didn't spend the extra money because I was pretty sure they would discover the mistake and take it back. But they never did. Sometimes bureaucratic errors work in the favor of the soldier.

In the summer of 1976 I began taking classes at the University of Washington in Seattle and stumbled upon a reserve Special Forces company tucked away discretely at Sand Point Naval Air Station on Lake Washington. I stopped in to see whether I could transfer in, but met the usual objection: I wasn't airborne qualified. They weren't willing to send a new recruit to jump school. Too many didn't make it, so it was a waste of money. They weren't short of soldiers and had no problem with retention.

I was talking to Sergeant First Class Rusbolt, the administration NCO. He was cordial enough, but the "no legs" policy was firm. From the look of him, Rusbolt had been a Special Forces soldier in Vietnam and was wearing badges and medals I'd never hope to own. SF isn't a "come one, come all" kind of organization. Only the best get in and just wanting to be a Green Beret isn't enough.[28] Not by a long shot.

So I played my trump card. In the office and in the presence of Sergeant Rusbolt, Sergeant Major Peck, Captain Costigan the Personnel Officer, and the overtasked civilian technician Mr. Carter, I announced, "I can type eighty words a minute."

Silence fell over the office.

All heads turned in my direction. You would have thought I had just proclaimed I won the Medal of Honor.

Mr. Carter turned around, straightened his back in his chair, cleared his throat and said, "Show that young man in."

Special Forces was nothing at all like the conventional Army. Everything was different in SF. It was exciting, challenging and fun. The men I served with were people I liked and respected, even envied. They were all in it for the right reasons. They didn't care about medals, promotions or pay. (Well, maybe just a little about pay.) They put in at least as much time during the month preparing for weekend drill as the drill itself. My time in Special Forces is something I wouldn't trade for anything.

In 1987 I went to medical school in Hungary (worthy of its own book) and came back to do a residency in Psychiatry at the University of Washington in 1994 (also worth a book). I tried to join the Army Medical Corps, thinking that since I already had over ten years of service, I might as well finish out my twenty for retirement as an Army doctor. It was there I encountered the jaw-dropping incompetence of the Washington Army National Guard (WANG) for the first time. The medical recruiter had no idea what he was doing and we spent over a year submitting the

28 Special Forces, popularly known as the "Green Berets," was created in 1952 to be the Army's unconventional warfare proponent. We generally refer to ourselves as "SF." The term "Green Beret" actually had a pejorative connotation when I joined. We almost never wear the beret and those who do risk appearing hungry for attention in an organization that prefers to keep a low profile. Special Forces, which is an exclusively Army organization, should not be confused with Special Operations Forces (SOF) which encompass Special Forces, Airborne Rangers, SEALS, CAG (formerly Delta Force) and others. And Special Forces should never, never, never be confused with Special Services.

mountain of paperwork and then resubmitting it over and over for small corrections.

I was wasting time so I decided to come back in as an enlisted soldier and apply for a commission in the Medical Corps from there. Even this was not without difficulty. My original personnel file had been lost when I got out in 1976 and had to be reconstructed to get back into the Army Reserve. When I transferred to the Individual Ready Reserve (IRR) in 1987 to go to medical school, it was lost again. The only document I had that verified that I had ever been a soldier was a DD-214[29] from 1976 and a language test that erroneously recorded my rank as Staff Sergeant E-6.[30]

I had never been promoted to E-6. I made E-5 in Special Forces but then accepted a direct commission as a captain in 1980 and reverted back to E-5 later when the regulations governing MI officers in SF changed. I presented my documents to the Army recruiter, who was refreshingly proactive. No, I didn't need to come in; she would come to my home with the necessary paperwork. No, I didn't need to show up on my own at the AFEES station for in processing; she would drive me personally. She got me right in as a Staff Sergeant and in 1995 I soon found myself back in my old unit which had been taken over by the National Guard.[31]

It was great to be back in SF. Many of my old friends were still there from ten years before. I made many new friends as well. I was soon promoted to Sergeant First Class (E-7) and then, two years later, to Master Sergeant (E-8). The WANG stood up an Information Operations (IO)

---

29 The DD-214 is the official discharge document to prove a soldier's service.

30 In the Army we often use our pay grade interchangeably with our ranks. E-1 and E-2 are privates, E-3 private first class, and so on.

31 In the early 1990s the Army restructured itself to transfer all combat arms out of the Reserves under the theory that if we went to war and activated the Reserves, it would be to support the Active Duty combat units. The Reserves were limited to support units, which were not attractive to many reservists. The National Guard, seizing the opportunity to take in large numbers of highly trained and motivated soldiers, made room for SF. The Reserves' loss was the Guard's gain. This was a full decade before the country transitioned to perpetual wartime footing where Guard and Reserves units would deploy to combat twice as much as Active Duty units, demonstrating the folly of taking combat arms out of the Reserves.

battalion, a brand new concept at the time. Because IO is also a Special Forces mission, I was offered the position of Group Sergeant Major.

It was a rapid rise from buck sergeant to sergeant major in six years. And these were six National Guard years. It takes at least fifteen years, or 5000 days of active service as an NCO, to make E-9, if one makes it at all. Less than one percent does. I had 275 days of service as an NCO. I may not have succeeded in getting commissioned as a medical officer, but as an enlisted man, things were going extraordinarily well for me.

Then 9/11 happened.

We went to war and in 2002 I was whisked out of my unit to deploy with 5th Special Forces. That lasted about two weeks when I got grabbed by Special Operations Command. That lasted a day or two when I got tagged to be the Information Operations Sergeant Major at Intelligence and Security Command (INSCOM) at Ft. Belvoir. From there I got loaned to a three-letter agency where I served for the duration of the war.

The Iraq invasion of 2003 afforded me the opportunity to view the profiteering of the defense contractor industry to the detriment of the military up close for the first time.[32] Contracting out for support in every field exploded when we went to war after the September 11 attacks in 2001. The sheer volume of required support forced the big companies like SAIC, Mission Essential Personnel and Raytheon to sub out much of what they provide. Thousands of small companies comprising no more than a handful of people sprung up to get in on the flood of cash.

One of the first problems I encountered as Sergeant Major of the 1st Information Operations Group was the difficulty in getting my people

---

32 While Secretary of Defense in the late 1980s, Dick Cheney commissioned a study to answer the question of whether a single corporation could meet all of the logistics needs of the US military. That task fell to Halliburton, who determined that the needs could indeed be met. They were then, inexplicably, allowed to bid on the very contract they had studied and were awarded the LOGPAC. Since then the military has never been able to free itself from dependence upon contracting companies for support. Indeed, it was next to impossible to even switch companies. Halliburton subsidy KBR is firmly entrenched as the entity that supports virtually everything we do militarily abroad.

reimbursed for travel expenses. The volume of travel vouchers quickly overwhelmed our permanent staff, which until then consisted of an elderly lady with medical problems and a young, drug-addicted single mother. The older lady missed not weeks but months of work due to illness and the single mom, who was also a racial minority, would not even make it in to work one or two days a week. It is very difficult to replace such employees who are shielded by laws that defend protected minorities from discrimination along with ensuring fairness in hiring. Her regular absence afforded us the opportunity to go to her desk and do her work for her. She did not do the work well when she was present and generally had no idea what she had done the day before, making it difficult to even trace her actions. It would have been much easier for us if she would have just stayed home all the time. We could have just done her work correctly rather than having to undo it and then redo it right.

The Finance office was overwhelmed, so INSCOM subbed out the processing of travel vouchers to a small company in Cincinnati, as I recall. We sent them hundreds of vouchers, virtually all of which were returned to have errors corrected. They never noted exactly what those errors were, so we were left to try to figure out on our own what we had done wrong. If we submitted the same travel vouchers through Finance at Ft. Belvoir, they got paid. The unpaid travel vouchers stacked up over 2002 and 2003. Mine went unpaid for 18 months, but that was nowhere near the record of 36 months of unpaid travel vouchers from one warrant officer. The average number of submissions until they got paid was eight to ten.

If the travel vouchers were processed at INSCOM, I could just walk over to Finance and talk to somebody to solve the problem, but I could only do that in rare cases, not routinely. The Cincinnati office was far away and very difficult to reach, even by phone or email. But as the weeks turned into months, I eventually learned that their clerks were instructed to send every travel voucher back that had even the slightest error no matter how insignificant. A brief paragraph near the end of the contract stipulated that they could send travel vouchers back that contained errors and charge us, the customer, an $85 fee for each. Over the year I was at

INSCOM, we spent some $850,000 in unbudgeted money on those fees alone in addition to the amount paid to the basic contract.

The profiteering is outrageous enough, but the harm done to our soldiers was much worse. Information Operations deals with complex and vital functions including computer network defense. All of our people need Top Secret clearances. One of the most common ways to lose a clearance is to have financial problems. Of the first team we deployed of ten operators, five had to return due to financial problems. Of the next twenty, 19 had to return. By the third iteration, there was only one soldier in the entire battalion still able to deploy. Failure to reimburse soldiers in a timely fashion for obligatory expenses related to their training disabled the entire group in 2003, leaving us critically vulnerable to cyber-attacks, especially from the Chinese.

The fiasco had further repercussions. Because the government credit card would be permanently revoked if the expenses were not paid, the soldiers had to find some other way to pay for their hotels and travel. Some took out credit cards that were being unscrupulously marketed to the poor and desperate. They would typically have a $200 limit, but as soon as the soldier activated the card, initiation fees and first year's dues put them $135 in debt. Moreover, the card could not be used to reserve a hotel or rental car. It was worthless.

When the soldier deployed with such a card, they found that they could not cancel the card until the $135 was paid plus the late fee. The late fee put them over the limit, so an over-limit fee was also imposed. While away, the companies piled on legal and collection fees. It was not uncommon for my soldiers to accumulate several thousands of dollars of debt for a card they never used and at a time when they were saddled by huge obligatory military expenses and not getting paid very much, if at all. The entire initial ten-man team we deployed in January of 2002 only received their first paycheck in August, a full seven months into their deployment.

It got worse. There was a collection agency that, according to their website, specialized in "hard to collect debts." They engaged in the odious practice of waiting until the soldiers were deployed to war, serving papers to their home addresses knowing they would not be home, and obtaining default judgements for thousands of dollars. My soldiers were naturally reluctant to talk to anybody about these problems, but I made it a point to dig into the details of their personal financial problems when I could. Most were highly paid computer security experts, systems operators and the like as civilians. They shouldn't have financial problems.

But the combination of being reduced to a soldier's salary, which was often unpaid for long periods, and being forced to charge expenses related to their service on private credit cards put some of them into extreme circumstances. Several simply refused to obey orders and deploy. Technically, that's desertion in a time of war, but under the circumstances who could blame them? Are we really going to line up hundreds of weekend warriors and shoot them as deserters? Several hundred Washington National Guard soldiers refused to deploy, forcing us to turn to the California Army National Guard to fill our rosters.

The Soldiers and Sailors Relief Act of 1940 protects deployed soldiers from debt collection until they return from the fighting. Serving papers to an address known to be vacant is also illegal. It was a pleasure to help several of my soldiers fight this, during which I managed to get at least one attorney disbarred. The infamous collection agency is no longer in business, either. Several of the predatory credit card companies were targeted by class action suits and ceased those destructive programs.

While at INSCOM in 2003 I was also able to discover why we were hiring linguists when we had language-qualified soldiers we weren't using. I located the office responsible for the linguist contract. INSCOM had agreed to use linguists supplied exclusively by one of the big contracting companies. In the contract was a paragraph in which we agreed not to use our own military linguists. I remember thinking out loud, "Who's the Einstein who signed this?" A clerk typist nearby informed me of the identity of the warrant officer who was the contracting officer.

I asked where I could find him. Would he be in soon?

No, the clerk told me. He was on terminal leave and about to go work for the very company for which he had signed that lucrative contract.

This type of profiteering and revolving door hiring surprises no one. It happens every time a nation goes to war. In 2003 there was very little oversight. Any congressman who suggested that we take a closer look at spending was shouted down with accusations of not supporting the troops or being soft on terrorism.

We often went to war without the best equipment. In the Guard and reserves, we were especially dependent upon our own wiles to scrounge the equipment we wanted to take with us to combat. But the logistics problems of the 2003 Iraq war were almost never due to a lack of equipment. It was a distribution problem. The equipment we had was simply not with the units that needed it. Throwing millions of dollars into buying more and better equipment does no good if it isn't distributed efficiently.

Before I deployed, I received a full complement of clothing and equipment from the WANG. Then I received another at the mobilization station. Finally, I got a third full complement of clothing and equipment at my receiving unit. In the end, I had a dozen duffle bags of helmets, body armor, boots, clothing for every possible climate, and even two laptops. I served most of my time in the Washington DC area, which may not be the safest city in America, but I really did not need five helmets and three sets of body armor. All of this took place against the media drone of how soldiers in Iraq don't have body armor so Congress better open their checkbooks and buy some. Or the terrorists win.

After the Iraq invasion I tried to retire in 2004 and return to the life of a doctor and family man. I finally had twenty good years in and could lock in a modest retirement when I hit age 60. I had failed to get a commission as a medical officer, but my experience in Special Forces and promotion to sergeant major was a good trade. I wrapped up my affairs with the Washington Army National Guard, transferred my records to the IRR, rejoined my family in Hungary and waited for my 20 Year Letter.

And waited.

And waited.

Finally, a year later I got a form letter from the IRR notifying me I had 19 good years in and should prepare for retirement from the National Guard. I contacted the IRR to find out what had gone wrong but was told they had no record of my transfer from the National Guard to the IRR. I contacted my old unit who assured me they had sent the records and I no longer belonged to the WANG.

Neither the WANG nor the IRR could correct the problem because I did not officially belong to either. While all this was dragging on, my term of service expired, so I was no longer even in the Army at all. But with no unit owning me, I wasn't officially discharged either. I was neither in nor out. I had no DD-214 besides the one I got in 1976, so I couldn't even get back in the Army because there was no record of my discharge.

I contacted the US Embassy in Budapest for help. They recommended contacting my congressman. But as a permanent resident of Hungary, I had no congressman.

I stayed in limbo until I was visited by a blessing disguised as treachery. I received a letter from the WANG reducing me from sergeant major to master sergeant because I had not finished Sergeants Major Academy (SMA). The reason I had not finished the final two weeks of SMA was because the country went to war and all schools were cancelled. The Sergeant Major of the WANG knew this but initiated the reduction anyway. That particularly malicious deed puzzled me. He knew the situation and he and I had always been on good terms.

It continued to puzzle me for another six months until I got the news that he had died of a brain tumor which had apparently been responsible for a whole swath of erratic and malicious actions. Because those actions were indistinguishable from the usual behavior of many crotchety old sergeants major, they failed to raise an alarm that there was serious pathology at work inside the man's skull until it was too late.

With the demotion came the opportunity to appeal and the appointment of someone finally officially responsible for listening to my story. I would be allowed to keep my E-9 for retirement provided I attended and passed the next available SMA course.

The WANG was now responsible for cutting orders to send me to SMA and of course they couldn't do it. They notified the IRR who couldn't do it either, but with a legal decision from their own command they couldn't ignore, they had to trace what happened to my records. When they could not find evidence that they had been sent to and received by the IRR, they resorted to reconstructing my records to reflect things happening the way they should have.

The reconstructed record of my final six months with the WANG that was sent to the IRR is completely fictitious. I left the WANG in November of 2004 to resume residence in Hungary with my wife and kids. My record reflects that I left the WANG in March of 2005 and attended drills each month up until then. This created potential problems with my taxes which I had filed indicating no income after November 2004. The reconstructed record had me earning money and not paying taxes on it into 2005.

This would also create problems with my security clearance. As recently as 2014 I had to undergo a Periodic Reinvestigation to clear up discrepancies between my reported service record and the official record. I spent many tedious hours with the investigating officer deconflicting records that have been lost and reconstructed no fewer than three times (1976, 1987 and 1996). Almost everything on my military record is not only a reconstruction, it's a reconstruction of a reconstruction of a reconstruction.

Reconstructing my records and transferring them to the IRR solved the problem of my missing final year necessary to get my 20 Year Letter and lock in my retirement. Since the records were a sparse fabrication, they included very little of my actual accomplishments and time in service. Missing the records for many of my correspondence courses and three Soldiers Medals along with any record of my commission as a captain in Military Intelligence would leave me with a smaller retirement check than I had earned, but I was just happy at that point to have one at all. Career and retirement had never been a goal for serving in the first place, so I looked upon any future retirement money as a bonus.

My next problem was how to attend the last two weeks of SMA. The IRR sent me orders on a Monday to report to Ft. Bliss on Thursday. They arranged a plane ticket from the nearest international airport, which was in Budapest, three and a half hours away by taxi and leaving at 6:00 AM Wednesday morning. That meant no sleep Tuesday night after a mad scramble to explain the situation to the professor, hand off my patients, find a substitute to teach my classes and get my stuff together for a two-week absence.

A major obstacle was having to pay all expenses up front using the government credit card and being reimbursed later. I did not have a government credit card.[33] Neither did I have a military ID card to get on base and I had no way of getting one before I arrived. I would also need uniforms and the IRR had no money or authority to provide them.

---

33 The "government credit card" is an Orwellian term meaning "not a government credit card." It is a credit card from a private company like Bank of America with which the soldier is required to pay for expenses related to his own training, especially hotels and rental cars. These expenses can easily exceed the soldier's own salary and he is obligated to repay them within 30 days out of his own pocket. Theoretically, the soldier should submit a travel voucher and be reimbursed within five working days, but I never saw a travel voucher reimbursed in fewer than four months. Now the soldiers can just have the reimbursement from the travel voucher sent directly to the bank issuing the card, but that wasn't the case back then. Financial problems created by the government credit card crippled the Information Operations unit I served in and sent many a good soldier into financial ruin.

CHAPTER 3

Sergeants Major Academy

I ARRIVED AT Ft. Bliss in the early hours of a Thursday in June of 2006, caught the Army shuttle to the hotel I would be staying at with my colleagues and planned my survival. I had $100 in cash and no credit cards that worked in the States. I needed a uniform and procured that through an Army surplus store near the main gate run by a Korean lady. I didn't have enough money to pay for everything I needed, but negotiated a discount on a used uniform and boots with the promise I would bring them back in two weeks. I would be out of uniform with no name tags, rank or patches, but it was a first step.

Next was the difficulty getting onto a secure base in a time of war without an ID card. Fortunately, gate guards don't harass a van full of sergeants major. In fact, I was able to get through the gate every day without showing my ID card even after I got a valid one a few days later.

Another problem was that we were all on per diem and separate rations. That meant we couldn't eat in the mess hall without paying. I would not be getting paid for several weeks, maybe months, and had no cash. So I lived eating one meal a day at the hotel, which had a complimentary continental breakfast. It wasn't much, but it had to do.

Upon arrival I was informed that my advisor had disappeared. Nobody knew what happened to her and she had certainly not informed me of the four research papers that were due the day I arrived. These papers are weekly assignments on various military topics and would be presented in class. Not having the papers is grounds for immediate dismissal.

My instructor said he could allow me 48 hours to write the papers before the first one was due for presentation. Fortunately, research is my life's blood and it was not difficult to knock out four papers to military standards by working through the breaks and lunch, which I wasn't eating anyway. I got the papers done just under the wire.

Next we had a weigh-in and Army physical fitness test (APFT). I was surprised to find that I was ten pounds lighter than I had been just a few days before in Hungary. I don't think it was entirely due to the McChrystal diet.[34] I strongly suspect that they purposely set the scales lower to help the marginal candidates pass. There are a lot of pretty fat sergeants major in the Army.

I passed the APFT easily, which isn't very hard. Being over 50, I needed to be screened and medically cleared to take the test for record. Ironically, one does not need to be cleared to exercise or take the test when not for record. But for the APFT to count, I needed an EKG and blood test showing no serious cardiovascular conditions. Once in a while, an older and out of shape soldier has been known to suffer a heart attack while exercising just as sometimes happens with civilians. The panic of having to get in shape quickly and pass the test can lead to a soldier pushing himself too hard. In my experience with conventional support troops, even *thinking* about the APFT can induce panic attacks.

Along with my advisor deserting without a trace, the SMA had no idea where my medical records were. I had sent them when I enrolled, but

---

34 General Stanley McChrystal, who was at that time commander of Joint Special Operations Command, limits himself to one meal a day to stay fit. As I aged, I came to appreciate the wisdom of limiting calories and the difficulty in resisting the temptation of four unlimited meals a day available to combat troops overseas. Today, soldiers commonly come home from combat deployments *fatter* than when they arrived.

McChrystal brought much of the agility back to Special Operations that allowed them to gather intelligence and react quickly enough to have a decisive impact on the insurgencies in Iraq and Afghanistan. When Special Forces got its own MOS (the 18 series), it went down a path leading to careerism and bureaucracy that cost it much of what originally made it special. In the 1990s emphasis shifted to SR/DA (special reconnaissance and direct action) and SF drifted further away from its core skills in unconventional warfare and counterinsurgency. By 9/11, Special Operations units of all services were isolated and stove piped with Rangers, Marines, SEALS and Green Berets competing to do the same raid and recon missions while no one was preparing for the guerilla wars we would soon have to fight in Iraq and Afghanistan.

they were missing along with everything else. I had learned long ago not to trust the Army with my records, so I hand-carried my medical records from Hungary which had all the required test results. The SMA, however, refused to accept these; they needed real Army records done on Army forms by Army doctors. I considered this ludicrous. EKGs and cholesterol levels don't change depending on the forms or who performs the tests.

I went to speak with the base surgeon doc-to-doc. She agreed completely that the regulation was stupid, was wasting money to hold up my graduation and demanding the tests be repeated. I had already completed the APFT days before and couldn't possibly die of a heart attack as a result. She could use her medical authority to sign off on my civilian EKG and lab records as valid.

She refused. She said that if it were discovered, she would be relieved of her gluteus maximus, or words to that effect. My suggestion that this was moral cowardice was not well received. I would have to get an Army physical at Army facilities in accordance with regulations and repeat the APFT.

This, of course, was impossible. I had no authorization to do anything but attend SMA and return home immediately afterward. The plane ticket was already bought. Even obtaining the required ID card and basic issue of uniforms had not been authorized. In the end I wound up with the highest academic score in a class of over 600 but was not allowed to graduate until I performed a valid APFT administered by an officially recognized military school while on orders and only after I had a proper Army physical clearing me as healthy enough to take the test. I was "counselled" (the new Army term for "disciplined ") for not having my medical records and not passing the APFT. I would be required to submit an official record of a passed APFT from a military school within 90 days or not get my diploma, be reduced in grade, and barred to reenlistment for having failed a required military school.

I was in a quandary. What to do? So close yet so far. I couldn't get the required physical or APFT at Ft. Bliss. My orders would run out the following day and I had to be on the plane back to Hungary. I would be reduced to Master Sergeant for retirement purposes. This called for desperate measures.

The nearest NCO Academy that was not at Ft. Bliss was at Ft. Huachuca, my old nemesis, four and a half hours away (three if you drive like the locals). I had an old friend there working as a contractor, so I gave him a call to see whether he could put me up for a day or two, just long enough for me to get an APFT. He said yes, so I hitched a ride with a classmate going that way and by nightfall was back in Sierra Vista.

CHAPTER 4

My First Job as a Contractor

FT. HUACHUCA HAD changed a lot since 1975. Gone were the WWII barracks I had stayed in along with the old classrooms of the same era. The government had poured tons of money into the fort which is the home of the US Army Intelligence Center and School (USAICS). Much of that went to pay for contractors to fill out the Army's colossal intelligence deficit.[35] Contractors with no more than a GED and one enlistment were starting with huge salaries and had lots of cash to throw around Sierra Vista.

My friend raved about the job. It not only paid well, it was the easiest job he had ever had. It was illegal to work one minute more than forty hours a week.[36] Employment was "at will," meaning the customer, i.e. the Army, could fire you any time they wanted without cause or notice, but you could also quit any time you wanted and the market was such that other similar jobs were always available. He strongly encouraged me to try it. And he would get a $2000 bonus if I signed up.

I had some trepidation about taking such a job. It would mean delaying my return to Hungary and my family. Also, I was completely unqualified to teach anything at the military intelligence school. I didn't have

35 By 2013 nearly 70 percent of the nation's intelligence budget was outsourced to contractors. A half a million civilians possess Top Secret security clearances.

36 There are good reasons for limiting work to 40 hours and forbidding employees from working extra unpaid hours, even voluntarily. This can have the effect of delivering more to the client than the client paid for and unduly influence him to award the contract to that company. Fundamentally, that is unfair competition and exerting inappropriate influence, much like offering perks and gifts. It can also have the effect of imposing unspoken obligations on employees and lead to unfair hiring and management practices. Defense contractor companies can lose their contracts and even their privilege to bid on future contracts if employees get caught working extra unpaid hours or working outside the job description in the Statement of Work.

the required MOS, had never deployed in military intelligence and never done the job I was trained to do so long ago. I had never interrogated a single prisoner and as a licensed medical doctor wasn't even allowed to. Nor did I have the necessary certification as an Army instructor.

But I was destitute. I had no money and had just missed my chance to fly back to Hungary. I was stranded. And I really needed to get that APFT and with it my diploma to lock in my E-9 for retirement. The situation was dire and called for bold action. It was the Fourth of July weekend, so nothing much would be happening for a few days and I had some time to think. My friend loaned me his car (he preferred riding his motorcycle to work) so I had wheels, a place to stay and food until I got back on my feet.

First order of business was to walk into the NCO Academy and have the First Sergeant administer the APFT for me. He was only too happy to oblige. When I passed, he helped me fax the results to SMA and within a few days I had my diploma in hand. Mission accomplished.

Next, on the first morning after the holiday, my friend delivered me to the office of Anteon, the contracting company he worked for. All they needed was a copy of my DD-214 proving I had the necessary MOS and verification of an active Secret security clearance. The company would fund my training at the next available Army Basic Instructor Course (ABIC). My clearance was still active but the only DD-214 I had was the one I got in 1976. It was enough however. It verified my MOS as 96C, POW Interrogator. An obscure clause in the contract with the Army allowed Anteon to hire contract instructors with the MOS 97E *or equivalent*. Since 96C had long ago been changed to 97E, it was considered equivalent despite the fact that much of what was taught to Human Intelligence Collectors – huminters for short – had not been taught to interrogators in 1975.[37] So all that was required was to fill out the necessary application. I held the pen; they moved the paper. I had not experienced such pro-active recruiting since chancing upon that rare National Guard recruiter back in 1995.

37 Even the MOS 97E was in the process of being converted to 35M, Human Intelligence Collector.

The very next day I was delivered to my new boss, John Rostow,[38] who would orient me to my job, which was teaching Human Intelligence Collection. Our particular project was called Enhanced Analysis and Interrogation Training (EAIT) which was later changed when the buzz word "enhanced" became associated with interrogation techniques that bordered on torture. It was a great concept, to pair up an analyst with an interrogator in order to get better information faster. So it didn't really matter that I hadn't interrogated before – what we were teaching was new to everyone.

John sent me to the lecture hall to observe the classes in session. My first day at the back of the classroom gave me a jolt. I had no doubts about my ability as a teacher and lecturer. I did that for a living. But the first instructor I saw was Derek Rex, a fluent Arabic speaker with lots of real world experience in Iraq and Egypt. He was a superb lecturer, knowledgeable and skillful. The students hung on his every word. I knew I wouldn't be able to teach with the same authority Derek did and wondered how long it would take before I was unmasked as a phony with no real world experience at all as a huminter.

What I didn't know was that Derek was the best we had. He was more than once named Instructor of the Year. No one was better. He was followed by an average instructor who stumbled through the PowerPoint slides and demonstrated only very shallow understanding of the subject she taught. I felt better after that. And Derek and I quickly became good friends.[39]

I was given a work station in one of the new buildings which consisted of a desktop computer on a folding table. About two dozen of us contractors shared this big open room divided into sections with portable dividers and into cubicles for the more important people. There was very little for us to do during the lecture phases of class. I set about studying the classes I would eventually teach, but found the workplace distracting. With nothing to do, our 8-hour days were spent mostly socializing. Even

38 Not his real name.

39 Sadly, Derek died of cancer not long ago. It is to his memory I have dedicated this book.

though we weren't working, playing games on the computer was still forbidden during work hours, as was anything else healthy, fun, restful or educational. We were there to work and anything but work was strictly taboo. So it looked like I was back in the same military environment I left in 1976 that whiled away the hours in idle conversation until something related to our jobs appeared.

The one thing we did every day that was crucial was the timecard. We were required to record our hours worked at the end of every work day. The Site Lead was responsible for checking to make sure everyone did his or her timecard every day and did it accurately. It seemed like nit picking. The timecards weren't submitted until Friday (and with some companies, every other Friday). What did it matter when a person actually did his or her timecard? But the timecard is virtually the only objective evidence of work that can be audited. It is the vehicle through which the company gets paid. So Site Leads catch hell if any of their people are not doing them properly, hell which they readily pass on to timecard delinquents.

The inefficient use of personnel was so blatant that both the Army and the contracting companies were continually trying to find ways to employ us more effectively. Although we spent most of our time sitting at our desks or in the back of the classroom observing, the Army couldn't use us for anything not specified in the Statement of Work (SOW). Soldiers can be given make-work details just to keep them busy, but they couldn't do that to civilians.

Not that they didn't try. At times we were directed to sit in the back of the classrooms and observe. But that took up too much space. Often we were ordered to work on our roles, but it really only took a few minutes to learn them and most of the instructors had already played all of the roles of captured detainees before.

Several times the Army tried to gather statistics on how much time we spent doing the different aspects of our jobs. For a while we were required to record what we did every hour of every day. Predictably, the statistics showed that we spent most of our time recording how we spent our time, so they stopped having us do that.

Since the concern of the customer over how little time we were spending doing anything useful suggested that we might lose our jobs if the truth got out, people predictably recorded that they were doing things related to the job that could not be verified, like doing research or assisting with a class.

In truth, there was no danger of the Army cutting back on instructors. The one phase where all of us were needed all the time was Booth Phase when the students actually try out what they learned in lecture. The Program of Instruction (POI) for the basic Human Intelligence Collector course stipulated that one instructor was required for every two students. Booth Phase was only a few weeks out of the whole three-month course, but it was crucial. Outside of Booth Phase, most of the course required only a few of us to deliver lectures or run teams.

There were ways to cut costs and make more efficient use of contract resources by modifying the POI, but in 2006 nobody was really interested in cutting costs, only in justifying them. The one-to-two instructor-student requirement justified hiring large numbers of contract instructors. Changing that ratio would only reduce to money allocated for the program.

The EAIT program was staffed entirely by contractors. There was not a single military instructor or supervisor on our project. The contractors were supplied by a collage of companies including Anteon, General Dynamics, Oberon, Lockheed Martin and SAIC. All paid basically the same salaries and there was a gentleman's agreement between the companies not to vie for talent by negotiating salaries. There was enough money and plenty of business to go around. Competitive bidding would serve no one (except the taxpayer) and cutting back on personnel or expenditures would only result in lower allocations the next year.

My first experience with Booth Phase came a few weeks into the job but before I was sent to ABIC. I was eagerly anticipating revisiting this experience, which had been so traumatic for me 32 years earlier, from the other side of the table. In looking at the curriculum, I recognized most of the approaches. We no longer taught "False Flag" or "Mutt and Jeff," but little else had changed.

We were also in the throes of revision in the wake of the torture scandals at Abu Ghraib and elsewhere. The whole interrogation manual had been rewritten and reviewed. Protesters at the front gate with signs reading "Stop Teaching Torture" were a regular sight at Ft. Huachuca in 2006. In point of fact, we never did teach torture, nor was it ever in the manual. The scandals that made the news were universally prompted by interrogators who were either not trained or who acted in violation of policy. What's more, the Army was serious about remedying the situation. Over my stint at Huachuca between 2006 and 2008, several of my colleagues were called upon to testify in investigations relating to allegations of torture. Regardless of how richly we felt terrorists deserved some rough treatment, almost all of us believed strongly that torture had no place in effective interrogation.

An iteration in the booth phase has five parts: Planning and Preparation (P&P), Approaches, Questioning, Termination, and Critique and Retrain (C&R). On the training schedule, a certain amount of time is allotted to each part and someone announces when each part begins. The time schedule is just for instruction purposes and not related to how much time should be spent on each part in a real interrogation which, as you can imagine, varies widely.

The roles were carefully written to be realistic, complete, and free from contradictions but fell far short of that goal. They varied in length and difficulty. They were supposed to be based on one overarching story and proceed from short and easy to long and complex. It was the same idea used back in 1975 when they based the story on a fictional conflict in the fictional Latin American country of Armanda. In 2006 the story was set in Iraq. In 2011 it was switched to Afghanistan. The instructor was to play the role and give up the information in the story, point by point, if the student asked the right questions in the correct manner.

The idea was to teach the student to ask questions correctly and systematically, but in doing so, the students tended to sound mechanical and impersonal, precisely not what is needed to build rapport and trust with the detainee. Many of the rules by which a student was graded and often flunked were completely arbitrary. For example, the student couldn't ask questions out of order or go back to another section if he forgot something. In a real interrogation it would be irresponsible for an interrogator not to go back and ask about something he had missed, but in the schoolhouse, doing so could earn the student a failing grade. I shudder to think how many students failed for reasons that had nothing to do with the ability to question a detainee effectively.

I got paired up with a very likeable contractor named Don.[40] I wondered how he had even managed to pass a course where cruelty was considered an essential skill. Don dressed himself in an orange prison jumpsuit and handcuffs. He showed me the role, which was that of an older, quiet Iraqi businessman who had been detained on suspicion of funding terrorists. The role prescribed which approaches would be acceptable, how the role player should act and respond, and of course what information he had. Don had played the role several times before, so he wouldn't need to look at the role until after the Approach phase when systematic questioning would actually begin.

At the bell, Don as detainee and I as invisible observer, were escorted to the booth and ushered inside by the "tiger team." (We called the interrogator-analyst pair "tiger teams" even though tigers don't hunt in teams. Chimps do, but "chimpanzee teams" just doesn't have the right ring.) The EAIT program was for interrogators and analysts who were already trained and experienced. We would not have to teach them the basics. The student interrogator began with the prescribed initial instructions to the prisoner and questions. It was clear the interrogator and analyst had done their homework. They hit the prescribed approaches on the money.

I expected Don to "break" (i.e. begin to cooperate), but instead he continued to resist. The team tried other perfectly valid approaches, but Don did not respond. Indeed, Don began to behave completely contrary

40 Not his real name.

to his role, flew into a rage, then into a sulk, and then became personally insulting. He continued on until a half hour was up and the signal was given to begin Questioning phase, at which time he suddenly became friendly and cooperative.

The tiger team asked all the questions correctly and systematically and Don ticked off all the items of intelligence they were supposed to collect. This felt more like the experience I had gone through except that the students were good. Later I asked Don why he hadn't responded when the interrogator ran the correct approaches.

"Approach phase lasts 30 minutes," he answered.

"But what if they do the right approach in less than that?" I asked.

"You still have to run it out to 30 minutes. You can't let them start questioning before Approach phase is over."

"Why not?"

"It wouldn't be fair. It would give them extra time to do the questioning. They could get more intel than the other students because they had more time."

"We don't want them to collect more information?"

"It's not that. We need to be sure all the students get the same amount of time. Otherwise, some will get higher scores and that wouldn't be fair," Don explained.

"That seems confusing, though. I mean, I remember as a student doing what I thought was the right approach, but the instructor didn't break. I thought I was doing it wrong."

"Me too. I'm sure glad those days are over!"

"So you just keep on going until time's up, then break and start to cooperate?"

"That's how I was taught. Besides, I just like to mess with the students," he said with a grin.

I wanted to ask about playing the role but wasn't sure how to do it without hurting Don's feelings. He hadn't played the role at all like it was written. He should have been quiet and polite, not ranting and insulting. I suspected the answer would have been "That's how I was taught." And perhaps he felt he had earned the right to give forward a little of the abuse he had received when he was a student.

As booth phase continued, I got to spend some time observing several instructor role players. Most performed pretty much the same as Don, giving no clue to the students how their approaches were going and running out the clock with anti-American tirades and personal insults to the students.

There was one particularly outstanding tiger team that became aggressive during Approach phase after none of the perfectly reasonable approaches worked. At the end of the iteration during Critique and Retrain (when we go over the student's performance and advise on how to improve), both the interrogator and analyst took issue with the instructor not breaking. The interrogator became visibly angry and the instructor had to tell him to calm down.

"If you can't maintain control in a school setting, you won't be able to when you have to do this for real," said the instructor.

"I've done real interrogations," the student answered.

"Then you should be able to control yourself."

"In a real interrogation, the detainee would have broken on the right approach."

"No they don't. Sometimes they never break. I interrogated at Guantanamo for over a year and not a single detainee broke."

"You've never run a successful approach and you're an instructor?"

The instructor's face took on the appearance of a thermometer plunged into hot water. "And you're a student. You're about this close to getting counselled, so I'd suggest you remember that," he said through clenched teeth.

On the way back to the office, he groused to me about how he'd never tolerate insubordination, how a student who can't maintain control has no business in this profession, etc. The student had really struck a nerve. I remembered back how Pappy had been able to get under the instructors' skin, incurring their wrath.

Not all of the instructors were on a power trip, but most believed that part of their job was to weed out students that shouldn't be huminters. The flaw in this mindset was that we had instructors of dubious skill doing the weeding and often colored by their personal biases. Tension was increased by the fact that many of the EAIT students were more experienced at interrogation than their instructors.

Nothing much had changed in 30 years, but I had. In 1975 I was a junior enlisted soldier with a couple years of college. In 2006 I was a Special Forces sergeant major with a doctorate, training in psychiatry, and decades of experience teaching at the university level. Now, sitting on the other side of the table, I could see that the abuse, then as now, had nothing to do with effective training or even screening out those students unfit for this rigorous profession. The instructors in 2006 were abusive because they had been abused and being surrounded by people of the same experience only reinforced the maladaptive practices. No professional teacher would ever get away with this kind of behavior in any high school or college.

As should be blatantly obvious, this is not teaching. It is letting the students try their best to feel their way through the exercise and letting them sink or swim.

Mostly sink.

It was not uncommon in 1975 nor in 2006 for students to fail every iteration and go into the final test with no confidence in their skill or knowledge. The course then as now commonly failed 50 percent of the class. That so many of the instructor cadre did not see this as evidence of failure on their part spoke volumes about the inadequacy of the course and the incompetence of the instructors who taught it.

Not all of the instructors were closed-minded, but it was hard to break out of the interrogator mindset that perpetuated itself. Among the fallacies perpetuated by generation after generation of instructors were:

1. This is a hard profession. Most students should fail.
2. A hard course equals high standards.

3. If you help the student learn, you are making it too easy.
4. If a student finds the course too stressful it means they are not emotionally suited to this profession.
5. The instructor, being the subject matter expert, has the responsibility to cull out the students that are not fit to serve in this line of work.

Human intelligence collection is indeed a hard profession to do effectively, but the skills needed to do it are not. In fact, we all use many of these skills in everyday life. Anyone of average to below average intelligence can master all of the tasks a huminter must master in the time allowed at the school. Whether or not they ever use them effectively is more a matter of latent talent and opportunity.

The job of the teacher is to make the subject matter understandable and impart the required skills to the student. Good instructors make hard material easier to understand; bad instructors don't. Intentionally making material difficult to master is inexcusable, yet I saw this over and over.

Good instructors like Derek Rex not only got better results, they got better reviews from the students. The bad instructors who got poor results and bad reviews consistently justified their failures by blaming the students and defending their conduct as maintaining high standards.

Another thing that bothered me was the assessments. Accurate assessments are crucial to good teaching. They not only gauge what the student has learned but how well he is progressing. They are an important part of the learning process. They can also help us identify weaknesses in the program and the individual instructors. Performance in the booth was impossible to grade objectively and instructors could adjust the difficulty and slant the grading to pass or fail whomever they wanted. Although the instructors were periodically evaluated, those evaluations were just as flexible and subject to the same biases as the student assessments.

The truth is that the instructors commonly made snap initial judgments of the students as to which ones should pass and which shouldn't and adjusted the difficulty of their instruction and their grading to fit their initial impression. On one occasion one of the senior instructors objected to me awarding 100% to a student who achieved all that I had required of her on that particular iteration. It was only the third or fourth of nine iterations and most students were still expected to flunk.

"Why did you give Jones 100%?" he asked.

"She achieved 100% of what was required from this iteration," I answered.

"Does Jones look like the perfect interrogator to you? Nobody is a perfect interrogator besides me," he said with a stab at self-deprecating humor.

"She's not a perfect interrogator..."

"But by giving her a perfect score, you just said she is."

"I'm still learning this job," I said. "Do you want us to score them based on how good they are compared to perfection or how well they did with each iteration?"

"Their score should be an honest reflection of how good they are. That's how it's done. I don't know anywhere in the world where a score should reflect anything else."

I was used to teaching at the university level where each lesson has a list of points of performance the student is expected to master. If an instructor could not tell the student exactly what his expectations were for complete mastery of the lesson, the student had every right to complain that he wasn't getting the education he was paying for. Here, by contrast, I saw that the instructor decided what the trainee deserves and adjusted the score reflect that. It was extremely difficult for a student to succeed by sheer ability in the face of a hostile instructor. Neither was there any viable recourse to unfair treatment. The only person to complain to was the instructor himself or perhaps the Course Manager, neither of whom could be expected to be sympathetic.

Paradoxically, that little incident was comforting to me. I had labored for many years under the assumption that I was just not cut out to be an intelligence collector when in fact the training staff had instilled that into me through bad teaching. Actually, the fact that I passed was an indication that in the staff's opinion I at least had the minimal skills or I wouldn't have even graduated. From their point of view, making it hard just made me a better collector. Instead, it left me with no positive belief in my ability at all.

There was really no excuse for this. The military courses all have lesson plans just like other institutions of higher learning. Each course has a Program of Instruction (POI) with a list of items to be taught as tasks or points of performance. The mindset of the instructor that he is somehow at liberty to decide who should pass and who should fail and adjust the instruction and grading to achieve that perpetuated this travesty.

As I mentioned earlier, the POI of the booth phase of interrogation course is broadly divided into five sections: Planning and Preparation (P&P), Approaches, Questioning, Termination, and Critique and Retrain (C&R). Afterwards the students write up reports, which must be in the proper format and include the intelligence they collected.

In P&P the student gets some information on the detainee supplied by the guards and capture documents. This should allow the student to plan appropriate approaches to the detainee. This was also where the insanity of the grading system began to manifest itself. The student had to do everything required in P&P but could be graded as 3 (Exceeds Standards), 2 (Meets Standards), 1 (Needs Improvement), 0 (Does not meet standard/Not Done/Not Applicable). For most of the requirements, it was not possible to exceed the standard. For example, the student had to have his map with him to meet the standard. But how could he exceed the standard? Bring two maps? This meant that it was difficult to score more than 66% even when satisfactorily meeting all of the requirements of the section. But passing score was 70%.

Part of P&P is selecting approaches that would likely work, given the information known about the detainee. An "approach" in this context means trying to get the detainee to talk based on a specific motivation. The student is supposed to choose three possible approaches and explain to the instructor why they might work. This was another point at which the prejudice of the instructor could be brought to bear. If the instructor didn't like what the student chose, he could fail the student regardless of whether or not the student could defend his choice.

Knowing the approaches the student would take also introduced an unrealistic element into the effort in that it made it easy for the instructor to counter the approach if he chose. But often the instructors didn't even bother to counter the student; they just refused to respond or responded inappropriately until the 30 minutes allowed for approaches were up. The instructors were expected to drag the Approach phase out for 30 minutes regardless, which explained why I was so confused when I was a student. I would try the correct approach but the instructor wouldn't respond, so I thought it was the wrong approach and tried something else. It is pretty easy to go through all the likely approaches in less than 30 minutes and find yourself stabbing in the dark with ridiculous choices merely because those are all that are left. Trying inappropriate approaches out of desperation can also be used to justify failing the student.

Once the detainee is "broken" (i.e. cooperating), Questioning phase begins. There is a precise way and order in which to question a detainee. Proper questions used stock phrases that were slavishly adhered to even up until a few years ago. The purpose was to develop the habit of asking precise questions that would elicit clear answers, but they often came out stilted and unnatural. A very, very common exchange went like this:

Interrogator: "What is your name?"
Detainee/Instructor: "Mohammad."
Interrogator: "Spell it."
Detainee/Instructor: "I, t."

The Interrogator is supposed to tell the detainee to spell "Mohammad" even though it would be obvious, especially in a conversation not held in English.

Even worse:

Interrogator: "Could you please spell you name?"
Detainee/Instructor: "Yes, I could."

Interrogator: "Spell your name."
Detainee/Instructor: "Y, o, u, r, n, a, m, e."

Teaching precise questioning is important and these games that illustrate the imprecision of everyday speech would be entertaining but for the fact that the student is being graded down for his mistakes and often ridiculed at the same time. In a real interrogation if the detainee behaved in this manner, the proper action by the interrogator might be to upbraid him rather forcefully. But that is something the student wouldn't be allowed to do to an instructor who is just teaching the way he thinks questioning should be taught.

In the Questioning phase, there is also a section known as "map tracking." In this section the interrogator asks the detainee to describe a route from a known place to an unknown place. The interrogator has to follow his description of the route on a map and find the correct location. As you might imagine, there is a lot of room for the instructor to make this part hard or easy. But map tracking is an obligatory part of the interrogation. If the student fails to find the location within 50 meters, he fails the entire iteration no matter how well he does on everything else.

There was also a new section added since 1975 called "Fishing." In this, the student has to ask a long, boring question over and over, hoping something will turn up. "Between point A and point B, what did you see, hear or know of that might be of interest to Coalition Forces?" This section could go on for a long time and students got used to rattling it off fast even though in real life it would not be used like this. It just ate up precious time on a timed iteration.

Finally, the interrogation ends with Termination. Certain points have to be covered to pass including "reinforce the successful approach." This point is always iffy when the student has no idea which approach worked in the first place.

So right from the start I struggled with trying to balance teaching the way we had been taught and teaching effectively. I liked teaching in the booth. Playing the role of the detainee and teaching questioning was a lot like teaching medical students to take a medical history. It also provided the opportunity to share some insight into the psychology of motivation. Similarly, I found my forte in certain lecture classes related to my training in psychiatry and clinical experience. I liked teaching "Detecting Deception" and "Critical Thinking."[41] I often taught "History of Islam," "Cultural Awareness" and "History of the Middle East" as well.[42]

In 2006 there was a plethora of instructors. There were so many that the Army could afford to maintain a policy that all instructors after completing ABIC must observe each class. (This would be the second time for most because they had all been through the course at least once just to get the MOS.) After that the new instructor was expected to assist in teaching each class. That consisted of pushing the button on the machine to advance the PowerPoint slides. A certified instructor had to sign off that the new instructor had both observed a class and assisted to certify that he was ready to teach the class as primary instructor. The first time teaching as primary instructor one had to be evaluated by a certified instructor authorized to evaluate other instructors.

It was not unusual for a paid contract instructor to sit through eight months of classes before doing any actual teaching.

41 In the wake of the weapons of mass destruction fiasco used to justify the invasion of Iraq, the Army began to require a block of instruction on critical thinking skills, especially in the Intelligence MOSs. All instructors had to be certified in Critical Thinking in order just to teach it. I loved to teach that class and always hoped to find a student (or even and instructor) who would actually put the skills to use. The first thing a student of critical thinking should do is research the curriculum on critical thinking, which would reveal that there is no evidence that teaching critical thinking actually produces better thinking. People like the subject and the skills do seem important, but the brain doesn't work in a way that can be programed to think better. It can recognize elements of critical thinking and perhaps apply them by analogy, but it doesn't use them to actually think differently.

42 In the ramp up to the Iraq invasion of 2003, I attended an excellent week-long course on Cultural Awareness which included History of Islam and History of the Middle East. It was taught by university professors and former diplomats who were expert in the subjects. By 2006, these classes were shortened to less than a day and taught by military or contract instructors rather than experts. In 2011, the course had been relegated to one former infantry officer on a Mobile Training Team who manifestly knew and cared nothing about Islam or the Middle East.

With all this layered certification, one would think that this would ensure that only the most skillful, competent, highly qualified instructors would teach the students. Actually, it never worked that way. The paperwork and filing generated an enormous record-keeping and record-inspecting requirement that created yet another three layers of bureaucracy for USAICS to maintain in the name of accountability. The military unit that controlled the school had precisely the same requirement as well. In addition, the contracting companies were also tasked with ensuring that the contractors met all the standards imposed by the military. The result was a mountain of incomplete and incorrect records that had to be corrected (i.e. falsified) prior to every inspection. Nothing worked as it was intended but a façade had to be maintained that it did. Just maintaining the façade devoured huge amounts of time, work and expense.

As I pointed out earlier, the only objective measure of work was time spent at the workplace. Doing one's timecard every day was the most important thing we did. There were several companies involved in the EAIT project and each company did them a little differently, but the correct and timely timecard compliance was paramount even though it bore no relationship to actually teaching the course effectively and producing competent Human Intelligence Collectors.

Added to the constant vigilance of the Site Lead was the need of the Course Manager to ensure that everyone was at the job and on time. If the Course Manager is a military leader and has military instructors, he has to do a morning report for accountability. But civilians aren't counted on the morning report even though the military customer is theoretically accountable for everyone on his project. They don't attend morning formation and the best the Course Manager can do is ask the Site Lead whether everyone is present who should be and how many people that is. Larger projects sometimes assigned an individual to maintain a sign-in and sign-out sheet. This only worked with projects that worked regular eight-hour days at a single location. When multiple locations were involved with irregular hours, it became unrealistic. There was simply no satisfactory way to maintain accountability for every contractor or what they were actually doing beyond taking the Site Lead's word for it that everything was fine.

The need to do a timecard that bore no relationship to the value of work being done and documenting time at the workplace that no one could physically verify generated the predictable cynicism among the staff. As with any military project involving long periods of inactivity, a major unspoken task was to appear to be doing something. Or, more importantly, to avoid looking like you are making improper use of time. Playing video games on the computer was prohibited. Doing personal business on the computer was prohibited. Anything enjoyable – especially if it involved pornography – was prohibited. Paradoxically, because we were teaching the skills of gathering information from terrorists, our jobs required us to research terrorism, which was also prohibited.

The perfect storm hit when Sean Nelson decided to research a Philippine terrorist organization, the Moro Islamic Liberation Front, abbreviated MILF. The ensuing investigation ate up several days, but as I said, when not in Booth Phase we weren't doing much anyway...

The hyper-prudish behavior of the military in 2006 made for some hilarity. In 1975 soldiers had very little privacy. There were no dividers separating the toilets. All showers were communal. We even encountered casual nudity during training when an instructor would fake mental retardation and let his pants drop or a female instructor would demand to be strip searched. But that was the '70s. At Ft. Huachuca in 2006, one could be disciplined for being naked even in the men's locker room. There was a sauna at the fitness center I often used and just wrapped a towel around myself. One day someone actually complained.

"There's a man in the sauna and he's buck naked!" I heard the unidentified voice complain to the manager.

"Well, he isn't supposed to be," the manager responded.

"Are you gonna do something about it? People can't use the sauna if there are naked people in it."

"Well, they shouldn't be."

It ended there, disappointingly. The time I was hauled away in handcuffs by the MPs for being naked in the men's locker room would have been a great story for a chapter entitled "you can't make this shit up."

Though I was not impressed with most of the contractors, some were brilliant exceptions. One of the brightest among us was Sean Nelson, an impish redheaded kid who had grown up homeschooled in a Christian fundamentalist family but went on to college and postgraduate study in Liberal Arts in programs with no fixed curriculum and no grades. He was largely in charge of his own education, guided by the faculty. Sean's intellectual superiority and wit couldn't be dampened and he annoyed the management to no end.

Sean had an intellectual's openness to fresh ideas while simultaneously maintaining his own opinions which he was happy to share unbidden. One of his favorite classes was "Empire of Liberty," a class designed to be delivered as if by someone from a foreign culture who hates America and is intellectually prepared to defend that hatred. It is supposed to give the students exposure to the kind of attitudes they can expect when they start interrogating detainees for real, but also to develop some thought and capacity for argument. It is an interactive class in which the students are encouraged to argue with the instructor even if only hypothetically.

It was entertaining to see the occasional student who could not endure the anti-American sentiments spewing from one of our own instructors, forget that it was just a class, and call Sean a traitor and condemn him to the gallows if only he could. Unfortunately, some of the instructors couldn't stand how convincingly Sean presented the class either. One older, conservative gentleman, who considered himself a historian because he liked to read about history, took over the class and changed the delivery entirely. When I asked him why he changed it, he said he felt it was doing too much damage to the students when delivered unpatriotically. It might shake their faith in America.

It is not surprising that the contractor force would consist of large numbers of conservatives. The force is drawn from career military, often retirees, who derive their core identities from military tradition. But many contractors were also liberal-minded and disappointed in the direction the Bush-Cheney administration had taken the country. Many of my colleagues, independent of age, considered themselves open-minded or progressive if not unabashedly liberal. Their conservative colleagues certainly thought so. In 2006 we were losing badly in Iraq and the full scope of the invasion fiasco was still fresh. It was not the proudest of times to be an American.

I was nevertheless envious of my colleagues who had actually interrogated, whether tactically in Afghanistan and Iraq or strategically at Guantanamo. I never had a chance to use my skills and, now as a licensed doctor, never would. Although it is something I wouldn't relish doing, part of me really felt the need to have at least experienced the interrogation booth for real to deserve the attention of the students. Most of my instructors in 1975 had never interrogated either and my entire, brief active duty career had been pretty much pretending with other pretenders. But here I was, surrounded by experienced interrogators, many of them in their early twenties.

Not that the majority were stellar examples. Most of them at least admitted to never having obtained any information of value and only a few like Derek Rex even spoke the target language well enough to actually use it. The summer of 2006 was a time of soul-searching for the military in general and Military Intelligence in specific. It was for me as well. We were in the middle of a huge revision of the rules governing interrogation in the wake of the torture scandals. The fort was being picketed regularly by protestors demanding we stop teaching torture. Although we weren't teaching torture, we nevertheless all felt that revision was necessary and that gave us a sense that we were involved in something important.

As I settled into life in Sierra Vista and my job as a contract instructor at Ft. Huachuca, I got reacquainted with the desert, which is breathtakingly beautiful. From the sky to the terrain to the plants to the animals and insects, the desert is gripping in its wonder. It is both sensually captivating and terrifying. Everything in the desert is hostile. Frying, frigid, hard, sharp, pointy, poisonous, biting, stinging...

I took to hiking in the desert every weekend which provided me the opportunity to reassess my life. The desert was good for my soul. I was suffering the qualms of leaving my profession of medicine and being away from my family, especially when my little girls needed a father at home. Was I doing the right thing? Could I say at the end of every day that I had done something good, something to be proud of?

I was ambivalent about having a good-paying easy job with maximum benefits. I had never worked a 40-hour week before. Sixty hours is a light week for a doctor. I was making decent money and not paying for malpractice insurance or having to deal with billing medical insurance companies. My starting salary was $86,000 and the cost of living in Sierra Vista was still low. I had time for leisure and study. I wrote a few books. I could live comfortably for the first time in my life and still save most of my paycheck. This really helped my family. Building a private practice in America had been tough and the income was never steady. I struggled to clear $1000 a month in Hungary as a doctor. As a contractor I could stash away a couple of thousand every month even after all the bills were paid and be pretty sure my income would be the same or higher next month no matter what I did. My pay was even better than my pay had been at the University of Washington as a house staff physician. Almost three times as high, in fact.

The Army was in the process of revamping the way we did interrogation and before long it dawned on me that I might eventually be in a position to contribute to that effort. By the end of 2006 I was confident I understood thoroughly what was wrong with the way we trained intelligence professionals. Given the chance I was sure I could dramatically improve the instruction methods we were using. The threats the country faced in 2006 were quite different from those of the Cold War. The Geneva and Hague Conventions as well as the laws of warfare needed fundamental reconsideration. What to do about the detention center at Guantanamo was on everybody's mind.

Contractors were being used everywhere and huge salaries were being offered to work in combat zones. The laws of war offer protection to soldiers and innocent civilians caught up in conflicts, but contractors, although civilians, are not innocent if they take part in the fighting effort. Traditional laws governing warfare do not adequately address people who are neither soldiers nor non-combatants nor mercenaries in the traditional sense. Even though the main motive of the contractor is money, they are supporting the military of their own country, not some foreign power. Not usually.

I used a lot of my free time to take distance learning courses and become familiar with international law. I made contact with lawyers and organizations that were involving themselves in precisely these questions. Both the Army and the contracting companies subsidize education, so I embarked upon a doctorate in law. I eventually wrote my dissertation on trying detainees at Guantanamo using military tribunals. Although this was taking me farther and farther from my profession of medicine, it seemed to me the right course at the time.

In 2007 the military radically changed policy in Iraq, bringing General David Petraeus out of career exile and putting him in charge.[43] The previous policy of conquest by superior firepower was replaced with winning the hearts and minds of the people. I was greatly heartened by this decision. Petraeus's success while in command of the 101st Airborne in Iraq was due to his understanding of unconventional warfare,

43 Petraeus commanded the 101st Airborne in the 2003 invasion of Iraq and is credited with exceptional success in the Mosul area using counterinsurgency and nation-building policies that were neglected by other US commanders. Mosul collapsed after Petraeus left when troops were drawn down and the effective policies discontinued. Petraeus was assigned to Ft. Leavenworth, Kansas, where he continued to develop doctrine on effective counterinsurgency. The US continued to operate ineffectively in Iraq until the Bush administration finally faced the seriousness of our failing policies and brought Petraeus back to command in 2007.

precisely the bread-and-butter of what Special Forces was originally designed to do. This would have huge implications for the profession of intelligence collection.

Winning the hearts and minds would require our soldiers, and especially our intelligence professionals, to engage more closely with the citizens of the countries we invade. To be effective, they would have to know the languages and culture. Up until 2007, these concerns had been mere afterthoughts and easily ignored. "Heritage linguists" – American citizens who are native speakers of the languages we need – would be extremely valuable. The Army eventually created the MOS 09L returning to the policy of training and sustaining linguists as an independent specialty. Soon it would introduce a realistic incentive for soldiers in language-dependent MOSs to maintain their proficiency.

But institutional paranoia runs deep. One of the truly amazing ways the military defeats itself is in its policy of prohibiting native speakers of a language from working in their country of origin. This policy was expanded to prohibiting people who have spent a lot of time in some country and developed a keen understanding of the culture along with fluency in the language from working there. The reasoning is that they might develop conflicting attachments and relationships which would compromise their loyalty to the US or make them more vulnerable to blackmail and coercion to spy against America.

These are reasonable concerns which history has shown to be manageable. It may be true that foreign intelligence services have recruited and blackmailed people in this category, but this risk can be minimized by prudent counterintelligence measures. Moreover, putting native speakers to work in cultures they understand opens the opportunity to not only collect much better information but potentially deceive the adversary with disinformation. The best foreign intelligence services in the world operate this way and consider the risk acceptable. The more knowledge and skill a Russian agent has, the more time that agent is allowed to spend in the US. Our policy is the opposite.

The result is our legendary ignorance of foreign languages, cultures and countries in the presence of plenty. America is a land of immigrants. We have a vast treasure of representatives from every culture in the world consisting of people who have immigrated and become citizens by choice. When we should be the best at understanding the rest of the world, we bar the very talent we need and possess from working in the areas of their expertise.[44] Instead, we deploy soldiers who speak no languages and know nothing of the local cultures. They need translators and these translators are recruited from the local populace, a pool of talent the adversary has even better access to than we do. If you were an Al Qaeda or Taliban commander, you could not pray for a better situation than for the Americans to put your sources, and in some cases even your agents, right next to the very people who know what the American commander intends to do, what he knows and what he needs to know.

In other words, the Americans give you everything you need to defeat them and pay you to take it.

We are not unaware of this phenomenon. We saw it happening way back in Vietnam.[45] We knew the Viet Cong and North Vietnamese intelligence service had infiltrated our command to the highest tactical levels and saw the results over and over. It had to be the translators we

44 At this writing, the country is embroiled in hysteria over the question of Syrian refugees. All concern seems to be focused on the possibility of a few terrorists slipping through the screening process while the treasure trove of knowledge and skills these refugees bring is being completely ignored. The rabid paranoia further serves only to alienate Muslim and Arab Americans who would otherwise eagerly serve in the fight against extremism.

45 The Vietnamese were so aware of the necessity of infiltrating the command of the invaders, they began preparing young people for this work a full ten years before American military forces began to operate in Vietnam in 1965. They had endured invasion and occupation by the Chinese, the Japanese and most recently the French. In the 1950s they speculated that the Americans would probably be the next invaders they would have to deal with and began sending young students to the US to learn English and get degrees in areas like journalism that would one day put them in a position to gain the trust and dependence of the Americans. An example of this is told in "Perfect Spy: The Incredible Double Life of Pham Xuan An, Time Magazine Reporter and Vietnamese Communist Agent" by Larry Berman. I would also recommend any of the excellent books by John Plaster, particularly "SOG: The Secret Wars of America's Commandos in Vietnam."

relied on, but we never succeeded in eliminating the agents. This single phenomenon is one of the key reasons we lost in Vietnam despite overwhelming military superiority and consistent tactical victories. When they can speak our language and we can't speak theirs, it puts the enemy at a decisive advantage.

We saw it in the former republic of Yugoslavia as well when, time after time, we barely missed capturing Persons Indicted for War Crimes (PIFWCs). It often felt like they knew we were coming because, of course, they often did. At Eagle Base at Tuzla, Bosnia, we had over 900 foreign nationals including translators inside the wire and our own people were prohibited from going outside the base except on missions. We isolated ourselves and were completely dependent upon local talent for translation.

And now we still see this happening even after over a decade of struggle in Iraq and Afghanistan. Even knowing we would be in these countries for many years, we refused to train linguists and cultural subject matter experts, choosing instead to rely on the enemy to provide them. The greater irony is that these translators are almost always hired through contracting companies, Mission Essential Personnel – the last company I worked for – being one of the most prominent.

It only takes three years to learn a language to near native fluency. I saw it over and over while studying and teaching at a university in Hungary. Students from every country in the world would come to Hungary not speaking a word of the language (and it's a hard language!). They studied the language formally for a year and by the end of that year could use it comfortably. After two years even without study they were completely at home and after three years, many of them you could not tell from a native.

I had the opportunity once to ask the three-star general at the Pentagon in charge of language policy why we continued to waive the language requirement when we know how essential it is to success. His answer was that we cannot predict where we will be sending troops in the future and therefore cannot plan which languages we will need. I disagreed, of course. Our extended involvement in Arabic-speaking countries and in Afghanistan were highly predictable and even after we committed ourselves, we knew we would be there long enough to justify supporting language and culture training. It is clear we will be dealing with the Chinese and the Russians for decades to come, yet at this writing we do not award Foreign Language Proficiency Pay (FLPP) for Russian and bar Americans of Chinese descent from working in Chinese at the highest levels.[46]

After a few months at Huachuca in 2006, I felt I understood the profession of Human Intelligence Collector well enough to do it and to teach it. I understood the major elements that were crippling our efforts in HUMINT. The one thing I still lacked, however, was field experience. I needed to gain actual experience as a huminter if I were to ever hope to position myself to contribute to significant positive change.

The only realistic way to pay those dues was to re-enter the armed forces.

46 There are exceptions, of course. One can get FLPP for Russian if it is one's primary language, one is in a language-dependent MOS, and one is in a job where using that language is required. The bar to Chinese working in China can be overridden, but the process is daunting. Qualifying for a high level security clearance involves extensive interviews by Counterintelligence agents who are selected for their innate skepticism and steeped in a professional culture rich in paranoia and xenophobia, if not frank racism. CI agents who are not white, Christian, monolingual males must at least reflect the behaviors and attitudes of those who are in order to advance in the profession.

CHAPTER 5

I Rejoin the Reserves

I HAD OTHER reasons besides my lack of field experience in human intelligence collection for joining the Army again. Although I had my 20 Year Letter that guaranteed my retirement at E-9 when I reached age 60, my personnel file with my record of service was still missing. I wanted a hard copy of my military records in my hands so that if anything were lost again, I could verify my service. There was nothing I could do but request them from the IRR and wait. That approach had so far proven fruitless. Joining a reserve unit would allow me to both reconstruct my records and to get some experience relevant to my contractor job. I started to look around for a unit to join.

When I moved to Hungary in 2004 I explored the possibility of doing work as a reservist at the US Embassy in Budapest, but was told they didn't do that. I was given the name and contact information of a DIA (Defense Intelligence Agency) warrant officer, Mark Rosen,[47] who was in charge of filling vacant jobs at embassies with reservists. The office of the Defense Attaché employed military personnel and there were always openings ranging from a few weeks to a year. Unfortunately, Mr. Rosen had nothing for me. If I could find an opening myself, I was told, and find the money to fund it, and do all the paperwork myself, I might be able to get myself on orders somewhere, but I had no idea how to go about that. He took my name and résumé but it was clear I would have to find another way to get myself back in uniform.

Although I couldn't join a unit while living in Hungary, now that I lived in Arizona things were different. On Ft. Huachuca, there was a US Army

47 Not his real name.

Military Intelligence battalion – the 5-104th Bn (MI) – and as luck would have it, the Command Sergeant Major had just quit. Not retired. Not transferred. Just walked away without so much as even taking his stuff with him. That should have been a sign that all was not well, but I joined up anyway and accepted the position he had conveniently vacated.

Indeed, all was not well. I walked right into the middle of a virtual mutiny against the commander. They badly needed a Sergeant Major who had no history with the unit to stabilize the battalion until some serious changes could be made.

Eventually the commander was relieved and the executive officer (XO) took his place. The unit was in shambles, statistically in last place out of 25 training battalions under the 104th Division, headquartered in Vancouver, Washington. I liked the XO and we set about putting the "Fighting Fifth" back on track. We looked at the areas in which we were behind and set about to improve the BFRR stats (Battle-Focused Readiness Review statistics, pronounced "biffer stats").

The 5-104th was in the paradoxical position of having the highest number of qualified personnel for its mission out of the entire division while having the fewest available to actually work. Almost everyone in the 5-104th worked on Huachuca as contractors. That was their real military mission and the battalion was little more than a pool of talent to feed that mission. Indeed, the mission of the battalion was to train military intelligence instructors and their members were already doing that full time as civilians.

At my first drill – dramatically referred to as "battle assembly" – the commander wanted all personnel to assemble in dress uniform for inspection to make sure everyone's medals were worn correctly. I didn't even have a dress uniform and performed the inspection in a business suit and tie. What really struck me, however, was that a large number of unit members were not present and their section leaders didn't know where they were.

"Battalion! Atten-shun! Report!"

Each section leader saluted and reported "All present or accounted for."

I questioned each one. "Sergeant Cosgrove, are you sure all your people are here?"

"They should be."

"Who's missing?"

"Uh, Sergeant Weslan...Sergeant Johnson...one or two others, I guess."

"You just told me they were all present or accounted for."

"Well, they should be here."

"Did you call to find out what happened to them?"

"No. They're big boys. They're responsible for getting themselves here."

"And you're responsible for knowing where they are and making sure they get here."

"We don't usually do that. There's no way I can keep track of a dozen people who live all over the state."

After falling the battalion out to start the scheduled training, I had the section leaders stay behind for a little talk. I made sure they understood that I expected them to contact their people every month before drill and know exactly where they were and what they were doing. Whoever didn't feel they could perform this most basic duty of an NCO could move aside and I'd replace them. Attendance improved after that.

Not only did attendance improve, I discovered a few chronic problems that, if handled, would significantly improve morale and readiness. There were the usual problems with pay and personal issues. Some just found it difficult to show up and opted for making up drill by coming in during the week at their convenience. But a major issue was language training and sustainment. In any MI unit, a popular reason for joining was language training. I understood that mentality well and was sympathetic.

In September of 2006, the Army made a dramatic improvement to Foreign Language Proficiency Pay (FLPP, pronounced "flip pay"). Up until then, linguists in the reserves could only qualify for a maximum of $20 FLPP a month extra (prorated from the $150 available for Active

Duty service members) if they stayed qualified in their languages. From September on, the maximum pay per language went up to $400 a month and not prorated. What was more, a linguist could get pay for proficiency in multiple languages, up to a maximum of $1000 a month in addition to their paycheck.

An extra thousand dollars a month. Now that's real money!

Our linguists now had sufficient motivation to maintain proficiency and take the language test, which had to be done on their own initiative and unpaid time during the week. I immediately scheduled myself for enough tests to max out the FLPP and spread the word to my linguists.

The first obstacle I met was that a number of soldiers had taken and passed the test and submitted the paperwork but not gotten paid. The unit tech couldn't explain why Division wasn't processing the pay. I made a few calls up to the 104th Division headquarters, but even the Sergeant Major didn't know who was supposed to be processing language pay. He did a little looking around and found the NCO, who didn't know it was her responsibility.

When, after a month with no FLPP forthcoming, I called again. The Sergeant Major assured me she was working on it, but I suspected she was probably just confused and didn't want to admit it.

Since Vancouver was my home town, I decided to take a little trip home to visit family and friends and along the way pay Division HQ a visit. Processing language pay is easy and I knew exactly how to do it. The Sergeant Major wasn't in, but I stopped by to introduce myself to the admin NCO and helped her with this task.

This naturally ruffled a few feathers, but in the end I got my pay and was satisfied that Division would be able to process everyone's paperwork in a timely fashion from then on.

Unfortunately, language pay continued to fail. There was such a backlog that the poor admin sergeant was overwhelmed by what she felt was an additional duty and not a priority. In addition to my linguists who were owed back pay – some for years – there were 24 other battalions with the same problem and I had opened a real can of worms.

A thousand dollars of extra money a month is a huge motivation. It is also a huge negative motivator when earned but not paid. Anger swelled up and manifested itself in complaints to the Inspector General, who was swamped. He thought they might be able to get it sorted out in a few years. Not surprisingly, several of my disgruntled soldiers quit in disgust.

Although my struggle for language pay showed few results, our efforts to bring the battalion's statistics up went better. We had a list of our deficiencies from the last inspection to work on. The former commander and staff had created a training plan that would address all the deficits. There wasn't much motivation to do more than present a plan to higher headquarters that we were working on improving our statistics. It really didn't matter to most of us whether we were first in the 104th Division or last. We weren't going to deploy, at least not as a unit. Our job was right at Ft. Huachuca training MI soldiers.

Nevertheless, the problems didn't seem that hard to fix. Retention could be improved by giving the soldiers, most of whom were contractors, something their civilian jobs couldn't provide, like training and certification in military skills. Being certified in more than one MOS widened one's possibilities for contractor employment. Getting an extra thousand dollars a month for language pay was another powerful incentive to stay in. We could also minimize the inconvenience of attending weekend drills and provide greater flexibility to USAICS by allowing soldiers to make up drill days during the week to better support the regular classes that were being held.

Fitness was a big problem, but most of our soldiers wanted to lose weight and be more physically fit. All they needed, in my mind, was an effective fitness plan that was fun and easy to maintain.

Weapons qualification was another issue. Many of the soldiers just couldn't shoot straight and we didn't have the money for extra bullets in our budget a combat arms unit would have. But there was a gun range and several soldiers not only had privately owned weapons that were similar enough to our M-4 carbines and M-9 pistols but air guns that were close replicas as well. A few family picnics to the range with a class on shooting thrown in with no pressure to qualify would help the worst shooters.

We really needed to focus on the problem areas down to the level of the section leaders and individual soldiers. Without some proactive involvement, things wouldn't improve. Just taking the whole battalion to the range more often and running more battalion-wide fitness tests wouldn't do it. The battalion wasn't that big. It was actually more like a company-sized unit with less than a hundred personnel. Most of the members were doing satisfactorily in most areas. Having everybody do everything that was already mostly satisfactory was a waste of effort, so I adopted a policy of leaving soldiers alone who were already performing at the required level and pouring all my attention into the ones with problems.

I started meeting with individuals who had fitness and weight problems every day before or after work (remember that most of the unit members worked on Ft. Huachuca) and started something of a fitness club that was actually fun. I got the poor shooters out to the range with extra ammo, even tagging along with other units, and helping them individually shoot better. I got some help with getting soldiers into the schools they needed. By the end of the year, our battalion was number one in the Division, up from dead last.

Once the battalion was back on track, I set about trying to reconstruct my records for the third time in my career. It was slow going. We had only one trained and experienced AGR (Active Guard or Reserve) unit technician and he was overwhelmed with the whole mess. Eventually he found himself in the crosshairs of an inspection and got blamed for some of it, so rather than fix it, he quit. That left us with no one who knew how to get soldiers paid, cut orders, or do any of the things necessary to keep a unit running. We brought in some volunteers and higher headquarters sent an expert out on Temporary Duty (TDY) orders. I was able to construct a skeleton personnel file for myself with barely enough information to meet the basics. My official legitimate MOS was 18Z, Special Forces Operations Sergeant, and I wanted to keep it. But my duty position was 35Y, Counterintelligence/Human Intelligence Senior Sergeant. To qualify for 35Y, an NCO should have the prerequisite MOSs of 35M (Human Intelligence Collector) and 35L (Counterintelligence Agent). I had neither but nonetheless found myself awarded the 35Y.

I was teaching a course to 35M (Human Intelligence Collector) and 35F (Intelligence Analyst) students and thoroughly understood both MOSs. Nevertheless, I tried to get permission to audit those courses along with 35L, for my own education and to legitimize the prerequisites. Permission was denied. Sergeants major are not allowed even to audit those courses because it might intimidate both the students and the instructors. I had to settle for doing the correspondence courses instead.

It was frustrating. I paradoxically felt like a superhero as the only Special Forces qualified soldier in the battalion and a paper tiger as the only soldier who had never been to any of the current MI MOS-producing schools. In addition, I had never deployed in a Military Intelligence unit or job.[48]

My frustration was cut short by a message from Washington, DC.

---

48 In the interest of full disclosure, I had deployed many times with Special Forces as both an intelligence officer and NCO. I had also spent a year supervising an Open Source Intelligence Collection unit at Ft. Belvoir during the Iraq invasion. I had completed both the Special Forces Operations and Intelligence Course at Ft. Bragg and the Military Intelligence Officer Basic Course at Ft. Huachuca back in the early 1980s. I was also trained and certified in Information Operations, Counterterrorism and Operational Security, all of which share aspects of Intelligence. I worked as an intelligence analyst for the Counterdrug Taskforce in Washington State. In addition, I did field work as a civilian out of the refugee camps in Thailand in 1976 looking for American MIAs in Laos and smuggled Bibles from 1977-1979 (see "Detour: My Brief but Amusing Career as a Bible Smuggler" by Lloyd Sparks). But strictly speaking, I was not a graduate of the required courses for my job at the 5-104th MI Battalion.

CHAPTER 6

Baku

"DOES ANYBODY KNOW where Baku is?" I asked.

I had been at Huachuca about nine months when I opened my military email one morning and found orders for the US Embassy at Baku, Azerbaijan. I knew where Baku was, but the absurdity of receiving an embassy assignment out of a clear blue sky was too delicious not to share.

"You mean Bagram?" asked Sean.

"Or maybe Basra?" asked Derek.

"Or Bosnia?" suggested Don.

"Nope. Baku. As in the oil capital of the Caucasus on the Caspian Sea," I said.

As I've already related, more than a year earlier, while trying desperately to solve the retirement mess from Hungary, I talked to the Defense Attaché at the US Embassy in Budapest about the possibility of drilling as a reservist at the Embassy. He said they weren't really set up to do that (which wasn't true) but perhaps I could volunteer through the Defense Intelligence Agency's Reserve program run by Chief Warrant Officer Mark Rosen.

I had contacted Mr. Rosen expressing interest, but he responded without enthusiasm. I would have to find my own slot and work out the details myself. And there it lay dormant until March of 2007. Although the efforts of Mr. Rosen and his assistant Sergeant First Class Allen went nowhere, a much more proactive Air Force Tech Sergeant named Tom Miller[49] eventually came on the scene. Through a complicated set of steps, he managed to get me orders and help me through the bureaucratic maze of the Defense Intelligence Agency.

---

49 Not his real name.

The foul-ups were many and serious. I alerted my supervisors at Huachuca and my landlady to the impending deployment and promised to formally apply for military leave as soon as the orders came. The orders failed to materialize on the appointed date, so I moved out of my apartment and spent a pleasant few weeks with my mother in Battle Ground, Washington. The orders finally arrived on a Friday night, requiring me to report on the following Monday morning. The orders required me to arrange air transportation through a military transportation office, the nearest of which was three hours away by car at Ft. Lewis and closed for the weekend by then anyway. The orders required me to use a government credit card to pay for the ticket and my lodging. I had no government credit card and would have to buy a ticket for which I would not qualify for reimbursement if I wanted to get to the DIA building at Bolling Air Force Base on the East Coast by Monday morning.

When I arrived at the housing office at Bolling, there were no rooms available, so I would have to lodge at approved off post housing at my own expense, though eventually reimbursable. The hotel they assigned me was two states and a four-hour bus ride away. Rental car was not authorized. Even taking the earliest available bus got me in after 9:00 AM, too late to attend the scheduled orientation lectures.

As it turned out, that didn't matter anyway. No one in particular was expecting me, so when I showed up I had to wait while the guards tracked down someone willing to escort me onto the facilities. Arranging for my training and orientation to my job with DIA fell to my own imagination, so I did the best I could. I spent my few days there mostly trying to fix problems and figure out what my job would require.

It was surreal, showing up like a tourist with no one particularly interested in why I was there. Tom Miller helped me a lot with directing me to the people and offices that could get me what I needed, but I wasn't even too sure what my job would involve. Active duty personnel go through a whole formal course lasting several weeks to learn to do the job of Operations Coordinator (OPSCO) at an embassy and it's an important job. The OPSCO coordinates permission for US aircraft to fly over or land in the host country, and arranges everything for VIP visitors, who were often at the level of senator or general officer. The OPSCO works directly for the Defense Attaché whose office gathers and reports information of a military nature. Training in this job was not authorized for me as a reservist. I had to figure it out myself by talking to people who had done it before and then finding the systems I would be using and finding someone to show me how they worked.

Experience had already taught me not to deploy without at least $20,000 available either in the bank or in credit cards. Pay problems and getting reimbursed are so common as to be the rule rather than the exception. With this particular assignment, I incurred over $10,000 in unreimbursed expenses before receiving my first paycheck. But when the money started to flow, it came in a flood. I got E-9 pay, hundreds of dollars a month in FLPP, a very generous housing allowance, and per diem at over $200 a day. For my entire deployment, the government paid for my hotel, food and transportation, so I had almost no overhead.

Half way through the tour, the Army would decide unilaterally to cut our benefits to save money, and I don't blame them. I was making over $8000 a month and didn't even qualify for all the benefits available to Active Duty, like Special Duty Assignment Pay, shipping of household goods, language lessons and a stipend for dress uniforms appropriate for embassy duty. The Army cut our per diem in half, so I only got $100 a day. That the cut only applied to reservists and not to Active Duty was grossly unfair, but how could anyone in good conscience complain about getting *only* $100 a day extra? Even with substantially lower benefits and support to reservists, the job was still extremely lucrative. I came home with over $80,000 in the bank after expenses from that deployment and used it to buy a couple of apartments for my kids.

It was odd how so much that was available to Active Duty soldiers was withheld from reservists on active duty doing the same job. We got half the per diem despite needing it more. We did not qualify for the

Special Duty Assignment Pay the Active Duty soldiers did even though we were doing special duty and the Active Duty people were just doing their normal jobs. Orders were written as Permanent Change of Station (PSC) in order to save money by not paying us full per diem even though the assignment was clearly temporary. We didn't get money for moving expenses. Full medical and dental benefits were not available to us. We had to buy our own dress uniforms which were required for our embassy assignments at a cost close to $1000. Active Duty and embassy staff got free language lessons while reservists like myself actually working in linguist jobs had to pay for those lessons.

This is one reason why reservists and guardsmen make up two thirds of our deployed forces. We're cheaper.

I was sent to a relatively safe and stable embassy in Europe for on-the-job training before reporting to Baku, which is a hotbed of international intrigue and in the Russians' and Iranians' back yard. At that embassy in Europe, I finally got some real on-the-job experience collecting intelligence in the Office of the Defense Attaché. There were nine collectors working out of that office, not counting embassy staff and CIA who had their own assignments. Of the nine military collectors, I was the only one who spoke the local language. I quadrupled the reports out of that office despite being a junior trainee. When my boss, the Defense Attaché, found out I knew that language because I had spent a lot of time in that country, I was immediately removed and sent on to my official assignment in Baku. As noted previously, no one with close ties to a country is allowed to work in that country or even in a nation that borders that country. The list of countries I am technically not allowed to work in includes Taiwan, Thailand, Cambodia, Laos, Vietnam, Holland, Belgium, Germany, France, Hungary, Austria, Czech Republic, Slovakia, Ukraine, Romania, Serbia and Croatia.

But I was okay to collect intelligence in Azerbaijan. I had never been there and knew next to nothing of the language, culture or history. Perfect.

My time in Baku and environs was extremely interesting and I wish I could relate some of the details here.[50] Unfortunately, much of the work is classified and in any case not really central to the theme of my work as a contractor. I will say, though, that I encountered contractors doing almost every job in the embassy that government employees also do.

At one embassy I was tasked with overseeing a small remodeling project that involved a secure area. The contractors hired to do this work all had to have security clearances and could only live in housing approved by the embassy. The OPSCO of that embassy put them up in a very expensive hotel and the leader of the crew asked me whether I would intercede on their behalf to get something cheaper. They had made the request but been refused without explanation.

I found the OPSCO to be a very agreeable Air Force chief master sergeant, the equivalent of an Army sergeant major. I asked her about the housing for the contractors. The embassy had put me up at the most expensive hotel in Baku, but I didn't have to pay for it. The contractors had to pay for their housing out of their salaries and wanted to spend as little as possible in order to take home more to their families.

"Chief, the contractors asked me to request you allow them to move into a cheaper hotel. Would that be a problem?"

"I know. They already asked and I denied the request," she answered.

"What was the reason?" I asked.

"They just want to pocket the money. It's pure greed," she said.

"But there's no obstacle to them living somewhere else? No security issues?"

"No. I just hate to see contractors fleecing the government for all that money."

---

50 For an entertaining fictional story that draws from my time there, see "The Baku Boy Scouts" by Lloyd Sparks. I wrote the book as a gift to the Boy Scout troop I helped with as an assistant Scoutmaster. Yes, there really was a Boy Scout troop in Azerbaijan made up mostly of the children of ex-pats going to one of the international schools.

"But it wouldn't change the money the government is paying for contractors to let them live somewhere else. Keeping them in the expensive place doesn't save the taxpayers a penny," I pointed out.

The OPSCO eventually relented and allowed the contractors to move, but it illustrated a common theme one encounters as a contractor. The resentment that full time government and military employees hold toward contractors often spills over into actions that have no other purpose than to hurt the contractor out of pure spite.

Even though I was living in comparative luxury at the Radisson Blue in Baku, I decided to move after a few months. It was too conspicuous. If terrorists decided to attack – and there was one foiled attempt while I was there – bombing a spectacular hotel that housed rich foreign businessmen and government officials would be more likely than going after one low-level embassy employee in a small, cheap hotel.

I enjoyed embassy work and wondered why I had never come across the field of Foreign Affairs Officer earlier. I would have loved a job that involved living abroad and interacting with diplomats and officials from all over the world. I looked into it and into other related careers while there, but at my age, it was too late to start. Sigh…

As it was, at least I got to work abroad out of an embassy in several foreign languages. I also got exposure to a much wider spectrum of intelligence collection than I would have as a tactical interrogator in, say, Afghanistan. When my year was up, I no longer felt I lacked the necessary experience to teach the subject with authority at an Army school.

I was properly paid FLPP for my work in the embassy as a linguist, but in only one language. The Army wasn't paying for German or Russian and had no tests for the obscure Central Asian languages I had studied like Uzbek and Kazakh.[51] Officially my language was Bulgarian because it was

51 At the University of Washington in 1979 I did graduate work in International Studies with an emphasis on Russia and Central Asia. During that time, I had the opportunity to study Mongolian, Uzbek, Tatar and Kazakh along with the obligatory Russian language. Many of the languages of Central Asia are closely related to Turkish, so when MI students ask me about which language to learn, that's what I recommend. There are very few speakers of these strategically important languages and if you learn one, you can pick up any of the other 35 related languages easily.

the first language the Army taught me, but a linguist's primary language could be either the first one learned in the Army, a language he spoke when he enlisted, or the language of assignment. In Special Forces, a soldier's primary language was determined by the mission and I was on orders in my Special Forces MOS of 18Z.

On September 11, 2001, the intelligence services had, counting me, only three Uzbek linguists clearable to Top Secret.

CHAPTER 7

Transitions

WHEN I RETURNED to Arizona in 2008 after a year of doing real world intelligence collection in a very invigorating environment, I found some substantial changes had taken place. The 5-104th Battalion had been moved out from under the 104th Division into the 100th Division. We now fell under the 1st Brigade (MI) along with only four other training battalions. The organizational structure would be better and more efficient. There was a chance for a fresh start.

At Huachuca the government was beginning to implement tangible measures to wean the Army off of contract support. Contract positions were being replaced with government civilian employee (GS, or General Schedule) positions. Several of my colleagues were applying for government jobs which paid a lot less but offered security. The contract for my job had been taken over by Oberon Associates, so I found myself working for my third defense contracting company doing the same job in two years. Oberon was a good company with good benefits for those who managed to stay with the company for more than a year.

The promise of leaner times was approaching. The floods of government money for anything remotely military were drying up. We could see that our easy jobs with bloated paychecks wouldn't last forever. I was junior and, despite my civilian education and recent deployment in the MOS, was still not competitive. I had less than a year of actual experience as a contractor and no seniority in any company.

So when Raytheon contacted me to ask whether I was interested in the job of Site Lead at Ft. Devens, Massachusetts, I listened.

That Raytheon would even contact the employee of another company was yet another sign that things were changing. Up until then there existed an unspoken agreement between the competing companies not to poach each other's employees and not to negotiate salaries. There was enough business to go around and plenty of money. Now the money was drying up, competition for top people was beginning to show, especially with so many making the transition to government jobs. Technically, the refusal to negotiate salaries to find the best people for the lowest cost was something akin to price-fixing and probably illegal. With all of the companies agreeing not to budge on the salaries offered, the customer – ultimately the taxpayer – had no voice in the marketplace. But by 2008 this had begun to change.

I was already making almost $90,000 as a Senior Training and Development Specialist. Raytheon offered to hire me as a Consulting T&D Specialist for $96,000. I didn't want to move to Massachusetts and I had a good position as Command Sergeant Major at the 5-104th MI Battalion which added another $20,000 a year to my income. Winters were unpleasant in Massachusetts and the cost of living much higher. I held out for more money and the condition of finding me an E-9 slot near where I would live and work.

To my surprise, they met my salary requirements and found me a position as Director of Instruction Sergeant Major with the 6/98th MI Battalion right on Ft. Devens. As unpalatable as moving from sunny Arizona and away from my friends was, it was clear that now was the right time. I was also pleased to see that I could negotiate a better salary. Just one year previously I tried that when General Dynamics took over the Anteon contract and was told flatly that the companies would not bid against each other. This suggested that Raytheon might be beginning to consider rewarding performance with bonuses and raises, something that had never been available to at will employees before. I wanted a job that rewarded performance and this might be it.

By then I already had strong ideas about how military teaching should be done and how people should be managed. I was eager to show what I could do and Raytheon offered me that opportunity. The project I was to support was a 35M reclassification course, a course designed to convert soldiers with other MOSs to 35M, Human Intelligence Collector. It was being run by a very focused, hands-on leader, Colonel Ralph Thompson,[52] commanding officer of the 1st MI Brigade. The Brigade ran the school and its headquarters was located within a hundred miles of Ft. Devens. That wasn't ideal, but it was a lot closer than Vancouver, Washington. I would have the ear of the commander both as the Site Lead and the Director of Instruction Sergeant Major at the local battalion.

General Martin Dempsey[53] had just assumed command of TRADOC (Training and Doctrine Command) and would be the catalyst to drastically revise the way the Army trains soldiers. He would soon draft the Army Learning Concept 2015 which outlined the new training philosophy to which the Army intended to convert by the year 2015. It was a radical departure from the military's pedagogical teaching style to one more suited to training adults using collaborative, student-centered learning methods. This doctrine was farsighted and long overdue. It was exciting and demonstrated that at least at senior leadership levels, the Army was ready to make important changes in the way they train soldiers.

I enrolled in a Master's in Education program with a major in Adult and Postsecondary Education. Training was now my profession and I intended to take every measure possible to become the best I could at it. I chose "Training Human Intelligence Collectors using Collaborative, Student-Centered Learning Techniques" for my thesis.

---

52 Not his real name.

53 General Martin Dempsey, Chairman of the Joint Chiefs of Staff from October 1, 2011 until September 25, 2015, was then Commander of TRADOC, the US Army Training and Doctrine Command. He is credited with creating the Army Learning Concept 2015 which revolutionized the way the Army trains and sustains the education of its soldiers. Although it does nothing to improve the quality and professionalism of Army trainers, it does pave the way for shifting the authoritarian role of trainer to that of a guide or facilitator, which is much more effective when training adults.

CHAPTER 8

Site Lead

"DELIVER THE PRODUCT and make the customer happy," Chuck Atkins told me, answering my question about my job description. "I can give you an eight-page detailed description of the job if you want, but it all boils down to this: Deliver the product and make the customer happy."

The US Army Intelligence Center and School at Ft. Huachuca is the Mecca of Army Military Intelligence. It has the advantages of economy of scale and close control of everything that happens there. But Huachuca and Sierra Vista were getting too big. With size comes bureaucracy and with bureaucracy comes a loss of agility. A recent study had found that the populations of Huachuca and Sierra Vista had already outstripped the ability of the water table to support the community. This along with the impending budget cuts was forcing training units such as the 100th Division to consider closer and cheaper places to train soldiers. One of the biggest expenses for units is the cost of travel and Arizona is a long way away from the East Coast.

Several smaller military schools existed that taught the same courses run by USAICS. They were generally easier to access and closer to the sponsoring unit than Arizona. It was often simpler and cheaper to send soldiers to these smaller schools and that was what was on Chuck's mind when he partnered with Colonel Thompson to staff the school at Devens. They would create a 10 ½ week 35M course run out of surplus buildings that taught the same material as the 16-week course at Huachuca for less money. If this pilot project were successful, Chuck hoped to duplicate it at four or five other schools. It would be a real money-maker for Raytheon by being a money-saver for the US Army.

Before accepting, I took a two-week annual training (AT) assignment at the military intelligence school at Devens as an instructor. I flew out in November, 2008, to get acquainted with what would be my new home and new workplace. The experience was decidedly mixed.

Fort Devens was a mere shadow of its former self. Once the home of the Army Security Agency, some chemical warfare labs, and the 10th Special Forces Group, most of the post had been sold off to commercial enterprises. It had virtually none of the core facilities a normal Army post would have like a medical clinic, a post office, a housing office, a PX (Post Exchange, i.e. store), a commissary (i.e. grocery store), a gas station, a Class Six (i.e. liquor store), a bank, etc. All of those were situated on land that no longer belonged to the fort. Inside the fence were a few buildings, a small shoppette, a dining facility (DIFAC, formerly known as mess hall or chow hall), some Spartan barracks, a motor pool and a supply building. There were a few buildings that housed the reserve units there, including a Marine Corps unit and my new battalion, the 6/98th MI.

As for it's potential as a school, Devens had none. There were no proper classrooms, no lecture halls, no library nor places to study. What served as classrooms were old warehouse buildings. The instructors' desks, if they had them at all, were in nooks off the hallway. The booths for interrogation training were too small and poorly ventilated. The recording equipment was entirely inadequate. Commercial Internet connections were unreliable and the military system didn't work at all. There were no fax machines, no reliable copiers and no printers.

The command structure was confusing. There was a colonel in charge of the post but he didn't control the schools, of which there were several. Mine would be the MI school, or more precisely, the 35M Reclassification Course.

My AT started out with some difficulty. Neither off post lodging nor rental car was authorized, even for a sergeant major. There was no one to meet me at the airport when I arrived, so I took the commuter train to Ayer, the town next to Devens. When I arrived at Ayer, I called Gary

Fraske, the Course Manager who called the supply NCO who dispatched the driver who had missed me at the airport.

The supply sergeant issued me some bedding and the key to a perfectly dismal room I might have to share with someone else over the next two weeks. He oriented me to the location of the chow hall and the shoppette which, miraculously, sold wine and beer. Ft. Devens had a no drinking policy, but that applied only to the students. There was a small exercise room which, judging from the level of fitness apparent in the full time military stationed there, went unused. There was an equally unused half-mile track. Most of what a soldier would need had to be found off post. A bank, a Dunkin Donuts, a dry cleaner, a gas station, a pizza take-out, a restaurant and a hotel were located in front of the main gate.

Devens had no housing office. Soldiers and employees who moved to Devens were on their own for finding a place to live. There wasn't so much as a bulletin board. The Ft. Devens website hadn't been updated in years. As a result, most newcomers found themselves renting places that weren't suitable and locked in to a one-year lease. As soon as practical, I took a hike down the road back into Ayer to see what might be available for me and my family when we moved there. Although there were several houses advertising rooms to let, I couldn't find the landlords. No one came to the doors when I knocked; no one picked up the phone when I called. Just as well, I supposed. My kids would have hated living there. Ayer – at least the part of Ayer I could walk to – seemed Appalachian. It was run down, poverty-stricken and without much in the way of infrastructure. Unfortunately, with no car to drive I couldn't see any more of the area than what was within walking distance. There were in fact some quite pleasant places not far from the areas visible to me on foot.

The next morning, I reported to Gary who assigned me to Sergeant Noelle Dattilo. They didn't need me to do anything in particular, so I just hung out with Noelle as she explained to me how the school ran. Soon I was helping grade papers.

Although Devens was completely unsuitable as a school, it was tiny and out of the way, which is usually a good thing. Despite the long list of inadequacies, Devens had one essential quality that outweighed all the negative: it was a pleasant place to work. The Course Manager and the supply sergeant had gone out of their way to come in after hours to take care of me and get me settled in. Gary was a competent and easy-going leader who trusted his staff and earned their loyalty. Noelle was uncommonly bright, an expert in Islam, Middle Eastern culture and history as well as a speaker of Arabic. The other instructors I met were either only teaching temporarily as part of their AT or at the end of their Active Duty orders and getting ready for their next job, whatever and where ever that might be.

I decided to accept Chuck's offer. My job in Arizona couldn't last forever and this was definitely a promotion. I had hated Arizona when I first moved there but grew to love it. Perhaps Massachusetts would be the same. So I said my tearful goodbyes to my dear friends in Arizona, knowing we'd inevitably cross paths again, and flew out just before Christmas to meet my family in Boston for that year's variation of the holidays.

With our family being scattered all over the globe, our Christmas tradition had become finding a new city to spend the holidays in every year. It has yielded some memorable experiences, usually due to the necessity of travelling around the world during winter holidays. This year, 2008, we managed to assemble in Boston during a blizzard. The family all arrived safely and got to the hotel before I did. The plan was that I would fly in last to pick up the rental van and then pick them up at the hotel from where we would drive the hour or so to Devens.

The family made it fine from Hungary and Hawaii and my arrival from Tucson was on schedule. But things started going wrong with the pick-up of the rental van. The GPS didn't work and I was completely unfamiliar with Boston. Worse, I didn't know the GPS didn't work until it led me astray a couple of times, running me through the same toll booth over and over until I was almost out of cash.

After more than an hour trying to get my bearings in Boston in the blizzard, I finally flagged a taxi and offered to pay the fare if he would lead me to the hotel, which he did. As it happened, there were two hotels by that name in Boston and he led me to the wrong one. I had to follow yet another taxi to the right one. By the time I met my tired but happy family, I was exhausted. My nerves were frazzled and I was so tired I just wanted to sleep. But we still had to find our way out of Boston and all the way to Devens and I was at a complete loss as to how to proceed. The GPS didn't work, I didn't have an adequate map and didn't know where I was anyway. Plus, it was snowing like mad.

That's when my kids sprang into action with their phones, plotting the route, finding stores along the way and even talking to customer service reps to find out if the stores had what they wanted. I can't even describe the relief I felt at having all that anxiety of getting us to Devens lifted from my shoulders. We drove the two hours to the hotel outside the front gate and the time flew, even with the stops for a little shopping.

The SpringHill Suites Marriott outside the gate at Devens is decent and we made it our base for the Christmas festivities which included shopping, skiing, shopping, eating, shopping, sleeping, shopping and marathon Family Guy episodes, all watched from a single king size bed. And then more shopping.

Work started the first week of January, 2009, but there were no classes until the second week. I made my way to the building that would be my workplace for the foreseeable future and found the Course Manager, Sergeant First Class Rodney Miner.[54]

Miner was a folksy, down-to-earth kind of guy who would be at home in the country, maybe farming or fixing cars. He had a brilliant and beautiful wife who outranked him by one stripe and they were deeply in love. They planned to retire together after this assignment and move far away to a home in the Midwest. He was very happy to see me.

Things had apparently not gotten off to a smooth start. He found the administrative requirements of the job tedious and taxing. His new military staff was not as reliable as he had hoped and in any case, mostly new

54 Not his real name.

to the job. This project would depend heavily on contractors and leaving control of the civilian teaching staff to me was something he was more than happy to do. Rod had not been the first choice for the job, but he needed an assignment to complete his final year before retirement and, despite the misgivings of the commander, got the job.

I introduced myself to the other eleven contractors as Rod showed me around. The first one I met was Roger Cohen[55] who impressed me as a very serious and stable individual with plenty of deployment experience. He and I became friends and remain so to this day. Everyone has their quirks and Roger had a miniature working medieval catapult on his desk. Roger was also most comfortable dressing in the unofficial uniform of the contractor: boots, cargo pants, T-shirt, safari vest and baseball cap. The official dress code required dress shoes, slacks, collared shirt and tie when teaching or company polo when not. He would grudgingly conform to the shirt and tie requirement, but I never did manage to get him to change his boots and cargo pants. I was sympathetic. Credibility with the students is important and the contractor uniform gave him more of that than a suit and tie ever would.

The next person I met was Jack Donohue.[56] Jack was a former Airborne Ranger and had served in the 2/75th Ranger Battalion, a unit I had trained with often when at Ft. Lewis. Jack was the only combat veteran among us who had actually fought as an infantryman. My first hint of his combat arms background was that whenever there was nothing scheduled for him to do, he would find a quiet place to take a nap. He was living in Rhode Island and commuting a couple of hours each way, which left him chronically sleep deprived. Policy does not allow for napping at the workplace and, although I personally didn't have a problem with people taking a snooze in their down time, I had to enforce that rule with Jack the first day.

55 Not his real name.

56 Not his real name.

Next, I met Charlie Foster.[57] Charlie was a fellow sergeant major and had served in MI support with the 10th Special Forces at Devens long ago. He was a Russian speaker and had a great deal of experience teaching 35M subjects both at Huachuca and at Devens. Charlie has a dour personality and his most salient trait is his pessimism. Once you get to know him, however, you discover a very competent and compassionate instructor. I wondered why I had been given the Consultant position and appointed Site Lead when Charlie was much more highly qualified than I was. Apparently he had applied for the job but Colonel Thompson denied him that position even while approving his hire as an instructor, which left him disappointed.

Three contractors – Pascal Valdez, Dick Hammond and Elliott Warner[58]– were sharing a rented apartment with Roger Cohen not far away which became infamous as a bachelor pad. The four of them could not have been more different. Roger mostly kept to himself after work. Pascal tended to oversleep and come to work unshaven and disheveled in a Navy pea coat and black wool watch cap which he wore indoors until I made him stop. Hammond was a big, garrulous, fun-loving guy who was easy to like. Elliott was a well-groomed black guy who wore tailored clothing and carried himself with an air of immense personal dignity.

Alice Davis[59] was a functionally single mom going through some frightening problems with a husband who did scary things when he went off his medication. In addition, we had a married couple – Philip and Jennifer Twain[60] – who had a delightful small child who had been conceived in a combat zone in Iraq. Philip, Jenn and Alice were part of the "Korean Mafia" – a group of contractors who had all shared the same experience of going to DLI for Korean language and getting deployed to Iraq when the Army in its wisdom deployed all the Korean linguists to Iraq and then sent the Arabic linguists to Korea to make up the deficit. Over the next

57 Not his real name.

58 Not their real names.

59 Not her real name.

60 Not their real names.

couple of years several more Korean linguists would enter and leave the instructor staff, including Ken Frickle, Denny Gee[61] and Kirsten Howard.[62] The Korean Mafia served to remind me every day of how bad the Army was at managing linguists, or personnel in general, for that matter.

Butch Mudslinger and Norm McMahan,[63] both family men, rounded out the complement of contractors. Noelle Dattilo was teaching in uniform and, when her orders finished, Raytheon hired her when a vacancy came open. Norm was prior service Navy and had interrogated at Guantanamo. A devoted family man and father, his singular purpose was to do a good job, work regular hours, keep his position for as long as possible and not make waves. Butch was a devoted family man as well, prior service Army and a Russian linguist. But he had a biting wit. While Norm kept his head down, Butch could not resist voicing an opinion when absurdities popped up, which was often. He was colorful and funny and one of the main reasons I looked forward to coming to work every day. Norm, Butch and Philip wound up sharing office space for most of the four years we were together and a visit to their cube never failed to entertain. Philip and Norm were home beer brewers. Philip loved soccer and opera. Butch had a penchant for punishing endurance events like Tough Mudder.[64]

In all, it was a colorful and competent crew. My first goal was to make sure the Raytheon staff could cover any task the customer needed. This meant making sure all the contractors could do all the jobs in the Statement of Work (SOW). This is both easy and hard. It was easy in that we were teaching a 35M course, a course all the contractors had been through to qualify them to teach. In addition, virtually all of them had taught this course before and most of them many times.

---

61 Not his real name.

62 Not her real name.

63 Not their real names. Anthony Davidson gave permission to use his real name, but approved the use of "Butch Mudslinger" as a pseudonym, to which I happily complied.

64 Tough Mudder is a 10 to 12-mile obstacle race with mud run events designed by some former British Special Forces soldiers.

But it was hard in that the Army's policy demanded that every instructor have some documentation that they had 1) been through the course, 2) audited the course again, 3) been an Assistant Instructor (AI) with every class, 4) taught every class as a Primary Instructor (PI) under supervision, and 5) been signed off as a fully qualified instructor for that course. None of us had all that documentation even though all of us had been teaching as PIs for some time. I was tempted to just ignore the requirement, but the Quality Assurance (QA) team would be coming out from Huachuca in the summer to inspect the documentation.

Technically, the certification requirement wasn't my problem. It wasn't my job to certify the instructors, just to employ the talent we have to best advantage. But I was strongly invested in the success of this project. If it failed, it wouldn't matter whose fault it was. I'd be out of a job with a blot on my résumé. I took the matter up with Sergeant Major Donna Ortiz, who was the Director of Instruction Sergeant Major at the 1st Brigade. She would be responsible for ensuring the 35M course passed the QA inspection.

Donna had written and provided me with an excellent little unofficial manual entitled "Don't Teach Without It." This handbook explained a lot of how things should work but revealed some ambiguities as well. There was no detailed explanation of how instructors verified that they had actually met any of the requirements between getting the MOS and teaching a class. A supervisor could just sign off on it.

I had the instructors each provide me a list of all of the classes they had taught so far. This yielded a table of who could teach what and we had all the classes covered in depth. Asking about the classes also revealed the preferences each instructor had for the work we would do. For instance, Noelle liked teaching History of Islam, Muslim Culture and all things pertaining to the Middle East. She and Butch Mudslinger gravitated toward grading papers. Roger Cohen thrived on Source Operations. Charlie Foster was particularly good as a small group leader.

This made it easy to compose the initial schedule. I just put the schedule up on the wall and invited the instructors to sign up for the classes they wanted to teach. The few that were left I simply assigned in roster order. This worked well and made it possible to gradually spread the experience around a little so that the instructors could expand their repertoire. The ultimate goal was for every contractor to be able to do everything in the SOW. Since I was going to sign off on everybody in my capacity as supervisor, I needed to feel confident we could actually deliver when it came down to it.

Another issue I soon encountered was that some instructors wanted to teach regular hours while others liked taking evening and weekend hours in order to stack their schedule to get three or four days off in a row whenever possible. This was an added blessing and softened the unpleasant task of assigning people hours they didn't like. Later, when we began to get overtime, I ran into a similar situation where some instructors preferred to work as little as possible to spend more time with their families while other wanted to work as much as possible to make more money.

I was confident that by the summer of 2009 we would have sufficient depth in talent and experience to assure the customer that there wasn't a job they needed doing Raytheon couldn't do and there wasn't a thing that could go wrong we couldn't fix. The customer could sit back and watch things run smoothly no matter how inept or inexperienced the military staff might be.

This story could have ended here with "and they lived happily ever after" but there would have been no book, and since you are at this moment reading this book, you can be assured that we never got to "happily ever after."

CHAPTER 9

The Mike Course

GARY FRASKE HAD been replaced by Sergeant First Class Rod Miner against all advice. No one had endorsed Rod and several, including Fraske, had warned that he wasn't suited to the job. Nevertheless, he got the position and was put on orders for a year. He was a nice enough fellow but was clearly not up to the task of managing something as complicated as a school, even an Army school. He had no vision for making the school a place of excellence, and if he had, would not have had the faintest idea how to bring that about. All he really understood was the time clock. Everybody should be at work on time and not leave until the end of the work day. In the interim, they should all be busy doing...something.

Miner believed, not unreasonably, that one of his duties was to make sure everybody in his charge was at work on time and doing something. Anything. It's a long and ancient tradition born of the belief that idle hands are the devil's workshop and that if not kept busy, soldiers will relax and enjoy themselves. Which is bad, for some reason.

The sounds of happy soldiers and contractors grated on Rod. He loved a quiet workspace and was known to shush grown adults for talking loud enough to be heard. If he could hear the sounds of a happy workplace from the office he and I shared, he'd grumble, "Listen to that, Lloyd! You know they're just screwin' off."

What they should be doing instead of "screwin' off" was unclear. We were in Phase 1 which is all lecture. Since there was nothing to do but warm a seat, he felt a gnawing anxiety that something was wrong and, because he was in charge, he should find something for us to do.

It didn't take long for Rod to piss everybody off to the point of threatening to quit. When class kicked off in the second week of January, 2009, the teaching schedule Rod had put together included almost no contractors. He scheduled the military instructors in as much as he could, but no contractors. I was aware that some of the military instructors had little teaching experience and I was all in favor of them getting it, but I was puzzled why Rod didn't ask me for contractor support right away. Why put the whole load on a bunch of new military instructors when he had a dozen seasoned Raytheon professionals to put to work?

Though there was no reason for it, he insisted that all instructors when not instructing or preparing to instruct seat themselves in the back of the classroom and observe. This met with no one's approval, but all grudgingly obliged. This lasted less than two hours until the hubbub of a practical exercise in the classroom rose to audibility in our office two doors away. Rod went in and shushed everybody.

After class all eleven contract instructors filed in to see me and inform me that either this treatment stops right now or they walk. Elliott led the delegation.

Elliott was particularly sensitive to any action that impugned his professionalism. He carried himself with dignity and expressed himself clearly and forcefully.

"I will not be spoken to in that manner," he informed me.

"How did Sergeant Miner speak to you?" I asked.

"I will not be addressed by my first name before the students. I will not be spoken down to. I will not be shushed like an unruly child. I will be treated as a professional."

"Did Miner shush you?"

The others quickly confirmed that Rod had indeed shushed them in the classroom.

Philip quickly explained that they had been doing a practical exercise with the students and there was a lot of discussion going on as a result. It wasn't as if they had been talking out of place during a lecture.

I diplomatically informed Rod that if he had any problems with the contractors to let me handle it for him. He was initially grateful that I would take that imaginary load off his shoulders. But when he sensed no urgency on the part of idle contractors to look busy, the feeling that something must be wrong welled up inside him again.

The workforce was idle. He must do something, but he didn't know what.

He took to examining the hours billed by each individual contractor. We of course uniformly entered forty hours per week on our timecards no matter what we did, but Rod was under the mistaken impression that we could only bill for hours actually spent teaching.

"Look at this, Lloyd!" he said, looking at Jenn Twain's timecard. "She billed for forty hours this week and I know *for a fact* she didn't teach more than six."

Rod not only felt it was fraud, but reasoned that he could save the government money by minimizing use of the contractors. This, of course, is nonsense. The government bought forty hours per contractor per week no matter how the customer used them. It didn't matter to Raytheon whether we spent forty hours teaching or forty hours sitting in a chair reading a book.

Raytheon did care about a few things, however. It insisted the contractors be on site for all forty hours billed. The company and the customer insisted that the contractors not nap on site, even during their lunch break. Raytheon insisted that all contractors do their timecards at the end of every work day. And it insisted that all labor performed be strictly within the Statement of Work. No cleaning floors or shoveling snow. No working unpaid overtime. Strict adherence to the SOW was necessary to avoid the appearance of providing added uncharged benefits, which could be construed as unfair competition. Working one minute over forty hours a week or cleaning a lavatory, no matter how well intentioned, could potentially cost Raytheon the contract.

It made for some uncomfortable experiences when the military instructors were required to work overtime (without extra pay) and do extra duty. It could look to the inexperienced eye like the contractors were lazy, unwilling to pitch in and help, or even unpatriotic. That sentiment would repeatedly rear its ugly head.

I had to balance customer satisfaction with protecting my contractors from abuse. Rod certainly had the right to demand that all the contractors sit at the back of the classroom eight hours a day and not teach, even if it was stupid. But he did not have the right to discipline civilians, even if they deserved it. Though my contractors were on the average better than the military instructors, not all of them were the cream of the crop. Most had had some deployment experience in the field they were teaching. Some had interrogated at Guantanamo and some had deployed to Iraq or Afghanistan. Few had done anything significant and most hadn't done well or if they did, it was prior to 2007 when policy governing intelligence collection changed radically. But all were competent instructors and, if managed properly, were well capable of doing the job for which they were hired. There was no need to make life harder for them just to maintain an appearance they were not idle.

One of the people Rod angered beyond what wisdom would condone was Jack Donohue. Jack, as I mentioned, was an ex-Airborne Ranger who had served in the 2nd Airborne Ranger Battalion and fought in Afghanistan. Jack was also a bit unstable, clearly a victim of PTSD and drank too much. His personal life was not in order and he struggled to meet the requirements of being a stable employee, even as a contractor.

In addition to being caught napping over lunch, Jack was suspected of downloading unauthorized programs onto a government computer and playing video games when he had nothing else to do. I don't really have a problem with any of that except that it's all against the rules. Miner pressed it to the point of threatening Jack. I told Rod to let me handle it, but his personal animosity toward Jack overcame his better judgment and he attempted on several occasions to sneak up on Jack and catch him in some unlawful online activity.

Sneaking up on an Airborne Ranger with PTSD is never a good idea. When Jack suggested to me that a knife across the windpipe might be what Miner needed, I started to seriously think about getting Jack some professional help for anger management.

I consulted with Fred Prince, my direct supervisor at Raytheon Chuck had put in charge of our project. He was most directly responsible for hiring and firing and I relied on Fred for advice on matters that might require action beyond my authority. I was pretty sure Jack would not actually threaten Miner, let alone carry out such a threat, but "pretty sure" isn't good enough when a life may be at stake. Fred advised watching Jack closely, which I was already doing, and keeping him informed. Although we both felt responsible for protecting the rights of Raytheon employees, that did not extend to killing customers.

Jack was a casual instructor, a sloppy dresser, and often used profanity while teaching. But that only endeared him to the students. He had real combat experience in the Rangers and that carried a lot of credibility. He had a way of making what they were learning real. Many of our students, far more than the instructor staff, had deployed in combat units before coming to be reclassified in what was after all a less dangerous job in Military Intelligence.

Unfortunately, Jack's standing did not improve as time went on. He began to upset the other contractors by taking too much time away from work for personal reasons. Anyone is allowed to use PTO (Personal Time Off) for any reason of their choosing provided it doesn't hinder the mission, but only three months into the project, Jack was already almost out of PTO. He had bought a boat with the insane paychecks contractors got in those days and was spending a lot of time doing boat-related activities.

Roger Cohen finally had it with Jack and told him off, calling him a slacker. Jack lost his temper and quit. I tried to calm him down and persuade him to wait until the next day, but he didn't. Of course, the next day he regretted it and tried to call Raytheon to undo the decision, but it was too late. Anyway, Chuck thought it best to replace Jack and if we didn't do it now, we'd have to do it later.

So Jack was dismissed before he could kill Rod or anyone else. Last I heard, he was in jail in Rhode Island, just another damaged veteran who fell through the porous cracks of the VA.

That left us down one employee. Although that wouldn't have any significant impact on our ability to support the customer, we wouldn't be able to bill for the entire contract until we found a replacement for Jack. Raytheon is a world-class, for-profit company. At full capacity, our twelve-contractor project generated something around $150,000 in billable services each month. Somebody at Raytheon, I'm sure, would notice the 8% drop in income and wonder what had happened. As relieved as I was that this problem had found a solution by itself, I was nevertheless unhappy that Roger had precipitated it. He wasn't apologetic. "It needed saying," he said.

Actually, it didn't need saying. Jack's difficulties were known to all, including Jack. You can't solve problems by just telling people off or firing difficult people. It's much better to work with what you have, correct the problems if possible and if not possible, transition smoothly to a replacement.

One of the things I like best about Raytheon is its personnel development policy. It focuses on correcting problems and developing quality employees rather than confrontational discipline. When a problem arises, the manager takes the employee aside privately and states the problem. Then he asks how the employee sees the problem and listens. This gets both people off on the same foot, agreeing on the problem and allowing a solution to be worked out satisfactory to both. I used that technique dozens of times while Site Lead and never got past the stating the problem part. The employee always acknowledged the problem and produced a solution. Only once did I ever have to advance to submitting a written reprimand for an employee's record and even that situation solved itself to everyone's satisfaction without anyone getting fired.

The problem with Raytheon's policy, if you can even call it a problem, is that because there is no public humiliation, coworkers do not know what actions have been taken to handle misbehavior. In Jack's case, every problem had been handled in accordance with Raytheon's policy, but neither Cohen nor Miner nor anyone else was allowed to see it. Roger wanted Jack punished for napping at the job site, for taking too much time off, or maybe for just being irritating. When you stripped away the veneer, the underlying motive was simple personal animosity. Jack just pissed Roger off. In point of fact, all of Jack's improper actions had been corrected quietly and without public shaming. Roger decided on his own to deliver some public shaming and the result was one less teammate to share the work load along with the loss of thousands of dollars to Raytheon, the company that paid our salaries.

Colonel Thompson had sold the Army on the idea of a cheaper 35M course at Ft. Devens. This project would succeed only if we could produce more MOS-qualified soldiers for less money than they did at Huachuca. He intended to deliver by cramming 16 weeks of training into ten and a half by scheduling ten-hour days and six-day weeks. We'd work long hours, evenings, weekends and holidays. This left little room to adjust when things went wrong. Winters in Massachusetts are brutal and there is rarely a month between November and April with no school closures due to snow storms. With the entire instructor cadre living off post, this virtually guaranteed having to reschedule classes both due to school closure and instructors being unable to get to work.

The Miners lived farther out than most but usually managed to get in to work on time despite the weather. Rod was rather proud of the fact that he and his wife had survived nine consecutive days without power the year before I arrived. If he could do that, then there was no excuse for anyone to be late to work. People should just plan on the bad weather, invest in snow tires, buy an emergency generator and get up earlier. I had a Jeep and kept a snow shovel in it, which got regular use, and was never late for work. But I also lived only 15 minutes away from the job site.

Living in rented apartments made the option of buying a backup power generator moot. Getting up earlier when it snows doesn't really help if the roads aren't plowed. Neither does it unclog the freeway when there is an accident. Or make your kid well when she's sick. No matter how well prepared one is, one cannot be ready for every contingency, so I learned to always have a couple of back up plans so that no single instructor would be indispensable.

One of the delicate aspects of managing contractors is that you have to keep your eye on everybody without them feeling like someone is looking over their shoulders. You have to build trust but you still have to monitor their performance. This required some judicious time management. Our training schedule was ten hours a day, six days a week, but I only had forty hours a week to keep an eye on everybody. Since it is expressly illegal to put in unpaid time, I had to identify key points at which I could monitor the most important activities and still not exceed my own weekly time limit.

I made a point of making the rounds to the entire staff every day around 3:30 to make sure people didn't forget to do their timecards, were getting their personal issues taken care of, and were prepared for tomorrow. I made sure everybody knew what the plan was for the next day and Plan B if something went wrong. I arrived at work early enough every morning to ensure that everything was ready to go and implement Plan B (and even on two occasions Plan C) if a problem arose.

In the two years I was Site Lead for Raytheon, we never failed to deliver a single hour of scheduled instruction.

Because of the inadequacy of Devens as a schoolhouse, I initially had to find creative, if not exactly kosher, solutions to problems that had the potential for stopping the project. We had no reliable Internet connections through the Army system, which we were technically required to use. We couldn't consistently do our timecards every day on the Army system and had no company IT support. I bought a portable wireless device and allowed contractors to bring in their personal laptops or just use mine to do timecards. We also had no fax, copier or printer, so I bought an inexpensive machine and brought it in everyday to meet that need. Raytheon had no official presence on Ft. Devens, no office, and no secure company communication system. We had no address at which to receive mail or store records, supplies and equipment. I took out a private post office box and found a desk with lockable drawers.

None of this complied with regulations or the contractual obligations of the military to supply us with the necessary support. But it was either this or stop the project and blame it on the customer. A fundamental truth of working as a contractor is that the customer will forgive minor breaches of the contract if it helps the project succeed. On the other hand, it is possible to slavishly adhere to every word of the contract and still fail. If the mission fails, along with it goes the contract. Failure is almost always the customer's fault, but you must never point that out. Not if you want more work in the future.

Along with the developing drama surrounding Jack, Miner was not doing so well in the spring of 2009 either. The job of Course Manager involved meeting the requirements of no fewer than four separate chains of command. It required doing a mountain of paperwork and Rod did not read or write well. His wife, however, who was a master sergeant in the same unit, was quite at home with the bureaucratic requirements of Rod's job and came in regularly to help him out.

Rod had found the Pearl of Great Price – a wife who adored him. They ate their lunches together every day and spent most nights at home by themselves playing board games. Love is a marvelous thing – not merely blind, but deaf, dumb and paraplegic. They had plans to retire later that year, move to their dream home in a small Midwest town on the prairie, and to live out the rest of their lives playing board games together in the evenings.

Unfortunately, both the Brigade and the 80th TTC had a problem with Master Sergeant Miner helping Sergeant First Class Miner. She was on orders to support another project and shouldn't be working at the 35M course. It wasn't her MOS either, so she couldn't be allowed to help even if the commander had been willing. Rod clearly could not do his job without help, so by the end of March, a council was held of the principal managers of the course to decide what to do about the Course Manager.

I sadly recommended that Rod be relieved. The contractors would not be sorry to see him go, but the relevant piece was that he clearly was not up to the requirements of the job. Master Sergeant Mike Bass, the Contracting Officer's Representative (COR, also called TOR, Technical Oversight Representative), spoke up to plead that some other job be found for Rod so he could run out the last days of his orders and qualify for retirement. After all, he had given 20 years of honorable service to his country, regardless of his failure at this most recent assignment. We should not forget that. We found a job for him as assistant to the NCOIC (the NCO in charge) of the schoolhouse where his duties would be nominal and there wouldn't be much, if anything, at which he could fail.

I, of all people, am sympathetic with finding ways for soldiers nearing retirement to achieve it. I had certainly been through the wringer myself. But intentionally creating a position for someone that produces nothing of value while maximizing expense to the taxpayer irritates me. A more honest thing to do would be to just let him stay home with full pay, but as I said before, in the Army, appearances are everything.

Over the early months of 2009, I also settled in to my position as battalion Director of Instruction Sergeant Major. This position entailed much less responsibility than I had anticipated. The Brigade Director of Instruction Sergeant Major, Donna Ortiz, was directly tasked with ensuring that the schoolhouse met the requirements of instruction. Donna was very knowledgeable and initially did most of the work necessary to ensure that we passed inspections when the Quality Assurance teams came out from USAICS.

Donna's biggest problem was that she lived far away and had a civilian job that prevented her from actually being present on Devens most of the time. She couldn't exert any direct control over the Course Manager, so that task fell to the TOR, Mike Bass. Mike was more available, but did not like being the go-to guy for problems originating from the Course Manager. The Course Manager was supervised by Brigade personnel who were too far away to do it well.

My position did, however, allow me access to the 6/98th Battalion's members when we needed extra instructors. This proved to be a real advantage to the schoolhouse. In order to deliver the product and make the customer happy, it was necessary to anticipate the customer's needs. Because half of my contractors were also reservists and the course had scheduled instruction every Saturday, we were often short of instructors on drill weekends. I could fill the anticipated deficit with my own reservists with the added bonus of getting them platform time as instructors. This synergy between my battalion and the schoolhouse worked out well for everybody.

My initial experience as the Battalion Sergeant Major in Massachusetts got off to a much smoother start than my previous one in Arizona. We had a decent commander, Lieutenant Colonel Rook, whom everyone loved. He was flexible, showed common sense and was not averse to good ideas. But his BFRR stats were low, partly due to the same reasons I encountered at Huachuca. We handled those problems in the same manner, focusing on fitness and weapons qualification while following up with individual problems. Unlike the 5-104th, we had competent unit techs and most of the battalion members did not work on post in jobs that distracted from their military responsibilities. We also enjoyed a great deal of flexibility in allowing unit members to make up missed drills by filling in at the schoolhouse. By the end of the year, Colonel Rook was singled out for praise by Brigadier General Patricia Heritsch, commander of the 100th Division, for bringing his battalion up from last place out of 25 battalions to first, edging out the 5-104th.

The 1st Brigade inherited my battalion's FLPP problems and one of the first things I did in 2009 was to contact one of the Brigade unit technicians, Steve Kilmartin, to ensure that it got the proper attention. Mr.

Kilmartin was cordial and assured me that he'd take care of it right away, which I took to mean right away.

My mistake.

With Miner gone, the job of Course Manager fell to the next ranking instructor, a cocky little NCO, Staff Sergeant Thompson[65] (no relation to Colonel Thompson). She was a competent squad leader and the job wasn't that hard, but no one had prepared her for having to suddenly jump into the driver's seat and run the entire course by herself. Sergeant Major Ortiz lived a hundred miles away and Master Sergeant Bass came around infrequently.

I say the job isn't that hard because if you have a cadre of instructors who have taught the course before all you really have to do is make a schedule of classes and fill it in with names. The course practically runs itself. The hard part is the paperwork that comes with it imposed from above. And the number of people and offices that fall into the category of "above" is vast. Reports have to be filed, counselling performed, evaluations completed and tasks assigned. There is a long list of items subject to inspection which Quality Assurance will indeed inspect regularly. Most of that paperwork is redundant, unnecessary and only there to meet some bureaucratic requirement, but if the requirements are not met, inspections are failed and careers are damaged. Regardless of whether the school is running and cranking out trained soldiers, if the paperwork isn't in order, commanders suffer and tend to pass the suffering on downstream. Sergeant Thompson was under the gun and did her level best to keep things flowing and classes continued run smoothly enough.

Until her replacement showed up.

The course is supposed to be run by an NCO in the grade of E-7 or 8. For some reason, neither officers nor sergeants major are allowed to be course managers. I long ago stopped trying to find reasons for the existence of insane regulations. With Sergeant Thompson struggling and no suitable candidate immediately available, I offered to take a two stripe

---

65 Not her real name.

cut in grade to run the course for Colonel Thompson but he balked. The Site Lead position was crucial. Who would replace me?

I suggested Charlie Foster. Charlie was still a sergeant major in my battalion but without portfolio. He didn't have any particular duties, but he had been in the battalion for many years and knew the unit inside and out. He was an excellent instructor and well qualified.

Donna Ortiz told me Colonel Thompson would not consider Charlie as Site Lead, end of story. The Colonel hand-picked everyone who would serve on this project and did not want Charlie in charge. Charlie could be a bit of a wet blanket, but was a very conscientious and reliable man, especially when students were involved. There is great value to having a colleague who can spot problems early and Charlie had raised pessimism to an art form. He wore his "curmudgeon" title with pride and I was sure no one at all would object to his replacing me temporarily.

Indeed, one of my major concerns initially was getting the project to run without me being physically present. By April, when everybody was comfortable with their new jobs, I began appointing deputies to take my place when I was gone. There were conferences and meetings to attend as well as my own time off, so my absence was something we had to deal with. From time to time someone else would have to make sure timecards got done and that people were prepared to do their assigned tasks. But whenever I left, even for a day or two, I was called every day by my deputy, whoever it might be, to solve problems and make decisions that really did not need to be handled by the Site Lead. Whenever the success of a project depends on a single individual, it's wrong.

There was another thorny issue. The Site Lead position doesn't pay extra for the extra work. The Site Lead is expected to teach just as many hours as everybody else in addition to doing the timecards and arranging the work schedule. My position as Consulting Training and Development Specialist did pay more, but did not specify Site Lead duties. As long as no one got any extra money for the extra work, there was no incentive to take over the extra responsibilities that come with Site Lead.

So I was pretty much restricted to my job as civilian Site Lead and not in a good position to exert any authority on the military side either as Course Manager or Director of Instruction. In any case, being both the military and the civilian manager would raise questions of conflicts of interest and the lines of authority were already blurred enough.

CHAPTER 10

Triple Start

In April Colonel Thompson announced that there would be a surge coming in the summer. We would be getting three times the number of students we had been expecting in order to support a push General Petraeus was planning in Afghanistan. All summer vacations were cancelled. We would all be working this project along with twelve additional temporary contractors. Our new Course Manager would be Captain Jordan Smith.[66]

Why Colonel Thompson had chosen Smith was unclear. For one thing, he was a newly promoted captain, so an exception had to be made to policy. I knew Smith when he was a junior officer in the 5-104th. He was intelligent and a quick thinker. Too quick, actually. He was prone to making snap decisions without fully considering the consequences. Smith's brain worked so fast that he didn't even know what he was thinking until he heard it come out of his mouth. This made for some amusement when he would say something that didn't make sense, realize it when he heard it but, having said it, go on to defend it rather than retract his statement.

Smith also had a very long résumé for a young man. He had a list of previous assignments that was pages long. He worked for a company that was marketing software to the military. Despite not meeting the standard requirements for Course Manager, he nevertheless brought a wealth of knowledge and experience to the assignment.

One of his first decisions as Course Manager was to rearrange the workspace. He wanted the contractors and military instructors working side by side. One team, one fight. He ordered the desks be rearranged. It took several days to uproot people from the workspaces they had

66 Not his real name.

grown accustomed to next to people they liked into new desks next to strangers. Smith had also failed to consider that not all the desks had Internet hookups, so many of the staff were suddenly paralyzed until IT (Information Technology, i.e. the guys who maintain the computers and communications systems) could set up some new drops.

This got him off on the wrong foot almost immediately. Not only were people unhappy with the new seating, we invested a week of unnecessary labor into fixing things that weren't broken to achieve a state of temporary paralysis.

Smith pointed out that the Ft. Devens IT people were responsible for ensuring all of our desks had working hook-ups, and he was right. It wasn't his fault the facilities did not meet standard. But his actions were perceived as taking something that used to work and turning it into something that didn't.

To add to the initial discontent, he decided to establish an obligatory, all hands staff meeting Monday mornings at 7:30. When on the first morning a few instructors came in a few minutes late, Smith demanded of me that all late contractors be counselled in writing and that the counsellings be on his desk by close of business. And as punishment, next Monday the meeting would start at 7:00. If people continued to show up late, he would keep moving the starting time back by half-hour increments until everybody showed up on time. Butch Mudslinger summed it up:

> "So if we show up at 7:30 you'll make us show up at 7:00. If we show up at 7:00, you'll make us show up at 7:30."

I informed Smith that Raytheon's disciplinary policy is private and no one outside of Raytheon is allowed to see whatever disciplinary measures are taken with one of their employees. He would have to settle for my assurance it would be taken care of in accordance with Raytheon's policy. He objected that this was insubordination and he would not stand for it. What's more, he wanted Mudslinger singled out for special counselling, whatever that meant.

At this point, one of the reservists there on temporary orders, Staff Sergeant Raymond Gosling,[67] inserted himself into the process. I knew Gosling from the 5-104th at Huachuca. He received very little attention from me because he met all the requirements important to the BFRR stats. He was a reliable soldier but showed no initiative nor potential for leadership. He claimed to have managed of over 70 contractors at Ft. Huachuca and informed Smith that he could in fact do whatever he wanted with the contractors. They work for him. He could have anyone fired at any time for any reason and should do so if they didn't comply.

Smith might have taken that course except that the next Monday, he was late himself, which generated a slew of jokes about him writing himself up. In addition to the ill will the early Monday morning staff meeting generated, it also threw a wrench in the schedule. Because the contractors can only work forty hours a week, the extra meeting time made it necessary to subtract time from the teaching schedule. Since most classes are two to four hours in length, even the half hour meeting time meant we couldn't schedule a contractor to teach a four-hour class for which he would only be available for three and a half hours. The price of the half-hour meeting was a loss of up to four hours of contractor availability.

Smith began taking Gosling way too seriously and started threatening to fire people right at a time when we needed every able body. Tensions rose. I had to take the situation up with Fred Prince, who explained to Smith and Gosling that military people not only cannot discipline contractors, they can't even schedule the individual contractors. The Site Lead schedules the contractors, period. He must refer all problems with contractors to the Site Lead and be content with that.

One of my favorite contractors was Jennifer Twain. She and I were the only instructors with actual academic degrees and certifications in the field of education. She and her husband Philip were both working on this Raytheon project and were two of the best we had. They had met in Korean language school and were sent along with all the other Korean

67 Not his real name.

linguists to Iraq early in the war. In a romance fit for a novel, she and Philip married and conceived their son in a war zone. Neither had been fully supportive of the Bush administration's justification for going to war. The absurd act of sending Korean linguists to Iraq and Arabic linguists to Korea demonstrated to them the folly of trusting the Army with their careers, so they both got out after one enlistment and went to work as contractors.

Jenn was given the responsibility of managing the classified material we had on site. Smith, who should have known better, decided to work on some classified material at his desk. He asked Jenn to bring him something out of the safe and Jenn objected.

"I'm pretty sure you can't do that," she said. "Your office isn't a secure site."

Smith had indeed been working on classified material in a place that had no guarded access and was visible to the road through the window and buildings across the street. Realizing his error, he became defensive and let loose a tirade of all the reasons the classified material was in no danger of compromise at his desk. Jenn wouldn't budge.

He took out a red cover sheet marked "Classified SECRET" and slamming it down on the laptop said, "There! Are you happy now?"

Jenn just walked away shaking her head.

"I want her counselled," he told me. "I will not tolerate insubordination!"

"Let me handle it," I told him. "Meanwhile, why don't you work on the classified material in a more controlled area?"

To my astonishment, he began typing out an email to me – though I was sitting in the desk next to him – "Surely, Dr. Sparks, you are not suggesting that it is acceptable for an employee of Raytheon to disobey a direct order when Raytheon works for the Army, this project, and me as commander." He went on for several paragraphs, ignoring my attempts to talk to him.

"Sir, I'm right here. Just say what you want to say."

Jenn was in no mood to deal with Smith's childish behavior and the chance that he might commit a security violation that implicated her was the last straw. She quit to go work elsewhere until leadership changed hands. I tried to talk her out of it; she was one of our best employees. "Just call me after he's gone," she said. "I'll think about it."

The contractors were my responsibility, but Smith had to manage the military instructors. These were reservists who were on orders which varied in length. Some were on for a few weeks while others had managed to get consecutive orders for several years. Their skill sets varied widely. Sergeants Dole, Marlin and Johnson[68] had been around for years and knew the job thoroughly. Sergeant Wilma Galena,[69] by contrast, had just come on with almost no experience at all. As Smith learned the job, he began to uncover the pile of deficiencies left by Miner.

These had been passed off to Sergeant Thompson, who had neither the knowledge nor resources to correct them. Smith was initially inclined to be understanding with Thompson, but we would soon be inspected by QA and he would have to shoulder responsibility for the state of the unit. He decided instead to counsel Thompson, documenting the deficiencies he inherited from her.

Sergeant Thompson came to me almost in tears and showed me the counselling statement Smith wanted her to sign. It was uncompromising and carried an accusatory tone. Anyone reading it would assume she had deliberately shirked her duties. She was angry and felt she was being grossly mistreated but didn't know what to do about the counselling. It would reflect badly on her and the extenuating circumstances of her performance went unmentioned. She had drafted a response that was both defensive and angry in tone, accusing Smith of personal bias.

I felt she deserved better treatment than this but couldn't inject myself into the matter. I was neither in her chain of command as Sergeant Major nor as civilian Site Lead and Smith hadn't done anything wrong. I advised her against submitting the response she had drafted. Its tone would not generate sympathy from anyone who might read it later. I suggested that

68 Not their real names.

69 Not her real name.

she simply non-concur and write "Captain Smith is in no mental state to counsel soldiers. I will respond when he regains control of himself."

This infuriated Smith and delighted Thompson. She thanked me profusely for the advice and left the course when her orders ran out never to return. I believe she eventually took an Active Duty position in a combat zone and was much happier.

Meanwhile I began receiving résumés from Raytheon to submit to Colonel Thompson for his approval as temporary instructors. As Raytheon's consulting representative, I was tasked with ensuring all of the applicants met the basic requirements for the job. Technically, the customer is not supposed to see the names on the résumés, only the applicant's qualifications, which should be the sole basis for hiring. Personal identifying data along with any information hinting at gender, race or religion is excluded by law. But the contractor world of MI instructors is very incestuous. Many of the contractors, myself included, were also members of the reserves and well known to MI commanders. Contractors often go back and forth between contract jobs and jobs on military orders. Colonel Thompson ordered me to send the complete résumés directly to him and cc no one on the email. He wanted to make sure no "trouble makers" got hired; there were certain individuals he would not consider for hire no matter how well qualified.

This is a reasonable concern and I was sympathetic. A commander should be allowed to hand-pick people for important assignments. But it was also expressly illegal. I struggled with how to support the commander without breaking the law. Trouble makers can be excluded from employment as long as one documents the trouble they have made. But I didn't have a long enough history with either Raytheon or the 1st Brigade to do that. I took my concerns up with Chuck who told me to just do what the commander asked, so I complied.

As it turned out, Colonel Thompson accepted all of the qualified applicants, so no one was subject to an illegal rejection. This time, anyway. By June I had a roster of twelve temporary contractors to round out the twelve permanent employees we already had.

The Triple Start was going to be way more difficult than we anticipated. We did not have enough space, so we had to find vacant buildings on Ft. Devens we could use as classrooms. We would not have enough booths and would have to rig something up to get us through Phase 2. I worked with Smith and two other contractors, Norm and Elliott, to try to work out the schedule, but it just wouldn't fit. There was a bottleneck at Phase 2 starting on August 10 when we would not have enough instructors to manage all the scheduled training. Colonel Thompson came around to see how the preparations were going and I expressed my concerns over our inability to staff the schedule. He assured me it would work; I just needed to try harder. Smith assured him we'd get it done as well.

Because Smith worked for a company that developed software for the military, he was quite proficient in the most up-to-date technology and in planning corporate projects. Smith decided we would do the whole schedule on Microsoft Project, which is an excellent program for this kind of thing. It allows multiple workers to contribute simultaneously and can get a lot of coordinated work done quickly from multiple work stations. Unfortunately, Smith was the only one who had MS Project on his laptop and we were not authorized to download it onto any other machines. In addition, no one but Smith knew how to use that software. So we found ourselves in the ridiculous position of having to pass around Smith's private laptop for each of us to do our share of the work. As a result, our planning team worked even slower than if only one person were doing it.

Finally, the day before we had to submit the schedule, Smith told me to enter the names – any names – into the schedule and we'd deconflict them later. He would submit it as a "working draft" and not the final schedule. Elliott Warner flat out refused to be a part of it.

"I've seen this all before," he said. "Somehow the working copy will become the approved copy and when the whole thing fails, we'll get the blame."

And eventually that's what almost happened. Poor Smith had to stay up all night creating a fully manned schedule that couldn't possibly work to get it to Colonel Thompson the next day.

As the new contractors began arriving for the Triple Start, things got off to a rough start. First, there was almost no time for settling in and orientation. Lodging was hard to find. I had just purchased a home and took in some of the temporary contractors. The boys at the bachelor pad also took in a few of the temps, as did Sergeants Dole and Marlin, two of the military instructors on full-time orders. The new staff had no place else to go.

There was much grumbling by the married contractors about having to cancel their summer vacations with their families. And there was bad blood between some of the temps and the staff, particularly with Gosling.

I knew Raymond Gosling from the 5-104th but not well. Because he was a competent soldier who had all his requirements up to date, I never had to focus any attention on him. I knew that he, like so many of us reservists at Huachuca, was a contractor. Gosling claimed to have managed dozens of contractors at Huachuca, but in fact he was only responsible for taking attendance at a major project on the fort and earned the enmity of many a contractor for reporting them late. Gosling was not well liked and welcomed any opportunity to make his personal enemies as miserable as possible. The effect on morale was not good. "I have no problem with being the bad guy," he informed me.

Neither do I, but that's not the first role one should employ when trying to get cooperation.

Our project had a large amount of money dedicated to supporting infrastructure, so Colonel Thompson was looking for ways to use it. The money would have been best used on overtime for contractors, but that wasn't allowed. Smith was lobbying hard for the Army to buy over $700,000 worth of laptops and software from his company. He insisted that the platform his company produced would be adopted Army-wide and was already in use in Iraq and Afghanistan. The soldiers would be best served by having it available at Devens to train on. The Army was using more than a dozen software programs to support intelligence gathering and analysis. Smith's looked promising but no one could say with certainty whether it would eventually be adopted.

Besides that, we were training collectors, not analysts. There was good reason to employ the kind of software the students would eventually use when deployed abroad, but there was no requirement in the Program of Instruction to train people on those systems and no time to squeeze it in. In addition, we did not have the qualified instructors to even teach it.

Colonel Thompson signed off on it anyway and we spent three quarters of a million dollars on laptops and software we would never use.

In addition, it was decided to buy some huge, high definition monitors for the classrooms and a high tech white board. These were equally useless because the classrooms were small enough we didn't need monitors and no one knew how to use the elegant features of the white board. We needed what we couldn't buy at Devens: more classroom and booth space.

Still, we got by. But August 10 loomed. I warned all my staff to be prepared to change course at a moment's notice, to come in expecting to do one thing and at the last minute be asked to do something else. Be flexible and do the best you can. Try to stay professional and positive. The schedule was so full that even Smith and I, the two people in charge, would be teaching full time and unavailable to attend to the duties of management. It would be utter chaos.

Then a personal tragedy struck. My wife's mother passed away. There was no way I could stay on the job and flew immediately to Hawaii where my wife and kids were enjoying what until then had been a delightful vacation. The process was draining in every way, as one can imagine, and I returned to Devens a week later on the 8th of August jet lagged and exhausted.

First priority was the schedule. When Phase 2 kicked off, who was scheduled to do what and where? I knew it was going to be chaotic but I wasn't prepared for the degree of absurdity that faced us. To meet the requirements of the Program of Instruction for three classes running parallel, Smith had scheduled the contractors in for almost 60 hours a week each, 20 unpaid hours over the allowed limit. There were many cases of instructors scheduled to be two places at once, classes scheduled to meet in rooms already scheduled for other classes, and absolutely no reserve in case somebody got sick or left. There was no time off and even he and I were scheduled to instruct the whole time, leaving no time for our real job of supervising everyone else. If things didn't run perfectly, there would be no way to correct the problems and the schedule had an abundance of problems built right into it.

Smith knew that he couldn't make a contractor work one minute over the forty hours stipulated in the contract. He knew, or should have known, that contractors can't even volunteer to work for free. If any of that happened, he could go to jail along with his commander. Any contractor involved in violating the Statement of Work would be fired and Raytheon would lose the contract and probably be fined and barred from bidding on other contracts in the future. When I confronted him with the 60 hours, he told me the contractors would have to work for free. We are at war and everybody is expected to go the extra mile. The soldiers do. Why should the contractors have it easy? One team, one fight.

Equally disturbing, Smith hadn't even published the schedule. The day before the chaos was to begin, no one even knew what they'd be teaching, when they'd be teaching it or where. I showed him some of the inconsistencies and asked him to allow me to deconflict the schedule and he acquiesced. He could see that even with the contractors working extra hours, it still wasn't going to work. If what I presented still didn't work, I could accept the blame.

That night I redid the entire schedule, limiting the contractors to forty hours per week each, fixed the conflicting locations by merging some classes together, albeit out of sequence, and double booked only the assistant instructors. They could be two places at once because they are really only backup. The primary instructors could push their own PowerPoint buttons.

It was still chaos and we didn't even come close to delivering all the required material, but most of the students passed. More than usual, in fact. It illustrated an important fact, that the instructors really don't matter much anyway. Highly motivated students pretty much teach themselves and do best when the instructors interfere as little as possible.

We also had a student population that knew they would soon be going to Afghanistan to participate in the surge. On top of being reservists who had deployed before, they were motivated to learn as much as they could. They deployed soon after graduation and made us proud.

Churning out a large number of huminters in record time and within budget put us in the spotlight. Colonel Thompson caught the attention of some people very high up at the Pentagon. Whatever corners he had cut and rules he had broken were forgiven and forgotten in the light of the fact that he had delivered the crucial intelligence collectors needed for Petraeus's surge and under budget.

I'm sure the Colonel must have known how close we had come to disaster. Even a cursory glance at the schedule Smith had given him would have revealed serious flaws. But he might have noticed less had Smith not complained to both the Colonel and my Raytheon boss regarding my "insubordination." Fred was quick to reassure me that I had done the right thing and contractors can't be insubordinate to someone they do not work for. I got high marks for saving that project and was rated "Far Exceeds Expectations" on my evaluation for 2009, my first year as Site Lead.

Jordan Smith wasn't stupid. Far from it. He was highly intelligent and knew a lot about IT and the field of intelligence collection and analysis. He simply lacked maturity and the skills to lead effectively. He took himself too seriously, frequently making himself an object of ridicule, which bruised his ego. His résumé revealed that he had been involved in a surprisingly large number of intelligence projects for a variety of agencies for someone so young. It also suggested that he might not have been welcome to stay very long at most of them.

Smith griped and complained about how the contractors had tried to sabotage the program right up to the end. He filed memoranda that fell on deaf ears and didn't manage, even with Gosling's encouragement, to get anyone fired. He was dismissed in the usual way: Smith was given an Army Commendation Medal and sent away to be someone else's problem, adding yet another brief assignment to his lengthy résumé.

As for Colonel Thompson, he narrowly missed going to jail. In personally insisting on vetting all the instructors he had overstepped his legal authority. Some thought he was showing favoritism, particularly in his selection of Captain Smith, who as an officer, was not supposed to be filling an NCO position. Thompson approved a huge purchase of questionable equipment from a company Smith represented.

To add to the list of grievances, three excellent instructors – Sergeants Dole, Marlin and Johnson– were all REFRADed (i.e. taken off orders and Returned From Active Duty) for failing height and weight standards. In the wake of our success, the Army authorized the expansion of our program. Raytheon could hire several more permanent contractors. I saw Dole, Marlin and Johnson as perfect candidates for some of those positions. They knew the job and were excellent performers. Since they already lived in the area, they didn't have to move to accept the jobs. Civilians do not have to meet the fitness standards of the Army, so failing height and weight and the AFPT were irrelevant. But Colonel Thompson did not want military instructors failing their fitness tests and after discharge turning around and getting their old jobs back as contractors for twice the money and half the work. He told Raytheon not to hire them. He was investigated, but the investigation was quietly dropped after his project succeeded in supplying Petraeus's surge with the crucial HUMINT collectors.

Our success was viewed as a mixed blessing by the contractors. On the one hand, we had saved the day and ensured Raytheon a favored position for the foreseeable future. On the other hand, we greatly feared we had set a bad precedent in managing the Triple Start pop-up. They might just do that to us again next year, ruining vacations and throwing family lives once more into chaos.

CHAPTER 11

The Devens Project Expands

When Smith left in September of 2009, we were presented with a new Course Manager, Master Sergeant Tracey Bovey.[70] She was a mother hen sort and we all breathed a sigh of relief thinking maybe we could get back to a pleasant work environment. Sadly, it was not to be. As pleasant as Bovey was, she had no backbone. She dreaded confrontation and one could never be certain she would follow through on matters agreed to. Her opinion was the same as whoever she talked to most recently, and that person often turned out to be Sergeant Gosling.

Gosling had mellowed a bit. He came to us originally on military orders, intending to return to his contractor job at Huachuca. Unfortunately for him, when his company was forced to downsize by cutting the least important people, his position was eliminated and he no longer had a job to go back to. Now all he had were temporary military orders to keep food on the table and was a little more cautious about calling for firing people. But he still maintained that the Course Manager could schedule the contractors directly without going through the Site Lead.

Fred Prince was a hands-on leader and visited us frequently at Devens. We sat down with Bovey and Gosling to educate them specifically on why they as members of the military must never attempt to direct civilians. They could go to jail if they do. They must deal with the company through the Site Lead. Bovey seemed to understand and readily agreed. Gosling put up a fight, claiming the military directed civilians all the time at Huachuca. Fred explained that it was either not what it appeared or it wasn't legal, but in any case, all scheduling of contractors

70 Not her real name.

must be done by the Site Lead, Dr. Sparks. Gosling finally acquiesced but without enthusiasm.

Raytheon had other reasons for sending Fred out as well. This project had succeeded beyond their most optimistic projections. We had not only delivered 100% of the product, we were singly responsible for the success of the Triple Start. We had turned out almost twice as many trained soldiers for the year as projected and kept it under budget. Our cost per soldier was substantially lower than Huachuca's. The Pentagon was now inclined to send more money Colonel Thompson's way and he had plans for expansion.

Big plans.

We would soon be starting up three more courses and bringing on up to forty Raytheon contractors at Ft. Devens. In addition to the 35M course, we would be adding 35L (Counterintelligence Agent Course, or CIAC), 35F (Intelligence Analyst) and 35G (Geospacial Intelligence Imagery Analyst). We referred to them in short hand as Mike, Lima, Foxtrot and Golf, with the 35G coming out comically as the "golf course." Even better, Chuck had big plans for duplicating what we had done at no fewer than five Army schools throughout the country. I hoped to help him pilot each of those projects once the Army approved. All we needed to do was continue to succeed.

Success was easy. The courses were already written and our instructor staff experienced and capable. All the Course Managers had to do was sit back and watch it flow. We had demonstrated that Raytheon could run every aspect of the courses and handle even the most daunting of challenges. Fred praised me to the Division commander, General Heritsch, saying we owed the success of the project to Dr. Sparks. The good graces of General Heritsch would pay dividends later.

If true, it wasn't comforting. I was confident I could handle the expansion at Devens, but if I began moving around the country with Fred to start up new schools elsewhere, the Devens staff would have to learn to function more autonomously. I was still getting calls to settle petty problems and not seeing enough initiative on the part of the staff to make decisions and move forward without seeking permission first.

Getting the staff trained to handle every aspect of the project had been my priority over the first year; my second year's priority would be training leadership capable of managing the project in my absence.

Finding enough temporary space for the Triple Start had been difficult. Where would we put four times as many students and instructors for permanent programs? It wasn't difficult keeping on top of everything at one course in one building, but soon we would be facing four courses in four different locations.

Fred was also investing more time in training me on Raytheon systems. Because Raytheon had no official presence on Ft. Devens – no office, no facilities, and no equipment – receiving mail and supplies was unreliable. I created temporary fixes by buying equipment out of pocket and opening a private box at the local post office, but we really needed a reliable way to get our mail and supplies without circumventing the system.

In having no space that belonged to us exclusively, I had no way to safeguard proprietary material. All our personnel files and information were open to anyone inclined to snoop around. The locked desk drawers were not secure. We had no place to meet in private and no secure communications. Everything we did through the Internet went through government servers or through our privately owned systems when the government server didn't work, which was most of the time.

Raytheon requires all employees to go through Six Sigma certification during their first year of employment and Fred got me started on it. I had encountered Six Sigma twice before, once in business school and once with the Army's Lean Six Sigma program. The basic idea is to find processes that are repeated over and over – millions of times – and find ways of making the process more efficient and error-free. Although on this project we had no processes that repeated millions of time, the principle still stood. I had to find processes that were inefficient and correct them.

It occurred to me that if I could persuade the post commander or maybe the Team Chief on Devens to let us have our own room, preferably in or near the headquarters building, it would solve several problems at once. I found the perfect room just down the hall from Tim Partin, who was the new Devens Team Chief, and put the idea to him. Whatever objections anyone else had to assigning the room to us were overridden and we soon had our own private area with a lock and key.

This gave us space to work in quiet when necessary, to meet in private, to store proprietary material and even some supplies. We had a phone, working computers and access to faxes and scanners on the same floor. Now our personally owned equipment wouldn't be needed except in an emergency.

That sufficed for my Raytheon Six Sigma project and I became officially certified.

MSG Bovey's new staff of military instructors appeared late in 2009 on a chilly autumn day. We went around the room and introduced ourselves. We listened to people talk about their military schooling, their boring deployments and hopes for a military career that might one day be less boring.

Gone were the most experienced instructors like Dole, Marlin and Johnson. To everyone's delight, Jenn Twain returned. Among the new instructors were Erwin Bayer and Wilma Galena.[71] Erwin had been one of our temps at the Triple Start and Wilma was his new wife. Although Wilma had no experience in 35M (she had been a medical assistant before transferring to the 6/98th and reclassifying), she had gained experience as an instructor while on orders over the previous year. Erwin came to us from the Georgia Army National Guard with experience running a similar course. He came prepared to work hard and do not only his job but any job needed to support the course.

I was only half listening when Staff Sergeant Kirsten Howard's[72] turn came to talk about herself. She seemed equally casual and bored by the process. She spoke Korean and Spanish, was working on her bachelor's

71 Not their real names.

72 Not her real name.

degree (a step above anybody else in the room), had a guitar collection (which indicated more than a passing ability to strum a few chords) and flew helicopters.

I suddenly woke up. She had me at helicopter.

I knew a little about her because I had been her Sergeant Major at Huachuca. She was fit, had just returned from a combat tour in Iraq, had all her schooling and spoke a foreign language. In fact, she had been part of the Korean speakers to Iraq and Arabic speakers to Korea fiasco along with the Twains. Since she already exemplified what I was trying to achieve in everybody else, I paid her very little attention back at Huachuca. In addition, she was both beautiful and married, not the kind of person to whom the Sergeant Major should be seen giving extra attention.

There was something else in her as well – an edgy bitterness. She didn't want to be here. It was a cruel thing for the Army to separate her from her husband Paul for yet another year, the fourth time in their six years of marriage. I understood her pain.

Of the uncounted costs of this perpetual state of "war" is the devastation of families, marriages and careers even for those lucky enough not to have been killed or wounded. We now have reservists and guardsmen who have spent more time away from their jobs and families than any soldier in WWII ever did.

We fell into business as usual under Bovey's leadership. Erwin Bayer made an immense contribution to helping her with her duties as Course Manager. Bovey was easy to work for and discipline among the military instructors was lax. She liked using first names and making sure everyone was happy with their jobs. The biggest problem was that she had trouble making decisions and the work schedule wasn't being laid out sufficiently in advance for people to plan time off.

At the end of the calendar year we ran into a problem we had created for ourselves when Colonel Thompson cancelled everyone's summer vacations. Most of my contractors now had PTO days they were obligated to use up before the end of December. We had also stacked our unused holidays onto Thanksgiving and Christmas, so we were short of contractors for the final days of the class that was to graduate in December of 2009.[73]

This dumped the bulk of the work onto the new uniformed instructors right before the holidays and generated some resentment. The sag in Raytheon support led to only 50% of the class graduating. Raytheon was still maxing its billable hours but the cost per graduate essentially doubled when the graduation rate halved. We would be able to excuse ourselves from the Army's failure to meet forecasts, but I would rather avoid such a failure in the future by good planning. Raytheon making lots of money off a failing project is not an attractive scenario even if it wasn't our fault.

Budgets and graduation rates are not things with which leaders at the lower echelons concern themselves. Most of the low level leadership in this field rationalizes low graduation rates by equating them with high standards. It's a hard profession and a hard course; only the best should make it through. Low level leaders take no thought for matters that concern the higher echelons, like cost per graduate and number of soldiers to fill the vacant slots in MI units. While the low level leaders pat themselves on the back for running a quality course, the school goes over budget and units fail to staff their manning tables and as a consequence fail at their missions.

I was very concerned about graduation rates and budgets. Ultimately, our jobs would depend on us turning out more graduates for less money, and for Raytheon delivering value, i.e. better results for a lower cost. This would happen only with prudent planning.

Jenn Twain created for my office what came to be called the Big Board, a giant calendar spreadsheet with everybody's name on it. It was

73 Raytheon did not allow us to cash in our unused PTO and we could only carry a small amount forward into the next year. In addition, we had ten paid holidays per year but, because we worked holidays when the military worked, we could only use those days when the customer was off, too. One key component to Colonel Thompson's plan was to work us on weekends and holidays to get the course down to ten and a half weeks. Practically the only way to use all ten holidays was to stack most of them up between Christmas and New Year.

a planning tool. I asked every contractor to pencil in the days in the future they were planning on being gone. I invited Bovey to extend that process to military instructors as well, so now the Big Board became the Really Big Board. We had 14 contractors and 12 soldiers to manage.

After putting their names on the board, the contractors still had to apply for leave if I couldn't just work the schedule around the requested time off. They would fill out a form and give it to me. I would get the approval from the Course Manager to ensure the contractor's absence wouldn't jeopardize something on the class schedule. Then I would sign off on it, make three copies and give one each to the Course Manager, to the contractor and put one in my files.

The weak link in that whole arduous process was that it depended on the Course Manager approving the contractors' absence. Without a firm class schedule more than a week or two out, Bovey wouldn't approve any contractor leave. If we continued like this the whole year, we'd never be able to prudently plan time off without stacking it all up in December again and leaving us short-handed. Requests for leave by the score piled up on her desk awaiting signature.

The (Really) Big Board was originally just a planning tool for my use, but it evolved into the official planning tool for the whole course. Eventually it became the approved schedule itself even though the days marked on it only represented desired time off, not approved time. As we moved into the early days of 2010, Phase Leads – individuals Bovey had put in charge of each phase – began filling up the teaching schedule with instructors, including contractors, without telling me. I had to continually remind them to bring me their schedules and have me fill in the contractors. I was sympathetic that this might seem an unnecessary step, but if we didn't, we risked scheduling someone who might not be available.

Gosling evolved into the permanent Phase 2 lead. He hated instructing and was always put in charge of Booth Phase for reasons no one could explain beyond him having done it last time. This phase is widely considered to be the hardest phase of the whole course, but in fact it isn't. It's just the phase in which most students traditionally fail. It is also the place they experience the most abuse in the name of "quality training."

Ray didn't like being in the booth. He liked supervising Booth Phase, which gave him hours of relatively free time with little to do but watch the clock and ring the bell. It put him in a bad light with the other instructors, making him look like the leader who would never do what he demanded of his soldiers. He was also in the habit of double checking all of the grade sheets looking for errors. This was perfectly within his duties, but it often resulted in failing students who thought they had passed and embarrassing instructors who had their evaluations countermanded. He never seemed to find errors in the student's favor, either. It reinforced Ray's paranoia that people really didn't like him and fortified his adversarial relationship with virtually everybody.

His scheduling the contractors right off the Big Board without consulting me resulted in my having some stern words with him. He shouldn't need to be reminded of what Fred Prince had so clearly pointed out. Ray continued to assert that Fred's position was incorrect and that Ray was completely free to pencil in the contractors by name if he wanted. When this resulted in scheduling a contractor during a period when the contractor had a doctor's appointment, it required some last minute juggling.

"Dr. Sparks, I'm scheduled to teach when I have a doctor's appointment," Laverne[74] told me one morning.

"Who scheduled you? I didn't put you on the board," I said.

"Gosling did. I just found out about it this morning."

"I'll handle it," I said. "Go to your appointment as planned."

I found Gosling and told him I would be substituting for Laverne. "Ray, don't schedule the contractors without talking to me first."

"It's not necessary. The contractors have to be available whenever we need them."

"Contractors are available, but I schedule them. I thought we were clear on that," I said.

74 Not her real name.

"We don't need anyone's permission to schedule the contractors, Mr. Sparks. I've been doing this for years."

"You scheduled Laverne for a time when she has a medical appointment."

"Did she clear that with Master Sergeant Bovey?" asked Ray. "I didn't see any paperwork on it."

"It's probably still on her desk if she did, but we really don't need to jump through those hoops when we can just schedule around things like this."

"I don't mind you filling in for her, but the fact remains that all contractors have to be available to work during normal working hours," said Ray.

"She can make that time up by just taking one of the study halls or a few hours on Saturday."

"But what if there are no study halls or classes on Saturday? She wouldn't be able to put in her full forty hours."

"That's my concern. I schedule the contractors," I insisted.

"Bovey and I can schedule the contractors. I don't care what Fred said."

"Ray, don't schedule the contractors without talking to me first."

"But..."

"Don't schedule the contractors."

I left it at that. Scheduling a contractor when she wasn't available should have illustrated my point, but Gosling insisted it was just another case of contractor insubordination.

Because Bovey hated confrontation, it was difficult to pin her down to a firm policy. She remembered that we had all agreed to leave scheduling the contractors to me, but the next day I would find her or Ray or someone else directly tasking contractors. When the contractors came to me for clarification, I would have to chase her down and straighten things out. When faced with Gosling telling her one thing and me something else, she would call Mike Bass or Donna Ortiz without telling me rather than resolve the issue directly. This often resulted in a call to Fred or Chuck, who would call me to ask what was going on. I usually had no idea, so I would have to ask Bovey whether she had some problem with the contractors. She usually brushed it off, denying there had been any problem and it had all been a misunderstanding. We have a great working relationship and everything is fine, she insisted. But it was unsettling to me and to my bosses at Raytheon.

Just as it was becoming more and more essential to keep a close eye on things at the Mike course, we started up the Lima, Foxtrot and Golf courses. Raytheon was now making more than three times the money on Ft. Devens it had in the previous year. Expectations were high. Raytheon hired two very mature individuals to function as Task Leads for the CIAC and Analyst courses, Will Richards and Sarah Sondheim.[75] I had never met Will, but I knew Ms. Sondheim, who was a senior warrant officer in the 6/98th. Henry Chan, who would lead the smaller 35G course, was also an NCO in my unit and was very impressive both as a soldier and a leader. I was happy to see we would have good talent right from the start.

We needed even more space now, so I approached Tim Partin – who by now was a good friend – and he gave us an additional room next to the new Raytheon office. I had been in the habit of making the rounds before work to make sure everything was in place and everyone present or accounted for. It would be easy to simply expand that to the room next door and leave the direct management of each course to the new leads. I continued to be directly responsible for the Mike course and to teach with the same class load as the other instructors.

Approving the timecards of three dozen contractors began to suck up a lot more time than it had with just twelve. One doesn't simply sign off on whatever time the contractor enters on his card. You have to check to be sure the hours were actually delivered and did not exceed the maximal amount allowed per week. The one thing I feared most was an audit of the timecards, so I made it a priority to check on everyone and keep a notebook to document whenever anyone put in irregular hours outside the normal eight-hour workday. We had a 60-hour a week training

75 Not their real names.

schedule at the Mike course alone which demanded stopping by on Saturdays and at evening study halls whenever contractors were scheduled to teach and occasionally visiting remote sites when we had practical exercises outside of Ft. Devens. Now I had four sites to check on every day and the Limas in particular did a lot of work off site.

Eventually we would get Will and Sarah approval authority for timecards, but I was still responsible for the entire project. It became more and more important to encourage the contractors to solve problems on their own. The biggest challenge was the nature of the problems that continually arose. Almost without exception they boiled down to personality conflicts. One senior NCO didn't like the newly-weds Erwin and Wilma, who he thought were too lovey-dovey. He didn't think that was professional behavior and wanted them counselled. Nobody liked working for Gosling. Charlie – Sergeant Major Foster – was frustrated with Bovey's inability to make and stick with a decision. The contractors with children needed to be accommodated when the schedule conflicted with the need to drop off or pick up their children from school. Elliott was touchy about perceived slights to his professionalism. Pasc Valdez and Roger Cohen kept showing up to work in dress that didn't exactly meet dress code. Butch Mudslinger had a biting wit that got under some people's skin.

I thoroughly enjoyed smoothing over the personality conflicts and keeping things running, but I was still limited in what I could do to influence the military side of the house. Unless Bovey's people outright broke some regulation, I couldn't just put on my Sergeant Major hat and bring things back into line.

But there were times when the Sergeant Major hat was called for.

Wind of a crass bet reached my ears. A bet was on between some of the male soldiers over who would be the first to bed Kirsten. A treacherous thread in the social fabric of any post is who is sleeping with whom. Trysts and affairs impact how everybody gets along and often go unaddressed because the subject is so delicate. And they can take bizarre turns.

Kirsten was as attractive as she was unavailable. She had made a commitment to stay true to her husband and missed the benefits of marriage terribly. Here was a woman who could have any man on post, would be hit on daily, but would go home after work, have her phone date with her husband Paul, and probably cry herself to sleep alone. I decided to keep close tabs on anyone who tried to win that bet.

Kirsten proved more than capable of defending herself. She didn't need anyone's protection and her caustic rejection was more than just reward for anyone who tried to seduce her. She was serious about fidelity and had my complete support, indeed my admiration.

Her looks and fitness unavoidably generated some ill-will out of envy. Although sweet to her face, Tracey Bovey hated Kirsten Howard. It seemed that everything Bovey struggled with, Kirsten did with ease. Kirsten was fit and beautiful, smart and witty, and men flirted with her at every opportunity. Bovey especially hated how Kirsten seemed to succeed at every task while applying minimal effort. Kirsten enjoyed respect Bovey could never hope to receive.

It wasn't until March when, during a company cookout, I found myself in the midst of a conversation – more of a running commentary actually – on the bizarre relationship between two of the most unlikely individuals on Ft. Devens. According to one of them, they were engaged, though no one was one hundred percent sure. There was nothing particularly attractive about the man involved and his putative fiancée didn't seem very attracted to him either. Anyway, Kirsten and Jenn were commenting back and forth on the most unpleasant picture those two must present during conjugal relations. And Kirsten was funny. Beer shooting out the nose funny.

I was thoroughly enjoying the repartee, when Kirsten mentioned she had grown up in, of all places, the very town in which I had a medical practice years ago! She had walked past my office many times and I knew where her mom and dad lived. Suddenly we had something personal to talk about and that led to her two passions in high school, cross country and band. I had been something of a band nerd myself. We both agreed that band camp was the best kept secret of high school. Band camp was of course not about music. It was about parties, underage drinking, strip poker and skinny dipping at night in the lake.

From that day on my whole attitude toward Kirsten shifted. She was no longer just a talented colleague and former subordinate. She was a kindred spirit I was now determined to protect like a little sister.

Kirsten wasn't the only person of whom I felt more than a little protective. Erwin Bayer had come to us in dire straits. Pride would not allow him to divulge just how much trouble he was in, but as his Sergeant Major, I knew something about why he had to leave Georgia and the National Guard. He had utterly failed at his last assignment as Course Manager. His NCOER (i.e. his military evaluation) was devastating. It included ethics bullets – negative comments on actions that had been unethical – including intervening to help a failing friend graduate and finding a job for an unqualified relative. It's very difficult to recover from a stumble that serious. He was also going through a painful divorce and, like so many Americans in those years, had a house on which he owed more than it was worth. He was strapped and had limited options.

When you give a man like that a second chance, you will often earn his undying loyalty and he'll give a hundred ten percent to the job. Erwin was a nice guy, a hard worker, a decent instructor and quite knowledgeable about Military Intelligence. He was a combat veteran. Most of all, he had found in Wilma the Pearl of Great Price, a woman who loved him and I was determined to see that he got every chance to get back on his feet.

Wilma was pregnant and they needed a real home. I had planned on moving my whole family to Massachusetts, but it didn't work out. I had a family home but no family. I took Erwin and Wilma in and we enjoyed many pleasant evenings together after work musing about how to turn the Mike course into a first rate project. Eventually I rented my place to Erwin and Wilma along with a friend who was also one of our new contractors at CIAC. I found myself a small apartment in a complex nearer to work where several of the other instructors also lived, including Kirsten.

Soon I was hosting little dinner parties at my flat. I invited Kirsten over one evening. "I'm trying to learn how cook and want to try it out on somebody, but it has to be people who don't matter if I accidentally poison them. Would you like to come over for dinner tomorrow night?"

"Sure. Mind if I bring a friend?"

"All the better," I said.

Before she and the rest showed up, I strategically placed my guitar in plain sight out of its case. She showed up right on time with Eric Kocen, a full-timer at the Devens MI battalion she had been palling around with. It wasn't hard to see why she liked Kocen. He was a nice guy, non-threatening, with a self-deprecating sense of humor and a never ending set of funny one-liners. ("I used to work for the Post Office. It's not as exciting as it sounds.")

I invited them in and offered them something to drink. We chatted while I put together the finishing touches on dinner. Spying my guitar, Kirsten went right to it and without a word, picked it up and started to play.

She played well and showed evidence of musical training. Best of all, she knew songs I knew and liked. At the end of the evening, I recommended that next time she bring her guitar.

There would be several next times. We began to collaborate on theme parties, carefully choosing the guest list. Soon we were inviting small, select groups of people over regularly for dinner, after which we would watch and discuss a thought-provoking film. Between the meal and the movie, Kirsten and I serenaded all present with dual guitars and a little singing.

What had begun in the winter as a perfectly dismal year by spring had become surprisingly enjoyable.

CHAPTER 12

Frustrations with the Brigade

At April's drill in 2010 a new soldier appeared. She was a sergeant living in New Hampshire and already serving in another unit, but she was looking for a new place to serve. She had been a photojournalist in Iraq and had no MI background. She immediately sought me out.

Her name was Kathleen Briere.

As Sergeant Major, I made it a point to welcome all new soldiers and get to know something about them. Sergeant Briere came right to the point: she wanted to deploy with Special Forces. I was the only Special Forces qualified soldier in the battalion and she figured that if anybody knew how to make that happen, it would be me.

I informed her of what she already knew. SF is restricted to males only and it's very selective. Wanting it badly isn't enough. Being in great physical shape isn't enough. And even if selected, it takes a couple of years of dangerous and demanding training just to become fully qualified and earn the Special Forces tab. Then you get sent into combat on dangerous, difficult missions.

There were, however, units that supported SF, but they were almost exclusively for men as well. Kat knew that MI supported SF in combat and was interested in being trained in an MOS that might get her such an assignment.

We could certainly do that, I assured her. What I didn't tell her immediately was that I was aware of a pilot program they were pushing through at Ft. Bragg called "Female Engagement Teams" (FET).[76] Afghan culture

76 Female Engagement Teams were pioneered by the Marines to interact with female populations of Iraq and Afghanistan. The Army adopted the concept, which

does not allow for men outside the family to talk to women privately. It's offensive even to refer to another man's wife and some normal courtesies in our culture can be insulting in Afghan culture to the degree of demanding blood. But the women know everything. They know who is involved in the insurgency, what they are doing, where they are and with whom they are working. The Afghan women are a trove of the kind of information we need and generally speaking want to see the violence cease.

The idea of Female Engagement Teams is to put a woman or two on a Special Forces ODA[77] and task them with talking to the women in the villages. These female SF soldiers should be skilled in healthcare and intelligence collection. But the biggest hurdle would be getting them through selection. They would have to be just as fit as the men and that was non-negotiable.

We had been talking about the merits of female SF since before I came in during Vietnam. Women can gain access to the women of indigenous populations that men can never achieve. But the obstacle had always been the question of fitness. How do you find enough women who can meet the high standards of fitness demanded in the elite units?

In getting to know Sergeant Briere, I soon discovered that this would not be a problem. She was a fitness fanatic. She was in the habit of getting up early to train. She did CrossFit, triathlons, and especially liked competitive rowing. At our first unit APFT, she blew everybody away. So the next month we discussed trying out for the FET. She was thrilled.

We made a plan to get her ready for SF selection and got up early several days a week to do the kind of fitness training she would need and to hone her military skills. We would have almost a year to prepare and in

---

evolved into Cultural Support Teams, or CSTs. For simplicity, I refer to all such teams of women supporting elite forces in combat zones as FETs.

77 The ODA – Operational Detachment Alpha – is the twelve-man basic unit of Special Forces also known as an A Team. It consists of ten mid-level to senior NCOs, one warrant officer and a commissioned officer, who is often the least experienced member of the team. The ODA was originally designed to be basically the general staff of a guerilla battalion and is staffed with experts in weapons, engineering, medicine, communications and intelligence.

the meantime, we'd put her through the 35M course and get her qualified in human intelligence collection.

One thing we needed was a body of natural water we could swim in, not just a swimming pool. Water operations are a big part of SF and all candidates must be at home in wild water. I'm a big fan of wild swimming as well and all spring I had been searching earnestly for a decent place to train. Massachusetts has no shortage of ponds and swamps, but finding a lake suitable for swimming was hard. All the decent ones within driving distance were built up on the shore and had either private or highly regulated public beaches.

Then I found Mirror Lake.

Mirror Lake is a crystal clear body of water on what used to be greater Fort Devens. The land around it still belongs to the Army, so it hasn't been developed other than being open to the public during the summer months from nine to five. But outside those hours, the pristine area is practically unused except by the occasional early morning angler.

After a thorough scouting of the environs I concluded that there was only one way down to the beach and if there were no cars in the parking lot, it was safe to assume there would be no one at the lake. Most of the time, I had the lake all to myself.

There is simply no way to adequately describe the experience of visiting the lake for a swim whether early morning or after dark. It was wild swimming at its purest. The flooding of all the senses, the feel of fresh air and water on bare skin puts me in a Zen-like presence of the Here and Now. Completely and simultaneously aware of all sensations. Open and focused. Ready. The experience helped me cope with the stresses that came with my job. When faced with a moral dilemma or a seemingly intractable problem, a swim in the lake often provided the solution. Swimming at Mirror Lake every day was my personal meditation practice, filling the void left now that I could no longer hike in the Arizona desert.

Kat didn't swim for pleasure; for her it was just training and she approached it with a "no pain, no gain" attitude. So in addition to training with Kat, I decided to share my secret swimming hole with Kirsten. I knew she liked to swim and had more than once expressed the desire to find a good place. One evening in May when we found ourselves doing laundry at the same time I broached the subject.

"I know a place we can go swimming nearby."

"Seriously?"

"Seriously. I go there all the time and it's beautiful."

"Really?"

"Come on. I'll show you tonight."

"You're serious? Tonight? What time? How far away?"

"I'll meet you at nine in the parking lot. It's five minutes from here."

"Okay. Nine-ish. But wait till I text you. I have my phone date with Paul at 8:30."

At nine sharp I got a one-word text: Swimming?

I met her in the parking lot and we hopped into my jeep. She had a towel and I had a bag with a towel in it, some bug spray and a swim suit.

She squirmed like a little kid at the thought of what was about to happen. We arrived at the parking lot just after nine and it was empty. It was still a little light out, but it would soon be completely dark.

We walked the quarter mile down the single road to the sandy beach, which we had all to ourselves. There was a small pontoon raft about fifty meters from shore and some floating ropes to mark off the swimming area for the public. We put our stuff down near the water.

The lake was exquisitely beautiful under the clear, starry sky and moon. We waded out into the cool water together and swam to the raft. I wasn't sure how strong a swimmer Kirsten was, but she showed me immediately. She dove off the raft toward the open water and I followed. We crossed the lake and back in an easy, leisurely glide, chatting about whatever came to mind. After about half an hour, we got out of the water, dried off, dressed and went back.

"Tomorrow night?" I asked.

"You bet!"

Wild swimming became our nightly ritual that summer. We had wonderful conversations and often mused about how no one would believe us even if we told them what we were doing. Swimming across a lake and back in pitch black night just for fun? Most of our colleagues wouldn't voluntarily climb into a chlorine-soaked public pool.

Looking back, my nightly swims with Kirsten was one of the highlights of my years at Devens and sealed a friendship that lasts to this day.

I came to look on Mirror Lake as my own treasure and I as her protector. I swam every morning before work until it froze over every year. I came to know every cove, every shallow. I would see the same mated pair of swans every fall, naming them Cygnus and Cassiopeia. I looked forward to its awakening every spring when the ice melted and it came to life with turtles, frogs and fish. She was my daily anchor to sanity.

In training Kat, I began to long for SF. My time in Special Forces was one of the most precious parts of my life and the grind of the conventional forces wore on me. The ho-hum, check-the-block training schedule, the adversarial staff and the "can't do" attitude of the conventional forces were constant reminders that my weekend drills had once been enjoyable. I took some pride in what we had accomplished both at the 5-104th and the 6/98th – twice bringing battalions from last place up to first – but it was pretty obvious I wasn't going to get any real authority over the school, which rested at the Brigade level and higher. I missed the camaraderie and the pride of serving with the best and I had reached as high as I would ever get in a conventional reserve training unit.

With our focus shifting back to Afghanistan, I felt it was important as an instructor to keep my experience current. I thought it would be a prudent investment in my career to get a combat deployment in Afghanistan with Special Forces before I retired and retirement was only two years away. While Kat trained for FET, I made discrete inquiries into possibly transferring into a Special Forces company in the Massachusetts National Guard in Springfield only an hour away. They would be deploying to Afghanistan next fall and needed a B Team[78] operations sergeant.

My interview centered mostly on what I had done in Special Forces and with whom. SF is a tight community and my reputation would carry more weight than my qualifications. Fortunately, the commander and the warrant officer I would be deploying with knew several men with whom I had served and that was all they needed to give me the green light.

With a combat deployment looming in six months, I felt it was time to take a more aggressive stance with the Brigade staff on the subject of delinquent language pay. After over a year of calling and being dismissed with "we're working on it," I decided to have a serious talk with Mr. Kilmartin's boss, Carmen Lopez.[79] In addition to her AGR position, Ms. Lopez was also a sergeant major in the Brigade and had all the authority she needed to make things happen. She had assured me language pay would get top priority and would make sure Steve Kilmartin kept on it.

But months went by with no results. I cornered her at a command conference in Phoenix. We had a drink together and I asked her how I could help with the language pay.

"No help is necessary," she assured me. "It's just that language pay is extremely complex and Steve is spending hundreds of hours trying to sort everything out."

Her explanation made no sense. Language pay is simple and easy to process. "Why don't you just submit the paperwork and let it go forward. See what happens," I suggested.

"We're researching the regs to see whether FLPP is authorized in your case. This is going to be a test case and if FLPP is authorized, then we'll proceed to try to get everyone paid. We need to make sure everything is well researched and supported before we submit the paperwork."

"Look, Carmen. I know FLPP inside and out. There's no need for a test case. I'm a certified CLPM (Command Language Program Manager).

---

78 Whereas the ODA is the basic unit of SF, the ODAs are grouped into companies of six. The company is staffed by the B Team. As B Team Operations Sergeant, I would have been responsible for managing the missions of the six ODAs.

79 Not her real name.

Language pay has been around for decades. Did you talk to the CLPM at Huachuca?" I had referred her to the CLPM of Ft. Huachuca who would do all the paperwork for us and do it correctly, so nothing could have been simpler.

"I gave the information to Steve."

"And?"

"He sent the paperwork up the chain but didn't hear back. I think he thinks he didn't do it right and just wants to make sure all his ducks are in a row before sending it up again."

"Well, let's go talk to the Division CSM (Command Sergeant Major). He's here. I just talked to him this morning. We can get to the bottom of where the holdup is."

"Just let Steve get it sorted out. There's no need to go putting any pressure on the Division staff. And don't you go talking to Division without going through Brigade," she warned me.

She hadn't reached out for help from Huachuca and Mr. Kilmartin was apparently spending many frustrating hours feeling his way around in the dark. I spoke to the CSM anyway and he told me he was completely unaware they even processed language pay. Wasn't that supposed to go through the 80th TTC? He sent me to the Division G-3, who was as obsessive/compulsive an individual as one might find outside of a psychiatric hospital, and he was quite sure nothing about language pay had ever been submitted to his staff. I checked with the Division personnel officer as well and got the same response.

I didn't know what was going on, but I knew language pay wasn't being processed at the Division or Brigade level and I wasn't going to get any more help than this from Carmen Lopez.

Just a couple of weeks later, the Division Commander General Heritsch made a tour of the school with Colonel Thompson. I brought up the subject of delinquent language pay. Colonel Thompson reported to her that the pay problem had been solved and everyone was getting paid. I spoke up to contradict him and Colonel Thompson was embarrassed. I think Lopez probably caught hell for that. In any event, I got even less cooperation out of her from then on.

She insisted that Mr. Kilmartin was putting in hundreds of hours trying to sort out language pay. I should be grateful they were even working on it at all. It wasn't his job. My pleas to take all that work off of Steve's hands fell on deaf ears. And frankly, I'm not impressed with fruitless effort; I'm much more impressed by people who get things done and make it look easy. I hate to threaten anyone with an IG complaint. If a sergeant major can't solve it, the Inspector General probably can't either. But in this case I was being opposed by another sergeant major up the chain of command, so I told Carmen I would be forced to file a complaint if this matter showed no more progress than it had up until now. Dozens of soldiers were owed thousands of dollars. Soldiers had quit before because of unpaid FLPP. This was serious.

Shortly thereafter I found myself under investigation. Nothing to worry about, I was told. Just a random audit of my language pay records. They do it all the time. Who else in the 80th TTC was being audited? No one. The audit, I was assured, was completely unrelated to my threat to go to the IG about delinquent language pay. My language pay was frozen until the audit was complete.

The audit of less than thirty pieces of paper, which could have been done in an hour, lasted over a year. The audit found a few minor errors in the paperwork. I had worked in a language, several in fact, other than Bulgarian without having my primary language officially changed. For having the audacity to work in other languages in addition to Bulgarian, $5,400 of my FLPP was revoked.

I took the matter up with Julie Ducklow, the pay analyst at the US Army Reserve Command who was responsible for revoking my pay. Why not simply correct the errors? Or if they preferred, why not change my primary language to the one I was working in? She told me they hadn't been able to locate the office in the Pentagon that did that.

At that time, I doubted any such office existed. The regulations required it, but it was often the case that the regs required things be done for which there was no money, space, expertise or personnel. And in any case, the soldier's Primary Language is simply defined, not awarded. It doesn't require any official action to change it.

Foreign language neglect continued to be an open, festering wound for me as it had my entire career. Our ability to speak to and understand not only the enemy but our hosts and allies as well is crucial to success. No other factor, in my opinion, has been more essential to victory and more responsible for our consistent failure abroad than our contempt for the languages and cultures of other countries. I do not exaggerate when I suggest that it would be better having no intelligence service than one that can't understand the target languages. At least we would only be blind. But we are forced to hire translators out of the pool of locals the enemy has even more access to than we do, allowing them to know more about us than we do about them. It provides our enemies and our hosts with the tools they use to manipulate and mislead us.

Cheating one soldier out of that much money is bad enough, but it reinforced the practice of cheating all the soldiers. Our battalion looked comparatively good compared to the other 24 in the Division, but we still needed a lot more soldiers than we had. We couldn't man all the instructor slots and found it necessary to continue to rely on contractors to fill the void.

While brainstorming over how to entice more soldiers into joining our battalion, Colonel Rook came up with a simple but brilliant idea. Why not just call all of the soldiers within an easy commute of Devens who were in the IRR and ask them to come back in? It couldn't hurt. We could offer them a pleasant place to serve doing something the country really needed right now. We could be flexible with drill and AT dates.

We divided up the list by MOS. I took the list of nearby 35M soldiers in the IRR and their contact info. There were over forty and that didn't count the 35Ls and 35Fs that others would call. I was able to make contact with most of them, but none were willing to come back into the Active Reserve. The most common reason I heard why they got out was their dissatisfaction with not getting the language school or language pay they had been promised.

Based on the attrition rates for all the MI battalions belonging to the 1st Brigade, I estimated we had lost about 60 soldiers due to failure to support foreign language sustainment. It costs the taxpayer about a quarter of a million dollars to train a single soldier in one language to basic level, and many of us speak multiple languages at higher levels. At the very least this neglect wasted some $15 million over the years I was in the unit. Never mind the effect on our missions overseas that failed for lack of qualified collectors. Never mind having to hire contract linguists at a cost of $200,000 a year as translators in addition to our own personnel.

I would be hard pressed to present an example of anyone in Al Qaeda or the Taliban who has done as much damage to our missions as our own staff had done in not supporting language sustainment.

CHAPTER 13

Staggered Start

In the summer of 2010 Colonel Thompson alerted us to an imminent a pop-up, a sudden unannounced class that would double our student load. Our fears that our success with the Triple Start would generate another vacation-cancelling emergency seemed to have come true. The Army needed an additional 24 soldiers trained in MOS 35M right away and were confident that Colonel Thompson could deliver once again.

This situation was different from the Triple Start, however. Colonel Thompson was acutely aware of how close we had come to disaster when Smith overbooked the contractors. Spending almost three quarters of a million dollars on fancy equipment and Smith's company's laptops and software had been a costly mistake as well. This time we would authorize extra hours and divert some of the money designated for infrastructure into human resources. The contractor work force would be temporarily doubled and budgeted for overtime. People's summer vacations would not be ruined and the opportunity to make even more money would, if not lessen the pain, sweeten the deal.

The Triple Start had been necessary to support Petraeus's surge in Afghanistan. This pop-up we now faced consisted of 09Ls (pronounced "Oh-nine Limas") who were Heritage Linguists. These are American citizens who are native speakers of languages we badly needed like Arabic, Swahili, Somali, Urdu, Dari and Pashto. Being citizens, they are clearable to Secret, even Top Secret, and extremely valuable. Not for nothing were they sometimes referred to as the "million dollar linguists." All had important missions waiting for them overseas and the success of their training was vital.

I got started vetting the new applicants for temporary contractor jobs. Several of the candidates had worked on the Triple Start the previous summer. As before, Colonel Thompson insisted on privately seeing the résumés with the names. No one else was to know.

This time I was aware of some personal history between the Colonel and a few of the potential instructors. He wasn't fond of some of the contractors who had applied for this temporary job. Sergeant First Class Sam Farmer[80] had a long and not entirely positive history with Thompson long before he was a colonel. Colonel Thompson never black-balled him from teaching, so whatever history they had couldn't have been all that bad and Sam was a fine instructor. If you gave him a job, you knew it would be done well and he was especially good at making complex subjects understandable to the students. But Sam was certain Colonel Thompson held a grudge against him and took every opportunity to mention it to anyone who would listen. I told him I felt he would be wiser to keep such opinions to himself.

Paul Sciavoni[81] wanted to come back. He wasn't well liked by some who had worked with him, but he was a competent and reliable instructor, dual qualified as both 35M and 35L. He had earned the Gold instructor's badge, which is awarded to expert instructors with a lot of documented experience.

There were other candidates as well, like Graham Donaldson,[82] who had just returned from a tour collecting intelligence in a combat zone. With his black, bushy beard, he could convincingly play the role of an Al-Qaeda terrorist or Afghan chieftain – until he opened his mouth and let his Louisiana drawl flow out.

Melinda Holly[83] was coming on board after having recently served supporting a Navy SEAL unit in Afghanistan. Dwight Delorean[84] had just spent 18 months in Afghanistan doing source operations. Ken Frickle,

80 Not his real name.

81 Not his real name.

82 Not his real name.

83 Not her real name.

84 Not his real name.

an intelligent and well educated man with expertise in tactical biometric technology was available as well.

I sent the résumés of all qualified candidates to Colonel Thompson, none of whom he disapproved except for Dole, Marlin and Johnson. Even though a year had passed, he still did not want them hired by Raytheon.

Now, after a year and a half on the job, I was acutely aware of the illegality of attempting to block former unit members from being hired by a civilian company. In the case of Dole, Marlin and Johnson, it did not involve the commander personally selecting the top talent – it merely served to set an example that as far as he was able, he would not allow soldiers who failed the APFT to benefit by taking the same job for more money as a civilian. I agonized over what to do until the problem solved itself. Dole, Marlin and Johnson were able to find jobs with other companies teaching at Ft. Huachuca.

Sergeant Farmer had to back out because of medical issues. As for Sciavoni and a couple of others, the unreliable Army communication system worked in their favor. I sent their résumés to Colonel Thompson but he apparently never got them. With no objection from him to ban their hiring, Raytheon okayed them for the job through a subcontractor. We got all twelve names of the temporary help vetted in plenty of time to plan ahead for the Staggered Start. Now all we needed was enough space to handle them.

Although we had two rooms in the headquarters building, ominously numbered Building 666, I asked Tim for a third. The room across the hall was empty and it would be perfect for housing the temps. He concurred and let us have yet a third room for the summer.

By June of 2010, I felt good about the upcoming pop-up. The 35L, 35F and 35G courses were running smoothly. We would have enough experienced instructors, overtime if we needed it, and adequate facilities. Raytheon instructors were now capable of carrying the entire course even with no involvement by the customer. Whoever took responsibility for any aspect of this course was going to look good and Raytheon would shine for yet a second year in a row.

With the contractor jobs gradually drying up at Huachuca, I knew the key to our success at Devens would be in continuing to produce more trained huminters for less money. Compared side by side, contractors are more expensive than soldiers, but when you look at the success in terms of trained soldiers produced per dollar spent, we came out much cheaper. The cost of travel, housing and infrastructure was lower at Devens. That, along with the course being three and a half weeks shorter, made us more economical.

Meanwhile Bovey, with the help of her old friend Donna Ortiz, was also preparing for a Quality Assurance inspection. Planning ahead wasn't Bovey's greatest strength and a number of administrative requirements had been neglected. Among the glaring deficiencies were the instructor evaluations. Instructors are supposed to be evaluated regularly, but she hadn't done any and needed to get them all done in less than two weeks.

The evaluation process involves a senior instructor watching an entire class or booth iteration while filling out a sheet and grading the instructor on every aspect of his or her performance. I was not happy with the evaluation criteria, which I thought were for the most part unrealistic. But I do support regular evaluations and everything they're supposed to accomplish.

Bovey presented me with DVDs of all the previous booth iterations and asked me to do an evaluation on each of the Raytheon contractors. With each iteration lasting over three hours, to do an honest evaluation would take all of my hours in a week and then some, leaving no time for anything else just as things were accelerating. An honest evaluation wasn't even possible using the DVDs because they didn't catch many of the things the instructor is supposed to be evaluated on. There is no opportunity to critique the instructor afterwards, either, which is the most important thing if the evaluation is to have any impact on improving performance.

My biggest objection, however, was that I as Raytheon Site Lead was evaluating my own people, a clear conflict of interest. I had every motivation to see that our people got the highest rating possible, thus enhancing my company's position along with my own evaluation at the end of the year. Could one expect any Site Lead to recommend that his own people be fired? I could in good conscience evaluate the military instructors – it was my job as Director of Instruction anyway – but not Raytheon contractors. She should do it herself or appoint another deputy.

She insisted she didn't have the time (as if I did) and felt confident I would be honest and fair. It was eyewash anyway for the QA inspection, she said. She just needed properly completed documents in each instructor's file for QA to check the box. In truth, I was quite sure the Raytheon contractors would excel in comparison to the military instructors, but it was still technically a conflict of interest and I said so to her and to Fred.

I didn't like taking the DVDs home and doing the evaluations on my own unpaid time. That's both illegal and against company policy. I didn't like giving my own people sloppy evaluations either, but there was no time to do real live ones. So I did the evaluations, making sure they were all done to standard and with as few bad or good marks as I could in good conscience include.

The contractors weren't happy. Most wanted and deserved excellent evaluations (90% or above), but each point of performance that receives a "superior/exceeds standards" also needs a comment justifying it. The same is true for any points that do not meet standard. Without being in the booth with them and actually watching them perform, I would just be making things up, which would be worse. I had to explain to them that this was just for the inspection. After the inspection we would do live evaluations and they could remove the lackluster evals from their files if they wanted.

I followed Bovey's instructions to the letter, my conscience paining me, and all the files were complete in time for the inspection.

I know the QA people from Huachuca. They are very helpful and not to be feared. But they also know when someone had pencil-whipped the files just for the inspection and said so to Bovey. All the files had the same handwriting, the same dates and looked very uniform. I drew the line at intentionally falsifying the evaluations. I think Bovey expected me to make the evals look more genuine by varying the dates and the penmanship, but I wasn't willing to go that far.

As we entered the final planning stages for the Staggered Start, Bovey divided the students into two classes, one run by Gosling and one by Howard. Gosling was happy to take the lead with his course but Kirsten was not. Kirsten's course would start a couple of weeks before Gosling's and would be one phase ahead, whence the nickname we gave it, the "Staggered Start."

Kirsten, with the firm conviction that nothing we do makes any difference, took the approach of making this the easiest she could on everybody, especially herself. She took the schedule of classes from the identical course at Ft. Huachuca and transposed it onto our calendar. Then she presented it to me as the contractor Site Lead.

"How many contractors do I have?" she asked.

I told her.

"How many contractor hours do I have?"

I told her.

"Pencil in every one of your contractors for every hour the taxpayer has paid for and have it on my desk by close of business today."

I said yes ma'am and I did as I was told. It would be a lot of work for the contractors and the military instructors would have it easy, but this is the way it should be. Her class would be staffed by highly experienced Raytheon instructors. I didn't anticipate any serious problems since the course was exactly the same as Huachuca's with which most of the contractors were familiar.

Bovey and Gosling by contrast spent a huge amount of time creating their schedule from scratch and maximizing the use of relatively inexperienced military instructors brought in on temporary orders. The remainder of the space they filled with contractors. They had a couple of weeks more time than Kirsten had and used every hour, often staying late at work.

The temps began to arrive a week before the classes started and had plenty of time to get settled. Permanent party instructors began teaching Phase 1, which as you might recall, is mostly lecture. Things went smoothly.

And just to ensure things went smoothly, Fred came out to greet everyone and reinforce the rules of working with contractors with the Course Manager Tracey Bovey, and the two Leads, Kirsten Howard and Raymond Gosling. "The Site Lead schedules the contractors," he reminded them. "All coordination of contract effort goes through Dr. Sparks. Treat the contractors as professionals. If any of them cause trouble, have Dr. Sparks deal with it. If he can't deal with it, either myself or Chuck will and are only a phone call away."

I was especially eager to get involved with the 09 Limas. Language proficiency is my hot button and this was a program I could get behind whole heartedly. I scheduled myself to teach as much as I could.

When Kirsten's class advanced to Phase 2, Gosling's class kicked off. I gathered the temps for Gosling's class together in their newly procured office and showed them the schedule. As anticipated, none had any problem with teaching any of the classes for which they might be scheduled.

"I expect this whole program to run a lot smoother than last summer," I began. Several of them remembered the Triple Start from the previous year. "Your place of duty is in this room between the hours of 8:00 AM and 5:00 PM with an hour off for lunch from noon to 1:00. If anyone needs to do anything else, see me about it. If anyone in uniform tells you to do anything other than what I've directed, have them see me. You work for Raytheon, not the Army."

"Is Bovey clear on that?" asked Paul Sciavoni.

"She's clear. Got it straight from Fred just a couple of days ago," I assured him.

Noelle and I had most of the classes the first day with the 09 Limas. It was invigorating! We were teaching courses like "History of the Middle East" and "History of Islam" to students who came from those places and grew up in those cultures. Our lectures were constantly interrupted with comments – which I encouraged – like, "That's not correct" and "I've lived there all my life and I've never heard that." I both wanted to finish up quickly because they obviously did not need their time wasted with those subjects and wanted it to go on for days for my own edification.

Less than an hour into my first lecture, the door to the back of the classroom opened up and in filed all the temporary contractors.

At the break, I gathered them together to ask what this was all about.

"Master Sergeant Bovey told us we had to come over here," said Paul.

"After what I just told you?"

"She said we could either come over here and sit in the back of the classroom and observe or be fired," he explained.

"I see. Don't worry. I'll deal with it," I said.

After finishing teaching, I sought Bovey out.

"Wasn't Fred clear about directing contractors?" I asked.

"I don't want them sitting over there lounging around doing nothing. Their place is in the back of the classroom when not teaching," she said.

"Then you need to tell me and I'll put them in the back of the classroom," I said.

"Okay. Put them in the back of the classroom," she said.

"Mr. Sparks, she doesn't need your permission to put the contractors anyplace she deems necessary," interjected Gosling.

"Nobody's saying she does," I said. "But the both of you need to have me do it, not direct them yourselves. Fred just said..."

"Fred's full of shit. I've managed over 70 contractors. I know what we can and cannot do," Ray said.

"I'm pretty sure Fred's right. Anyway, those are his instructions and I work for him. All the contractors work for Raytheon," I said.

"And Raytheon works for us," Bovey said.

"I thought we agreed I would schedule the contractors," I said.

"They were just sitting in the office doing nothing," she objected. "Some of them had their feet up on the chairs and were texting!"

"They weren't scheduled to do anything yet. I told them very clearly their place of duty was in that office unless they were scheduled to teach. I told them that if anyone but me tells them to do something not on their schedule, to send that person to me. You just negated everything I told them."

"I want them in the classroom observing instruction," she insisted.

"They don't need to be observing instruction. They know how to teach. They're here for only one cycle and there won't be a second time around to teach anything they observe anyway," I said.

"I still think they should be in the classroom rather than lounging around doing nothing," said Bovey.

Gosling broke in. "When I started at Huachuca, I had to observe for eight months before I was even allowed to assist," he said. "They need to observe classes before they're ready teach."

"Ray, they come ready to teach. Fully qualified," I said.

"No they don't. I'm not going to allow anyone to teach until I'm sure they're competent. That's the regulation," Gosling insisted. "We may let them work in the booth after I sign off on them."

This was crazy. They would be here for only one cycle but Gosling wasn't going to let them teach until they had passively observed each class. In other words, they wouldn't teach at all except for playing roles of captured detainees.

Bovey continued. "In any case, I want them in the classroom observing when they're not teaching."

"Then tell me and I will put them where ever you want them. But don't direct them personally. When Fred was here, he made that clear."

"Fred's full of shit," Gosling repeated. "It's completely legal for us to put the contractors where ever we want. I managed over 70 contractors for years. It's completely legal."

"No it's not," I said to Ray. I turned to Bovey, "I'm just trying to keep you out of trouble. And remember, I do have a law degree."

"And I disagree," Bovey answered.

"We'll put the contractors where ever you want them. Just go through the Site Lead," I insisted. "Anyway, it's easier for you. You don't need to be wasting your valuable time micromanaging the contractors."

"Tell them that unless they are scheduled to teach, their place of duty is in the back of the classroom," Bovey said.

"No problem," I said.

This wasn't getting us anywhere. It seemed so simple to me, yet Bovey and Ray were totally confused. I'd just have to roll with it. Putting the contractors in the back of the class may have been bad management, but it wasn't illegal as long as they directed me as the Site Lead to do it.

I called Fred to report what had happened. He had no kind words about Gosling, but reminded me that it was not Raytheon's concern how they used their contract resources. If they wanted to have them stand around all day doing nothing, they could do that. It might be stupid, but they could certainly do that as long as they didn't demand the contractors do anything outside the Statement of Work.

I conveyed that directive to the contractors the next morning. Everyone would be at the back of the classroom until assigned to teach. It was met with the expected comments but I asked them to keep in mind they were taking home $40 an hour for doing nothing.

Bovey and Gosling had trouble with the 09 Limas right from the start. There were a lot of objections that the content of the course was flawed. Some were practicing Muslims and felt their faith and culture was being demeaned. One insisted that he room only with a fellow Muslim. Others feared that the dining facility was not making the appropriate accommodations for Muslim dietary restrictions.

The contractors stayed in the classroom and mingled with the students, reinforcing the not-even-thinly veiled contempt all had for both Gosling and Bovey. Tensions escalated further when Bovey demanded the instructors not talk to the students between classes. There was a non-fraternization rule that forbade cadre from mixing with students outside of the classroom for which there are good reasons. The Army is serious about protecting students from the potential predations of instructors, especially in a military environment where rank increases the opportunity for abuse. But the restriction went way too far, in my opinion. College students learn the most outside of class when they can discuss things with the instructors informally. These students were mature adults and justifiably resented the restrictions on their personal lives. A no alcohol policy (which did not apply to the instructors) and marching to the dining facility and back made them feel they were being treated like children and did nothing to enhance their respect and devotion to the Army.

The escalating tension was in stark contrast to Kirsten's class, which was running very smoothly. All had passed Phase 1 and were well into Phase 2. Her determination to put as little effort as possible into managing the course gave me maximum freedom to employ my contractors the best way I saw fit. She refused to get wrapped up with petty matters and usually just texted me when something went wrong and expected me to fix it. The longest communication I had with her relative to work was a text message: "Where's Donaldson? WTF!" (I, of course, found Donaldson.)

Gosling's course began failing students immediately. Students don't usually fail Phase 1. It's pretty much all lecture and the written assignments are not difficult. I asked Bovey why we were seeing student failures this early.

"They don't speak English," she replied.

"What do you mean they don't speak English?"

"I mean they can't write. They make too many mistakes. If they can't write reports about what they collect, what good are they?"

I asked to see some examples. It was true that there were a higher number of grammatical and spelling errors than average, but rarely anything that obscured the meaning.

"Is it really necessary to flunk them on grammar and spelling?" I asked.

"The standards are clear," said Gosling. "I agree with Master Sergeant Bovey. If they can't write reports in correct English, it doesn't matter what they collect."

"The Army standard is '*generally* error free.' There's a lot of leeway for imperfect English. Most native-born Americans don't write well either," I pointed out.

"But this writing isn't generally error free. It is consistently full of errors."

"Errors which do not obscure the meaning."

"I sympathize, but my hands are tied. This is what the POI says. Any more than a certain number of errors per assignment and the student fails."

It was true that the grading standard set a limit on the specific number of errors. This too I felt was not helpful. It did not differentiate between errors that obscure the meaning and those that don't. The very reason these students were so valuable was that English was *not* their native tongue. We have a million native English speakers in the military but only a handful of Heritage Linguists. What's more, no collector is going to write a report alone and send it forward without it being checked by someone else. Every section has a quality control NCO and editor that would make sure the reports met standard before they were submitted.

Bovey and Ray stuck to their guns and failed a number of students on grammar and spelling.

The irony of Gosling failing students based on ability in English was not lost on the rest of us. I'm not sure whether he actually graduated high school or had come into the Army with a GED. In any case, he was not known for his intellect. He found reading difficult and study downright painful. College was not in his future. His passions were video games and softball. Neither Bovey nor Ray spoke any foreign languages but Bovey at least had some appreciation of other cultures and diversity. Gosling didn't.

Near the end of Phase 1 for Gosling's class, things came to a head and Paul Sciavoni precipitated it. He was bored and disgusted with sitting in the back of the classroom until Gosling deigned to allow him to teach. He called over to the 35L course and volunteered his services, or rather told Will Richards that we had several 35L-qualified contractors over at the Mike course who weren't doing anything. Will could request assistance from Dr. Sparks if he wanted.

This action showed initiative, was well intended and made sense in light of the wasted manpower. But it was not taken well by Bovey or

Gosling. Although she stood only to benefit from the truculent contractors like Sciavoni doing something else somewhere else, she had Sciavoni fired.

Bovey didn't even call me to deal with Paul. She called Fred and Chuck directly and demanded Sciavoni be canned. Fred gave me the bad news over the phone.

Paul flashed a three-letter text to me: "W T F?!"

There was nothing we could do. The customer can fire any contractor at any time and does not need to state a reason. Paul may have been a little obnoxious, but he was an extremely valuable instructor and dual qualified as 35M and 35L. I pressed Bovey for the real reason she had Sciavoni fired. Bovey hated confrontation. It didn't surprise me she would go behind my back to Raytheon – she had done that before – but it did surprise me she would initiate the release of a contractor. Bovey is at heart a very compassionate person. Paul had a family and needed the money. I don't know what Bovey had against Paul, but her actions were clearly personally motivated.

"It came to my attention that Paul Sciavoni took a rental vehicle down to Philadelphia over the weekend to visit his family. That's illegal. It's misappropriation of government equipment," she explained.

I knew Paul had gone to visit his family, but I doubted he would have taken a government vehicle instead of his own.

"Why didn't you tell me about it and let me handle it?" I asked.

"I didn't think you needed to be bothered with this. Anyway, the decision to fire Paul had to be made by Fred or Chuck."

"Feel free to talk to Fred or Chuck anytime you want, but talk to me first. My job is to solve problems here so they don't get to Fred or Chuck. I can't do that if you don't keep me in the loop."

Despite her reassurances to keep close communication in the future, I worried. This had been a pattern for her. She would agree to a plan, listen to another person, change her mind and then do something we hadn't agreed on without telling me. Then I would get a call from Fred asking about a problem, real or imagined, of which I was unaware. Fred appreciated the situation and advised me not to let Bovey out of my sight. Put my desk in her office and stay with her all day if necessary. She was also calling the Brigade staff with whom she was close and we were concerned they may be getting a negative impression of the contribution Raytheon's contractors were making.

Meanwhile I talked to Paul before he left. He was crushed. I asked about the Philadelphia trip. He acknowledged he had gone but had taken his own car. He hadn't missed any scheduled work. Was that the reason he was fired, he wondered? I told him what Bovey had told me, but that was off the record. She had no proof that Paul had done anything wrong, but didn't need it. That was the irony of work as a contractor. You couldn't be fired for false accusations but you could be fired for no reason.

Not only could you be fired, you could be blocked from further employment. Paul applied to the 35L course when an opening came up, but despite stellar qualifications, he didn't get the job. Someone of lesser qualifications was hired instead and no explanation was given or required.

Pablo Diego[85] was next to go. Gosling told Bovey that Pablo had had an inappropriate relationship with a student at Huachuca and been fired. He had recommended against Pablo's being hired in the first place, but as there was nothing in his record to indicate any history of inappropriate behavior, we hired him anyway. When Bovey found out, though, she reacted strongly. Having been the victim of infidelity herself, she had a sore spot for men who seduced women and then left them disillusioned and broken-hearted.

She called Fred to have Pablo fired. Fred called me to find out what was behind this. Again, I had to plead ignorance. I asked Bovey about it and why – again – she had called Fred without talking to me.

"It was serious," she said. "This isn't simply using a government vehicle for private use. Mr. Diego has initiated an inappropriate relationship with one of the female students."

85 Not his real name.

"All the more reason to let me know right away," I said. "And Paul didn't take the government vehicle."

"Yes he did. It had almost a thousand miles put on it over the weekend," she said.

"By someone else," I countered.

"Never mind that now. Diego is having an inappropriate relationship with a female student. I saw it with my own eyes."

"You were peeking in someone's bedroom?"

"No. I saw him talking to a student in the classroom during a break."

"What's wrong with that?" I asked.

"They weren't discussing class work."

"What were they talking about?" I asked.

"About meeting up together after class," she said.

"Are you sure?"

"I heard it with my own ears," she insisted.

"I need to investigate this. Who all were involved? I need to interview all parties," I said.

Bovey gave me the name of the student and arranged for me to talk to her during a break. The student was surprised at the allegation.

"I just asked Mr. Diego what there is to do around Devens after hours. A lot of us would like to go out after class and have some fun. He told us about some karaoke place called Chip Shots or Cheap Shots or something like that, but that was about it."

"Did he make a pass at you? Or suggest the two of you meet up?"

"No! Absolutely not. I'm married."

"Did anyone else witness this conversation?"

"Yeah," she said. "There were three or four of us involved."

I talked to the others who confirmed the substance of the conversation. The students had asked about places to go out after class and Diego had made a suggestion. All thought the idea of him starting an inappropriate relationship was ridiculous.

I told Fred what I had discovered and recommended Diego not be fired. I was also still upset about the lie that had gotten Paul fired. Fred said he would take it up with Chuck, but Chuck made a quick decision and Pablo was gone before nightfall.

Allegations of sexual misconduct are about the quickest way to get action in the military. Any such allegation has to be investigated promptly. We had done that, but Chuck still thought it best to remove Pablo immediately to demonstrate Raytheon's complete, unflinching support for the Army's policy. I'm sure Chuck was completely unaware of the subterfuge that accompanied the firing of Pablo and Paul.

I had some words with Bovey about this. It was not like her to be unfair. She was always willing to listen to everyone's point of view. But for some reason, twice in a row now she had acted precipitously without investigating and two innocent men lost their jobs.

"Talking to students on break in the classroom area doesn't constitute and improper sexual relationship," I said.

"I disagree," she said. "Just because they aren't sleeping together doesn't make the relationship any less improper. Anyway, Diego has a history of sexual predation."

"We don't know that," I insisted. "No one has complained and even if he did have an affair with a student, that would have been elsewhere. He's done nothing wrong here."

"I disagree, and I won't have people like that working here."

I failed to persuade her that her actions were improper and had to accept the situation. Chuck had made his decision in any case.

We were down two contractors, but with the loss of so many students, it didn't have much impact on the course. None, in fact, as Gosling was still not allowing the contractors to teach. But Raytheon was losing income.

Soon Gosling's class entered Phase 2 – booth phase – and Kirsten's group moved on to Phase 3. Booth phase, you'll recall, is where the students learn to question systematically. It is traditionally the hardest phase and the one where we lose the most students, but shouldn't be. The subject matter is straight forward. It's just a matter of practicing it correctly over and over to learn to do it right. The difficulty of Phase 2 was artificial. It was hard because the instructors made it hard, not because the subject matter was intrinsically demanding.

In Phase 2, the instructor is supposed to "realistically" play the role of the detainee. You can probably imagine what happened when the instructors tried to play the role of detainees to students who were themselves native to the culture the role player was trying to portray. The image of the Mike course – already at a record low for the ham-fisted manner in which these students had been treated and the summary firing of two innocent contractors – descended even further. Tempers flared and the cadre responded with intransience. By the end of Phase 2, half of the class was gone.

Meanwhile, Kirsten's class sailed through with no casualties. One hundred percent graduated – a first – and all the student evaluations of the instructors were positive – also a first.

The contrast upset Bovey and Gosling. Kirsten was taking it easy and getting excellent results while they were burning the midnight oil and failing. Even more annoying, she was trim and fit while Bovey struggled hard to keep her weight down and pass the APFT. (Kirsten had seriously contemplated intentionally failing the APFT just to get sent home, but her pride wouldn't let her do it. She would often run the half hour to work and home again, just for the enjoyment.)

Gosling hadn't taken an APFT in over a year. He had opted for a routine minor operation just before his last APFT and managed to get his medical waiver extended for over six months. (Time off to recover from that type of operation is rarely more than a week.) He loved softball and walked a thin line between actively participating in the ball games while maintaining he was still not medically fit to take the physical fitness test.

Kirsten had made friends with Tim Partin and the two of them shared the same thinly veiled contempt for the cadre of lesser ability who compensated by tormenting others. In addition to having a refreshing personality and saucy wit, Tim was an extraordinary marksman. He wore the

"President's Hundred" patch, earned only by the top expert shooters in the Army. In her down time, of which she had plenty, Kirsten often visited Tim's office both to socialize and to keep him informed of the real situation at the Mike course.

Bovey noticed this and tried to counsel Sergeant Howard for being away from her job and visiting the Devens Team Lead. It backfired. Tim counselled Master Sergeant Bovey for interfering with his open door policy. No one was to be forbidden from seeing him for any reason.

Kirsten had also taken a liking to Graham Donaldson during Phase 3. Phase 3 is all about Source Operations – the recruiting and management of agents and walk-ins who are not detainees. This is actually the hardest part of 35M training. You can't control the agent or walk-in like you can the detainee. The information they give you is harder to verify and it often involves giving money to the source for secretly working for the Americans. In real life, Source Ops can get your source killed. It can get you killed. One of Kirsten's most traumatic events in Iraq was the murder of one of her sources within earshot.

We had some really top-notch contractors available to teach Source Ops. Dwight Delorean was one who had just come back from 18 months doing Source Ops in Afghanistan. Graham Donaldson was another. Neither of them had much use for Bovey or Gosling. When Graham's friend Paul Sciavoni was fired, he did not keep his opinion on the matter quiet.

I got a call on August 4, 2010, from Kirsten.

"Lloyd, Donaldson just came in drunk. He's getting out of control."

Donaldson was a 220-lb rugby player. This didn't look good.

"Do you think he'll get violent?" I asked.

"I think he might," she said. "You'd better come right away."

If he got violent, somebody was going to get hurt. I had to get over there and take control of the situation immediately. On the way, I rehearsed in my mind what to do. I didn't want to escalate the situation by antagonizing Donaldson, for whom I had the deepest respect. But I had to come in large and in charge.

I took a deep breath and threw open the door.

"*What do we got*?!" I bellowed in my best sergeant major voice.

"Happy birthday to you,

"Happy birthday to you,

"Happy birthday dear (mumble, stumble, fumble…)"

It had all been a prank. I had completely forgotten it was my birthday and there on the table was a cake with a candle and some other treats. Kirsten and Graham wore ear-to-ear grins. I couldn't do anything but drop my jaw and my briefcase.

It wasn't long after that Donaldson got the axe. He stepped away from his post of sitting idly in the back of the classroom in order to get a haircut during a break and came back a few minutes late. Bovey had him fired.

Why? I wanted to know.

"He was away from his duty station. I didn't know where he was," she said.

"Why didn't you ask me? It's my job to keep tabs on the contractors," I said.

"He was scheduled to be in the back of the classroom and he wasn't there," she said. "It's not the first time people have wondered where he was."

"When you need to know where a contractor is, you have to come to me. That's my job, not yours."

"Well, you don't seem very good at keeping track of your people," she said.

"They are where I tell them to be. If they need to be somewhere else, they coordinate it with me and I coordinate it with you. That's the way this thing works," I insisted.

"And I disagree. I need to know where the contractors are at all times. He wasn't where he was supposed to be," she said.

"You don't know that unless you talk to me. I schedule the contractors."

"And I disagree."

This line of reasoning got us nowhere. Graham Donaldson was one of the best instructors we ever had. I assured him I would go to bat for him. This was the most outrageous firing yet.

"Don't bother," he said. "I've had it with this place. I don't want to work here anymore. Not as long as people like Bovey are in charge."

"What are you going to do?" I asked.

"Probably go back to Iraq or Afghanistan. Do something real."

Two more contractors were fired after Donaldson, making a total of five for the Staggered Start. Now Raytheon was taking a real hit in lost income. Fred asked Bovey whether she wanted them replaced and she said no. That was a huge mistake. It cut the available teaching staff down by a quarter. When we started Phase 4, which is the field exercise that runs round the clock for almost a week, we were really strapped for people. We had the money to pay contractors overtime, but were still short. The military instructors had to work 12-hour days for an entire week. Morale was grim.

I was able to wangle a few soldiers from the 6/98th just to play the roles of villagers. We also had more overtime money available, so any contractor who wanted to work 60 hours or more that week could. But the farcical mismanagement – keeping half the workforce idle during previous phases and firing instructors just in time to leave us short-handed in Phase 4 – became the symbol of Bovey's legacy. Bovey couldn't plan ahead more than a few days, couldn't delegate effectively, and was dangerously unclear on the difference between directing Raytheon and directing Raytheon employees as individuals. Being a "people person" is usually a good thing, but not when it leads a soldier to forget that fundamental legal distinction enshrined in the Constitution that protects the citizenry from the military.

Kirsten's program, by contrast, graduated 100% of the students she started with and received rave reviews. Commanders from the supporting units sent letters of thanks and called to tell us what a great job we had done. Best of all, Kirsten had created a Phase 3 that ran perfectly. All we had to do from now on was not change anything.

Although the Staggered Start had been a fiasco for the 09 Limas, it had also been the proof that when the Army uses Raytheon contractors, everything goes well. Kirsten had made maximum use of contractors; Gosling had sidelined them. This proved the value we brought to the table. These stats showed that the cost per graduate is far lower when you hire Raytheon. Rely only on military instructors and the cost per graduate not only doubles, quality and morale suffer as well.

Armed with these statistics, we could continue to sell value to the Army even in a climate of cut-backs. When money is scarce, value – bang for buck – counts even more. Chuck could market the programs under the slogan "When Raytheon is on the job, all is well."

But that wasn't the news that reached higher up.

CHAPTER 14

Repercussions

We had flunked out 50% of the Heritage Linguists, deflating Colonel Thompson's reputation as a miracle worker. These million dollar linguists had assignments waiting for them. Whole missions failed when the linguists didn't show up. At a cost of $50,000 a week to the taxpayer, Gosling sidelined enough instructors to privately tutor each failing student. The stench of it reached the level of the two-star general in command of the 80th TTC, Major General McLaren.[86]

I received the brunt of his wrath.

In September, just after the completion of the Staggered Start, I attended a planning conference in Virginia for the 80th TTC. General McLaren cornered me. He was under the impression that I had been in charge.

"What the hell is going on up there at Devens?" he demanded.

"Well, sir, the Course Manager sidelined the instructors..."

He shut me up with a wave of the hand. I locked my knees and heels at the position of attention.

"Do you know what went wrong?"

"Yes, sir."

"Do you know what to do about it?"

"Yes, sir."

"Are you or are you not a sergeant major?"

"I am, sir."

"Well, fix it, then!"

---

86 Major General John P. McLaren Jr. served as the Commanding General of the 80th Training Command (TASS) from 2008 through 2011.

That didn't leave much room for excuses.

My position was weak at the battalion level with the Brigade maintaining direct control over the Course Manager and the school. General McLaren tasked a staff officer in the person of Major Drake Sampson[87] to investigate the whole affair.

Major Sampson took a couple of days to thoroughly interview the main players in the Staggered Start and piece together the events. He was less concerned about the ongoing problem we had with military leaders directing civilians than about simple management of resources. The government had bought hundreds of hours of contract instruction. How had those hours been used? Why were military managers intruding into the management of civilian contractors? Why weren't the proper chains of authority being used?[88]

He gathered the leadership together for a meeting to elicit information from everyone involved. Among those present were Master Sergeant Bovey, Tim Partin, his assistant Jennifer Fogelman, Master Sergeant Bass and myself. Sidelining the contractors while failing half the class was, in his opinion, a major failing of the leadership. Why did Gosling sideline the contractors? Claiming that they weren't ready to teach held no water. Why did Master Sergeant Bovey allow this misuse of resources? She was the Course Manager. Why wasn't she managing the course? Why was she going around the Raytheon Site lead to personally direct civilians? And isn't the whole course overseen by the Brigade Director of Instruction? She was very familiar with what was going on at Devens, given her participation in the preparation for the Quality Assurance inspection. Why wasn't Sergeant Major Ortiz directing instruction?

Why had Bovey fired five contractors after the government had already allotted money to pay for them? Why hadn't they been replaced? She recounted how they had, in her opinion, violated various policies and needed to be removed. Besides, Colonel Thompson had specifically

87 Not his real name.

88 Indeed, Major Sampson's on-going responsibility was to facilitate the smooth operation of the schoolhouse at Devens. With the byzantine overlapping chains of command, operations often suffered just from the complexity of relationships.

instructed that Sciavoni, among others, not be rehired after the Triple Start of the previous year.

"You know Colonel Thompson specifically forbade hiring Sciavoni," she said to me.

I cringed. In fact, Colonel Thompson had not blocked Sciavoni and others from being rehired. As far as I knew, he never even looked at the résumés I sent. The Army email system failed. There was no hard evidence of Thompson black-balling Sciavoni, but now it was a matter of official record.

Unbeknown to most of us at the time, Colonel Thompson was under investigation for matters associated with the Devens project. Any documentation of wrongdoing would bolster whatever case was being built against him. These proceedings would be admissible in court if things went badly for the Colonel.

Up to this point, there was nothing on record to prove anyone had broken the law in firing contractors either. No official reason had been given because none was required with "at will" employees. But here I was able to recount in detail for the record how Mr. Sciavoni had not in fact committed the misdeed of which he had been suspected. Bovey knew who was putting so many private miles on the government vehicle in question. It was one of her own uniformed instructors and she did nothing to correct the misdeed. An apology to Paul would have been the least he was due.

My investigation of the allegations against Diego and the firing of Donaldson for getting a haircut also went on record. It also reached my ears that a couple of Bovey's military instructors had probably had sexual liaisons with students, though none were investigated. Bovey had turned a blind eye to her own staff while focusing her wrath on contractors. The heart-breaking difference was that she needed no proof – nor even suspicion for that matter – to fire a contractor. Investigating and punishing soldiers is much more complicated and requires due process.

Even the one evaluation she and Erwin performed on a contractor was a sham conducted to reach a foregone conclusion. Another of the temps,

Mr. McGee, who was a minority and a disabled veteran, had been fired after a process that clearly singled him out for special attention. Bovey had conducted an evaluation on him specifically to document a reason for firing him. In truth, McGee wasn't very good, but to personally target him for this purpose while not evaluating others was wrong. Moreover, racial minorities and disabled vets have robust resources to fight cases of discrimination and this looked like racial discrimination even if it wasn't.

"I hope Al Sharpton doesn't get wind of this," cracked Tim, never one to miss a chance for a little sarcasm.

Donaldson's and Diego's alleged misdeeds were brought to light and seen for what they were. A picture emerged of personal grudges motivating the firing of personal enemies on flimsy pretexts to the detriment of the mission. In fact, the only instructor to be let go for not having the official prerequisites – he had not been to an approved ABIC course but had been hired by a sub to Raytheon – was an excellent instructor no one wanted to see let go. But the QA inspection revealed this deficit and rules are rules, or so they say.

The petty behavior of the Course Manager and Sergeant Gosling contrasted with that of Sergeant Howard, who had made use of the same instructor pool and managed to achieve complete success. Kirsten demonstrated that leadership is more than strong-arming subordinates. It involves the ability to inspire trust, commitment and enthusiasm. In addition to inspiring people to get the job done, a good leader takes care of her subordinates. Kirsten's subordinates – instructors and students alike – trusted her. Gosling, on the other hand, maintained an adversarial relationship with virtually everyone. Bovey, in wanting to be liked, vacillated to the extent that she could not generate the trust necessary to command. Her habit of avoiding confrontation by going directly to Bass or Fred without talking to me gave us all cause for concern and annoyed Major Sampson who saw no need for the convoluted maneuvers she constantly made. The lines of authority at Devens were complicated enough. Why couldn't she just stay in her lane? Why all the hysteria?

"Somebody sneezes and she calls a Congressman," he remarked.

Both she and Gosling maintained that the real reason so many 09Ls had failed was that they didn't speak English. They were simply not able to do the job no matter how many instructors were available to help. Privately tutoring them wouldn't have helped. Major Sampson, however, did not feel this was an excuse for not trying. Besides, Sergeant Howard's team had graduated 100%. Did all of her students have perfect command of the English language?

Major Sampson needed no convincing that imperfect English is not an obstacle to working as a 35M. He had served overseas as an intelligence officer in a combat unit and worked with linguists. The translators the Army commonly hired – who were not US citizens and not clearable to Top Secret – never spoke perfect English either. But I think Major Sampson was also influenced by the fact that neither Gosling nor Bovey were fit or even willing to deploy. Kirsten and I were. Physical fitness and deployability mattered to him and his contempt for the degree of obesity he saw all around him at Devens was thinly veiled if at all.

"Some of these individuals here are just…enormous," he commented as we talked afterwards. "Isn't the command enforcing the Army fitness policy?"

"Selectively," I told him. Colonel Thompson had used lack of fitness to REFRAD Dole, Marlin and Johnson. But there was a large number of large soldiers at large not on any apparent fitness program. Gosling's medical waiver was wearing thin, especially in light of his enthusiasm for softball.

Major Sampson's report was succinct and clear. He recommended that Staff Sergeant Gosling be immediately relieved along with his supervisor Master Sergeant Bovey and her supervisor Sergeant Major Ortiz. He also raised the question of why Sergeant Major Sparks was not the Brigade Director of Instruction. I was senior, more highly qualified, more highly educated and physically present at Ft. Devens.

These recommendations were not welcomed by the Brigade staff. My transfer back into Special Forces was pending and I expected to be in Afghanistan before very long, but it was not to be. The chain of command delayed my transfer long enough for me to miss the deployment. It was hard for me not to see this as another example of spite in action. They gained nothing by preventing me from deploying. Indeed, they could have rid themselves of a troublesome sergeant major who was now recommended to replace one of them at the Brigade as Director of Instruction.

CHAPTER 15

Leadership Vacuum

Colonel Thompson's time as commander of the 1st Brigade was up. His replacement had already been chosen. Sadly, he would not advance further and never got his star, though he had certainly earned it. But neither did he go to jail. Whatever investigation he was under was quietly dropped and he was allowed to take his military retirement and enter the contractor world, as was a common practice for retired Military Intelligence officers still in their prime. Such was his value to the Army that he was eventually recalled to active service after a few years.

Two weeks before he was to take command of the 1st Brigade, the chosen successor to Colonel Thompson declined the job. General Heritsch would now have to find a new candidate and she was not happy. A colonel with a Military Police background by the name of John Pearson generously stepped in to be a caretaker commander and prudently resisted making any major decisions unless absolutely necessary. He let his staff continue to run the Brigade as they always had, so Major Sampson's recommendations were not carried out. With the pro-active Colonel Thompson no longer pushing for the success of the MI school at Devens, more work fell to Mike Bass as TOR, who only wanted peace and quiet.

Bass's job was to enforce the contract, not manage personnel. That responsibility properly belonged to Director of Instruction Sergeant Major Ortiz, who was even farther away and less available. The Course Manager runs the course and the Director of Instruction ensures that the Course Manager does her job. Instead, Mike Bass was constantly pestered with calls about problems Bovey could not or would not solve, mostly involving personnel management. I was frankly surprised that neither he nor Donna held the Course Manager to her responsibilities. Most leaders would have responded with "either you get the job done or I'll find someone who can." I suppose it was probably due to the long friendship they had with her and Bovey's sweet personality.[89]

The leadership vacuum at the Brigade prevented any serious changes from being made. Gosling stayed. Bovey rode out her time as Course Manager and a new Course Manager was phased in. Ortiz retained her position as Brigade Director of Instruction, unable to exert any influence over instruction at Devens, so far away.

Ortiz, Bovey and Gosling weren't the only one's briefly terrified by Major Sampson's recommendations. His remarks about the obesity of the full-time staff at Devens did not go unnoticed. Spurious charges were filed against him, alleging racism and sexism. He was cleared, of course, but the climate at Devens and the Brigade was less conducive to cooperating with anything Major Sampson recommended.

In the fall of 2010 the command of the 6/98th MI Battalion changed hands and our beloved Lieutenant Colonel Rook was replaced by Lieutenant Colonel Dean Rondeau. Rondeau had a leadership style that was the polar opposite of Rook. Where Rook was soft spoken and easy going, Rondeau was loud and intense. Rook had been in MI all his career; Rondeau had a Civil Affairs background and was a police detective in civilian life. I wasn't sure whether I was going to like Rondeau. Neither was anybody else. He had big plans for the 6/98th and contented reservists fear big plans.

Along with keeping our BFRR stats up, he also wanted to push our training mission harder. He wanted to get ABIC certified himself – a very reasonable idea. He also wanted to incorporate some adventure into our training calendar with perhaps some winter training or mountaineering. While I and perhaps three other soldiers in the battalion liked the idea of getting outdoors for some realistic training once in a while, MI also stands for "Mostly Indoors" and the thought of actually putting on a helmet and

89 She once closed a military graduation ceremony with "Let the hugging begin!"

equipment set off alarm bells. It was bad enough we had to do an APFT twice a year and go to the rifle range. Actually walking around in the woods was an alarming prospect. The woods are dangerous! You might get lost. What if you sprained an ankle? You might get bitten by a tick and get Lyme disease. The horror!

So Colonel Rondeau was welcomed with caution.

Any doubt about the suitability of Dean Rondeau to command an MI battalion quickly dissipated. He was very savvy about Military Intelligence and had a lot of real world experience in addition to his work in criminal investigation. He was very smart and his rough exterior housed a compassionate heart.

In the fall of 2010 we finally managed to get Sergeant Briere into the 35M course, but not without considerable resistance from Brigade. I didn't understand where that was coming from. We had openings for the next course, so there was no reason not to expedite the paperwork. One of us could hand-carry it if necessary. But for some reason, the Brigade staff resisted. "What's the hurry?" asked Bass.

The staff resented being asked to do anything outside of the routine, but this wasn't even that. Moreover, there was every reason not to delay. It would help our BFRR stats, to say nothing of getting a good soldier ready to deploy. Producing deployable soldiers was our mission. Every unit's mission, in fact.

Briere was well liked and was quickly appointed class leader. She was a natural leader and carried with her an infectious optimism. She had no problem with any of the course material and we kept up our early morning training program in addition to her class load.

We had a particularly interesting student in that class, a former Latvian police officer who had been trained by the Russians in interrogation. Their methods are quite different from ours and Pyotr Lyshenko[90] was a valuable addition to our knowledge base. His written English was atrocious, but he had no difficulty in establishing rapport and communicating. Plus,

90 Not his real name.

he was fluent in three very valuable languages and knew how things were done in the Russian military. He had almost failed Phase 2 because of his English, but I took measures to ensure he stayed. After the 09 Lima fiasco, I would not have escaped General McLaren with my skin intact had we flunked someone like Lyshenko for reasons of imperfect grammar.

I kept close tabs on Briere in Phase 2; I did not want her flunked out on a technicality, either. The class was entering Phase 3 when I had to travel to attend the annual MI training conference at Huachuca.

One of our first activities for Colonel Rondeau and me together as Commander and Sergeant Major was to attend the annual training conference at Ft. Huachuca. Rondeau and I, along with the other pertinent unit leaders flew out to Tucson, drove to Sierra Vista and rubbed elbows with everyone else involved in MI training. All of the Brigade staff were there as well, including Colonel Pearson, Sergeant Major Ortiz, and Master Sergeant Bass. Our new Course Manager, Erwin Bayer also came along.

Erwin was transitioning into his job as the next Course Manager. It would be refreshing to have a strong leader who knew the job and could plan farther into the future than Bovey had. He would also be in a better position to control Gosling, who had an annoying tendency to seek out reasons to flunk students and fire contractors.

Erwin had come to us as a temporary contractor during the Triple Start and then afterwards was hired on permanently. He was transferring to the Army Reserve from the Georgia Army National Guard and moving to Massachusetts to be with his new wife, Wilma Galena. His life had taken a pummeling with losing his civilian job, failing at his National Guard assignment, and going through a nasty divorce while being saddled with a mortgage for a house he couldn't sell. They needed a place to stay and I took them into my home until they could get back on their feet.[91] Erwin

91 This was not an unusual practice for me. Contractors often came to us destitute and in need of a little help until their paychecks started coming in. At one time or another, half the contractor force at Devens has been guests in my home.

and Wilma lived with me for over a year and had their first baby, Chris, in my home.

Erwin badly wanted the job. He had gone down in flames the last time he tried when he was in the Georgia Army National Guard and needed some self-validation. His previous assignment with the Georgia Guard had been as Course Manager, exactly the same job he was applying for with us. Poor leadership skills and ethical violations were specifically noted on his NCOER and the language was harsh. Just vouching for him would be difficult.

He didn't know that I was aware of the situation and I intended to protect his privacy. Nobody on our current project needed to know he hadn't done well before, but his bad NCOER would be impossible to hide when he put himself forward as a candidate for the job. I thought he had the potential to be a fine leader and if he ran into trouble, I was close by to help. My only concern was that he tended to be a little pompous and heavy handed when put in charge. I left him in place as my deputy once when I had to go to a conference and when I returned more than one contractor asked me never to leave him in charge again.

Erwin also had some problems stemming from his transfer over from the National Guard. His records were incomplete. The damning NCOER was missing and he did not have a current APFT either. He was clearly overweight and I worried that he might not pass the APFT he would need for his application. But somehow, he produced the necessary documents in time and was selected for the job.

When we announced Erwin as Bovey's successor, enough contractors privately expressed their misgivings to me that I mentioned it to Fred. In addition, there was the problem of his wife working at the same site under his authority. The military doesn't like to do that, to have a spouse working for a spouse. It's a conflict of interest and he already had an incident of nepotism on his record. But if Wilma could take a job as a contractor while he was in uniform, she wouldn't be technically under his command. So Wilma applied for one of the open contractor positions as an instructor and the Brigade commander did not object even though she lacked the requisite experience in the MOS and had never deployed as a 35M. She had at least instructed for a few months and would not have to adjust to the job.

I had a serious conversation with Fred about both Erwin leaving Raytheon to become the Course Manager and hiring Wilma. We agreed that Erwin should not forget that he would be coming back to the same job with Raytheon – Raytheon is very good about keeping jobs for their employees who deploy on military orders – and not alienate his coworkers with his leadership style. I for one felt having a more decisive leader would be a positive change and he and I had had long conversations at home about how to run the program more efficiently. We were confident there would be no problem with his leadership style since he was going to be leading friends and coworkers he already had a good relationship with. Fred did not have a problem with hiring Wilma as long as the customer didn't either.

Erwin phased in as Bovey phased out in the fall of 2010 and his wife Wilma came on board as a contractor.

At the conference at Huachuca I was mesmerized by an inspiring speech given by the commander of USAICS, General Custer.[92] (Yes, that's his real name.) He spoke of the urgent need to radically change our training methods. The Army Learning Concept 2015 – created by General Martin Dempsey, at that time commander of TRADOC – had just come out and it was as refreshing as it was revolutionary. He talked of harnessing all the power of the Internet, of distant learning technology, and of employing

92 Major General John Custer commanded USAICS and Ft. Huachuca until December of 2010 when he was replaced by another career Military Intelligence officer, Major General Gregg Potter. Custer retired to work at EMC Corp. as Director of Federal Missions and Programs. Potter left Huachuca in October of 2014 to take over as Director of Intelligence of the International Security Assistance Force (ISAF) in Afghanistan. In my brief personal contact, I found both men to be bright, forward-thinking proactive leaders dedicated to the daunting task of bringing the US Army into the modern Information Age. I let General Custer know I was eager to support his efforts and would count it a privilege to serve under his command. Unfortunately, the line of enthusiastic volunteers for any such job was long.

collaborative, student-centered learning methods. He recommended buying and studying "The Global Achievement Gap" by Tony Wagner,[93] a Harvard professor of education and advisor to General Dempsey. I was familiar with the work as part of my Master's in Education studies and bought five copies to circulate among the instructors I worked with. I even dared to hope I might meet Tony Wagner, who was at Harvard only an hour away and who had even done an education project at Devens some years earlier.

General Custer spoke of how we live in the day of the "strategic corporal." Instant access to what is happening in the world at any moment made it possible for even the lowest level soldier to have serious impact on the global missions of the Army. Foolish acts by low level soldiers such as photographing atrocities at Abu Ghraib and shooting at copies of the Koran had resulted in worldwide outrage. Such acts could only be prevented by educating and empowering low level soldiers capable of stopping them.

He closed the talk with the following statement: "If it's not immoral, unethical or illegal, if it forwards the mission of the warfighter, and if you are willing to take personal responsibility for it, don't wait for someone to give you permission. Go ahead and do it."

With this statement General Custer gave us, one and all, the authority to implement the steps necessary to improve the Mike course and begin applying the provisions of ALC 2015. I was ecstatic.

While we were away in Arizona, word came to us from the Mike course that all was not well.

First, I learned that they had failed Pyotr Lyshenko. His reports were not in perfect English, which had been the ostensible reason for failing him, but he had also taken some issue with the American policy of no use of torture ever. The Russians had used torture in Afghanistan and it

93 Tony Wagner has written, in addition to The Global Achievement Gap, a number of works on the theme of improving American education. At this writing he serves as Expert In Residence at Harvard University's Innovation Lab.

was very effective, he claimed. To take that position alarmed, well, everybody. With no one to serve as his advocate, he never even appealed the decision.

I talked to him on the phone from his home in Mill Creek, Washington. I couldn't talk him into coming back and trying again. He felt that if the instructors at the course were any indication of the quality of intelligence collectors in the US Army, he didn't want to be part of it and recommended I leave as well.

Secondly, Kat Briere had wound up on Elliott Warner's team for Phase 3 and she really liked Elliott. Because Elliott was in her (and my) unit, Erwin felt he should transfer Briere onto another team. Having a sergeant from her own battalion as the faculty team leader would give her an unfair advantage.

I took issue with that. We had several students from the same units as their instructors but Erwin was applying this logic only to Kat's case. Moreover, both Erwin and I were in Kat's unit anyway, so any bias toward her was not eliminated just by changing instructors. We shouldn't be worrying about unfair advantage in any case. An unfair *disadvantage* should be a concern but not an advantage. In fact, I think the students should be given every possible advantage, fair or otherwise. This isn't a contest to see who wins on a level playing field. It's war. Our job is to teach everything to every student any way possible and Sergeant Briere having a good instructor – and Elliott was one of the best – is a good thing, especially when they get along.

Erwin insisted that Elliott might pass her out of friendship, so he wanted her transferred. I argued that it was virtually impossible for one instructor to pass a failing student by himself, but if that were indeed a concern, let's just let Elliott recuse himself and have someone else test her. That's what we would do at the university.

Erwin wouldn't consider that option for an instant. I sensed a personal animosity toward Elliott driving the situation and saw storm clouds on the horizon. Elliott was sure to take this as an insult to his professionalism. Erwin didn't tell me that he and Elliott had served together in Iraq and there was some old tension between them, but Elliott would fill me in later. Erwin conceded that there was very little chance of Briere failing or of Elliott being the reason she passed, but said he didn't want someone coming back one day and raising the question of favoritism.

That someone might be more likely to raise the question of unfairly setting up a student for failure didn't concern him.

I should not have been in the middle of this at all. As the contractor Site Lead, I did not assign the students to the individual teams. Erwin had complete authority to switch the teams around, but I think he realized he was in for a show-down with Elliott.

With Sergeant Howard's orders almost up, Erwin had to find someone else to lead Phase 3. My recommendation was Dwight Delorean. He had done source ops in Afghanistan and had worked closely with Kirsten when she led the Phase 3 that had succeeded so well. He was well educated and a natural leader. Erwin wanted to put his wife Wilma in charge instead. There was no one less qualified than Wilma to run Phase 3 and no one more qualified than Delorean. What was Erwin's reasoning?

"Mrs. Galena knows how we run things at the school. Mr. Delorean doesn't," he said. Erwin had the comical habit of referring to his own wife as "Mrs. Galena" thinking it sounded more professional.

"Delorean knows how to run Phase 3. And if he has any problems, there's plenty of support. Besides, he has the street cred the student's trust. Wilma doesn't," I countered.

"Mrs. Galena is more experienced at the school, and that's what matters," he insisted. "Delorean can serve as her assistant until he's ready to assume the Phase Lead job."

"How about if Dwight leads and Wilma serves as his advisor?" I asked.

"Nope. I want Mrs. Galena as Phase 3 Lead."

We were right back at the obstacle that would just not go away. The Course Manager cannot choose which contractor to put into which position. He can only request that I put a certain contractor there. I was in the position of making the customer happy by giving the position to his wife or making the customer unhappy by choosing someone else. I opted for acquiescing to Erwin's demands even though it was, in addition to being foolish, clearly nepotistic. As long as they didn't change the Phase 3 plan Kirsten had perfected, it would still probably work out all right even with someone as unqualified as Wilma in charge.

I explained my position to Mr. Delorean and asked him to understand. I had hopes for him playing a leadership role in the expansion of the Raytheon projects as they grew. We would just have to be patient.

At Huachuca Colonel Rondeau and I spent a few evenings over dinner brain-storming how to put new and more effective instruction techniques into place. We were both fully ready to take General Custer up on his challenge to make changes without asking permission as long as we were willing to take personal responsibility for them. I knew exactly what I wanted to do the first day of class and had his full support.

I was sure Erwin was completely on board with the revolutionary changes that General Custer wanted. He had already begun to have problems the day he assumed the Course Manager position. People found him abrupt and overbearing. Shifting from being the central authority figure to one of a guide for the students – essentially a peer – would hopefully soften his style, which more closely resembled that of a dyspeptic drill sergeant. When Erwin stepped into a leadership position his personality switched from the jovial, hard-working, loving family man into a dictator, or so it seemed to his friends. Jenn Twain was particularly indignant.

"What's the problem with Erwin?" I asked.

"He's a pompous ass," she said. "He stands up in front of the students, posturing like he's the next General Patton, belly hanging over his belt, and spouting stuff like he wouldn't graduate a student that he wouldn't personally take into combat," she said. "These students have been in combat. They're wearing patches from the 82nd Airborne, Special Forces and Airborne Rangers. Erwin's not fit to wash their underwear."

"I just want the old Erwin back," said Butch Mudslinger.

"He puts the 'dick' in dictator! How did he ever get this job in the first place?" asked Kirsten. "You can't tell me he's fit enough to pass the APFT."

All that was true and what they didn't know was even worse. They didn't know about his previous history of failure at the same job. I talked with him about leading by influence, about how leading people you don't directly control isn't like leading an infantry squad. The modern military is a mixture of services and civilians and you can't simply order people around and expect results just because you're in charge. Even if it's the way things should be, it's not the way things are.

I was hopeful Erwin would learn and adapt. He was basically a likeable person. He didn't need to turn into a Mussolini to be an effective leader.

As serious as my concerns over his leadership style were, they were gradually eclipsed by the realization that he didn't really grasp our mission, which was to train as many huminters as best we could, not just run a hard school. Indeed, it was one of the most widely-shared blind spots of most of the instructors, not just the Course Managers. Making the training difficult does not make it better. Quite the opposite, in fact.

I returned from Huachuca full of enthusiasm for making some significant changes in the way we trained soldiers. My Master's thesis on training human intelligence collectors using collaborative, student-centered learning techniques had just been accepted and I had the blueprint for a training program that would both improve the quality of training and potentially reduce instructor costs. I say "potentially" because although we could do the job with fewer instructors, the Army wasn't going to let anyone go. We would have the same number of bodies; they would just have less to do.

There was also the potential for Raytheon that, because I had written the thesis while working for the company, they might be able to claim ownership of the intellectual property. If the Army adopted it, they would have to pay for it. My job title was Consulting Training and Development Specialist. Creating the training plan was certainly "training and development." I contacted a Raytheon representative from the head office on the matter of intellectual property, but she wasn't certain about ownership of my training plan and Raytheon took the matter no further. I was relieved. I feared that Raytheon would at least try to claim ownership of any idea or procedure an employee produced that was adopted by the customer. That would have made it harder to implement my ideas on my own.

On the first day of class after my return I shared something of my experience at the Huachuca conference with the students.

"I've just returned from four of the most inspiring days of my life. The Army has created something called the 'Army Learning Concept 2015' and we're not waiting until 2015 to start. This will revolutionize the way we teach and the way you learn. It will also more closely resemble the way you work and learn in the field. We instructors will be less the 'sage on the stage' and more the 'guide by the side,'" I said, stealing a line from Stephen Brookfield,[94] an authority on adult education.

I divided the students into six-person teams and took the main themes from the lecture's PowerPoint slides and distributed them.

"You have five minutes to research your topic using any resources available – your iPhones, laptops, the Internet, your own experience. Anything. In any of my classes, you are free to use whatever electronic devices you can get your hands on," I said.

This was a radical departure from the course policy, which forbade the students from using any resource other than the handouts we made for them. Using anything else was considered cheating and grounds for expulsion.

"After five minutes, one of you will present the topic to the rest of the class," I said. "I will choose who presents, so everyone has to be prepared. After the presentation, the topic will be open for comment from the whole class."

"Is this a graded exercise?" one of the students asked.

---

94 Stephen Brookfield is a scholar in adult education and critical thinking who at this writing holds the John Ireland Endowed Chair at the University of St. Thomas in Minneapolis-St. Paul, Minnesota.

"Nope," I answered. "You're free to fly or to crash and burn. I'll summarize each topic with the school solution, but the real learning process will come from you. From now on, you're the teachers."

I continued. "Don't be afraid to make mistakes or give alternative opinions. Dealing with different points of view and wrong information is part of this profession. We're trying to get away from the 'one right answer' approach and the 'school solution' being the only correct response. The real world of MI isn't like that."

Adult learners – especially soldiers who are already trained and experienced – do not come as blank slates. They already have a framework for understanding what they're being taught. They have to fit what you're teaching into what they already know, not build a whole new context like children do. They have to manipulate the new information, play with it and see what works and what doesn't. Seeing what doesn't work – making mistakes – is an indispensable part of the learning process and traditionally we had been penalizing the students for making mistakes. Essentially, the policy until now had been to punish learning and paralyze imagination and creativity.

From now on, they had permission to make mistakes without penalty.

They also had my permission – indeed encouragement – to access as many sources of information as possible rather than spend all effort combing through the handouts to find the school solution, the one right answer some faceless "expert" had declared at some point in time long, long ago in a galaxy far, far away.

To enhance learning, it is also important to take most but not all of the stress away. They may have to perform one day under very stressful conditions, but at the schoolhouse their mission was to learn. Make-or-break tests and threats from the instructors do not enhance education. Keeping things light and engaging in a little levity from time to time support the learning process. I did not want the students to worry about whether or not they would pass; I wanted them focusing on learning as much as they could in the short time allotted to us.

The biggest problem I had with this first hour of collaborative, student-centered learning was sticking to the time schedule. Presentations were enthusiastic, sometimes serious, often intense, and usually humorous. Anything but dull. Students wanted to continue discussions during the break. More than one student commented that it was about time the Army went to a more effective learning program.

My new policy lasted one hour. On the break, Erwin called me into our office.

"What are you doing?" he asked.

"Instituting the new learning methods," I answered. I got a blank stare in response. "Collaborative, student-centered learning? ALC 2015?"

"That hasn't been authorized yet."

I was taken aback. Erwin had sat through the same inspiring, persuasive lecture by General Custer I had just days before.

"Sure it has," I said. "USAICS told us to implement it right away. Don't wait until 2015."

"No it hasn't," he said.

"Erwin, the General looked us in the eye and told us to go do this."

"I don't care what the General said. We tried collaboration before. It doesn't work. We're not doing it. If he doesn't like it, he can relieve me."

I didn't know where to start. Pull out my notes and show him? Call the commander? This was both stupidity as well as flagrant insubordination. I couldn't ignore his refusal to follow the commander's intent, but escalating to a confrontation in front of the students wasn't good either. I decided to back off as gently as I could and give Erwin a chance to reconsider.

"You're the boss," I said. "What do you want to see happen?"

"Go back to giving the PowerPoint lecture the way it's supposed to be done. And have the students leave all electronic devices outside and close their laptops. This is testable material. I don't want any cheating."

"There's nothing wrong with them using the laptops we issue them. That's what they're for. Why shouldn't they keep their cell phones as well? They can't access classified information."

"They need to get used to leaving all electronic devices outside the classroom. If they get in the habit of bringing them in all the time, they might forget when we really do have classified material out."

This reasoning was as thin as the reasoning for transferring Kat. Take a student off a team because the leader *might* make it easier for her to learn. Take the tools away from the students because someday one of them *might* forget to leave it outside a secure area. Something bad *might* happen, so let's ensure nothing good does. Can't be too careful...

It was difficult to return after the break and tell the students that our experiment in collaborative student-centered learning had just been cancelled. There was no way hide what had just happened and that the Course Manager had just completely reversed something I had so enthusiastically endorsed as the policy of the Commanding General of USAICS.

The superiority of the new method over the old method couldn't have been illustrated any more effectively than by trying it and immediately taking it away. The students saw the power of the new method, but more importantly, saw clearly why the old ways were so bad.

It also put the Course Manager in a position from which it would be difficult to recover. He had not started off with much credibility, strutting about in front of a class of combat vets with nothing on his overly snug uniform to brag about. Now he seemed like a petty tyrant more concerned with maintaining control than with ensuring the students learned something relevant. They would soon be deploying to combat; Erwin wouldn't.

This incident, straight on the heels of returning from the conference, put the first serious strain on our relationship.

The second was right around the corner.

Erwin had directed that Sergeant Briere be removed from Elliott's team. That hadn't happened. Wilma blamed Mr. Delorean for not implementing her instructions. I talked to both Elliott and Dwight to get their take on what had or had not happened. Yes, they were aware that Erwin had directed the change. Dwight explained that he felt the move was wrong, especially right before the test. It would set Sergeant Briere up for failure, which he was sure was Erwin's intention. Elliott outright refused to carry out the change.

"Elliott, you know he has the right to do that. We have to do what he says," I reasoned.

"Yeah, I know. I just don't like the way he orders people around, to deliberately try to flunk students he doesn't like. And to put Wilma in charge just so he can take her along to all the conferences. Wilma! The worst instructor we have!"

Wilma had a sweet personality and was easy to like. The problems with her reputation as a bad instructor stemmed from taking liberties while teaching that inevitably resulted in bad reviews from the students. She was in the habit of bringing her child in to work and letting the students pass him around while she taught class. She would often get bored in the booth while she was supposed to be playing the role of a detainee and ignore the student while she texted. That her husband, the Course Manager, protected her when anyone else would have been fired, angered everyone, not just Elliott.

"How is Phase 3 going otherwise, by the way?" I asked.

"Totally effed up," he said.

"Didn't they just keep with the program Kirsten created?" I asked. "It worked perfectly."

"Not even for a second," Elliott said. "Wilma immediately started changing things around. I'm sure Erwin told her to do it, but she totally messed up the schedule. Now, every day we have to change the schedule and fix problems from the day before. We look like fuckin' amateurs!"

"And he's blaming it on us," Dwight pointed out. "It's all the contractors' fault."

"How is it possible to make it look like this is the contractors' fault?" I asked.

"I took over after Wilma fubarred[95] it. She quit and I had to pick up the pieces," Dwight said.

"Erwin made her quit?" I asked.

"No. She quit on her own. Just refused to continue as Phase Lead with all the criticism she was getting," Dwight explained. Wilma did tell me later she felt she was being attacked from all sides, instructors and students alike.

"Well, let's just get through this the best we can. Briere will be fine no matter where she goes."

"Don't be too sure," Elliott cautioned. "You heard about Lyshenko, didn't you?"

"I did. But I've talked to him and I think we can get him back after Erwin's gone and the new policies get put into place."

"Is Erwin getting replaced?"

"Not immediately. But the way things are going, we'll have to replace him."

Actually, it was beginning to look like Erwin might be REFRADed almost as soon as he started, but I didn't want to spread any rumors. He hadn't taken the APFT and was due for a new one. He had outright refused to take it the last time it was scheduled, saying he didn't need it. Now he was well overdue and Jenn Fogelman, Tim Partin's second in command, was very clear that he would take it and pass it or face the consequences. He was way too heavy to pass weight standards and nobody would put money on him passing any of the three events: pushups, sit-ups and the two-mile run. What's more, we were nearing Thanksgiving and Christmas season, not the best time to go on a diet.

After smoothing things over with Elliott and Dwight, things looked like they would simmer down enough for us to get on with the course. That night Erwin apologized for being heavy handed, but was sure he was

95 FUBAR – Fucked up beyond all recognition. The acronym dates back to at least the Second World War. My father gently explained it to me as "fouled up beyond all recognition" when I was a child.

right. In any case, as Course Manager he had the responsibility for delivering the course the way he saw best. If the General didn't like it, he could relieve him.

"Erwin, no two-star general a couple thousand miles away is going to personally relieve an E-7. But he might relieve your commander if he doesn't think the Colonel is implementing his policies."

"Let him. But I'm not going to follow a policy I know won't work. Collaboration doesn't work. We've tried it before."

"I don't think you completely understand what he meant by 'collaborative learning.' You should read Tony Wagner's book."

"I will when I get some time," he said. "Right now, I'm up to my ass in alligators."

He smiled. "And on that subject, I want to get this matter with Elliott and Briere cleared up. I want them separated."

"Why is that such a problem?" I asked. "This late in the phase will only set her up for failure. She's doing well. Why jeopardize it with a last-minute change?"

"Because Elliott is insubordinate. I ordered him to change. You ordered him to change. Yet, Sergeant Briere is still on his team. If I let him get away with this, all discipline will break down."

"I talked to him. He'll comply."

"He should have complied when I first ordered it."

"You know Elliott. Get in his face and he'll shove right back, even when it's not good for him. You used to be friends. It wouldn't hurt for you to talk to him like a human being. You know, treat him as a fellow professional."

"That's the difference between your style and mine. You just want to talk him out of it. I will make sure he complies whether he likes it or not."

"You don't need to come down hard on him. He'll comply."

"Yes. He will. I want us both to talk to him tomorrow."

"That's fine. Just remember that he works for Raytheon, not for you. Be professional. Don't antagonize him unnecessarily."

The following morning Erwin found a time for the three of us to meet behind closed doors. I could see immediately it was not going to go well when Erwin addressed Elliott directly.

"Mr. Warner, Sergeant Briere will be transferred off your team immediately and you will comply!"

Erwin looked my way. "Dr. Sparks?" He evidently expected me to allow him to directly order one of my contractors and to back him up.

"Now let's look at this problem from every angle…" I began.

Erwin broke in. "Mr. Warner, you will comply immediately. End of discussion. Dismissed."

Elliott didn't say anything. He just looked over at me, looked back at Bayer with a gaze that could melt steel, stood up and walked out.

Silence hung in the room and Erwin glared at me. "Lloyd, I am really pissed at you right now."

I paused, not sure how to begin. He had just lost his temper and was in no mental state to entertain a rational discussion. I tried anyway.

"Did you really not see that coming?" I asked.

Erwin remained quiet and glared.

"I told you I would get compliance. Elliott agreed to comply. Elliott works for me, not you. Now he's really, really angry. I wouldn't be surprised if he quit."

"You have no control over your people," he said.

"You *are* one of my people," I said. "Cool down and we'll talk later. Meanwhile, I need to talk to Elliott."[96]

96 I've never found it productive to humiliate a subordinate, even in private. It attacks a man's ego, against which he puts up defenses. The righter you are in your criticism, the more it hurts and the stronger he defends himself. If you do manage to bludgeon a subordinate into submission, from that moment on, you can never take your eye off him. He will move heaven and earth to exact revenge, no matter how long it takes and no matter what the cost. I've found it infinitely more productive to engage a person at his best self-image, to appeal to his noblest sense of self. This takes a lot more thought and self-control than simply berating a person because you are angry.

I tracked Elliott down and listened to a tirade about Erwin's incompetence as a leader, as a huminter and as a human being. He told me about how in Iraq Erwin was known for getting three pieces of insignificant information from a walk-in but write it up in three separate reports to pad his record. He didn't trust Erwin and never had. What's more, he's a hypocrite. He keeps putting down people like Delorean and Briere while he puts his wife Wilma into positions for which she is completely unqualified. "For cryin' out loud, she's got her desk set up like a mini daycare with a playpen and toys! She's passing the kid around in class! The latrine smells like baby diapers," he said. "How did she even get this job anyway?"

Bringing Chris, their new baby, onto the worksite was a thorny issue. I told Wilma she couldn't do that. It was against Raytheon's policy. She countered by saying she didn't bring him in; her husband the Course Manager did. It was against Army policy as well, so I reported it to Mr. Partin and Ms. Fogelman, but it got the same compliance as the APFT. Bass didn't want to hear about it, either, even though this was one area he was legally obligated to enforce as TOR. Bringing babies on site violated the Statement of Work.

Of course, both Erwin and Wilma had their jobs because of me. I had put my faith in them and it was becoming increasingly clear that that faith may have been misplaced. Wilma may not have been suited to the job of Phase 3 lead, but it was Erwin who insisted she be put there. Erwin wasn't doing well on honing his leadership skills, either. He had just one tool in his toolbox and that tool was a sledge hammer which got way too much use.

I recalled that his NCOER contained negative comments about his lack of effective leadership and attempts to put an unqualified friend or family member into a job. This put flesh to the skeleton.

These last couple of days had also revealed to me that Erwin was probably incapable of even grasping what the General had talked about. Erwin clearly did not understand collaborative learning. He was extremely uncomfortable with relinquishing authority or allowing the students any autonomy. The incident with Elliott also showed how far his need to control the people he worked with extended. This combination of inability to understand ALC 2015 and the compulsive need to control others forced me to consider that I may have been remiss. In trying to help Erwin back on his feet, I hadn't considered that he may truly be incapable of doing the Course Manager's job the way the commander wanted it done.

A pattern of deception and controlling behavior was gradually emerging. Erwin began to commit some truly counterproductive acts in addition to removing Briere from her team the day before the test. He was also preventing the students from going to study hall at night unless all went together. Allowing some of them to study when others didn't would give them an unfair advantage, he explained. One student was found to have material in her possession from a previous class. She was studying ahead. This little piece of initiative was interpreted as "cheating" and an ethics violation. She was sent home and barred from re-enlistment.

Studying ahead was not unusual. Prospective students commonly sought out recent graduates to find out as much as they could about the course and prepare for it. One student – Sergeant Jack – felt so confident he asked whether he could just take the tests and go home without staying for the whole 10 ½ weeks. This laudable effort was rewarded with extra harassment from a few of the instructors who felt he needed to be put in his place.

Flunking students for making extra effort to study ahead was insane. It not only retarded the learning process, it often eliminated the brightest and most proactive students. Any effort at collaboration was viewed as cheating. Using laptops to access the Internet along with the class handouts was not allowed. The class was forced to keep even their official laptops closed during lecture and passively watch whatever snail-paced PowerPoint presentation was read to them.

The Mike course was now batting 0 for 4 in good Course Managers since Fraske left. From Miner to Smith to Bovey to Bayer, all had failed badly and all for different reasons. The other courses didn't have these problems.

The 35L, 35F and 35G courses were all running smoothly with high graduation rates. They had good Course Managers who rarely raised a ripple. The 35M Course Mangers by contrast were sending constant tsunamis Mike Bass's way and he was wearing thin. What had been the common thread in the selection of a chain of bad leaders?

How is it that the military so often seems to pick not only a poor leader, but the worst of all available leaders? I've mused about this over many a campfire with friends. I once heard an explanation that made a lot of sense. The eternal conundrum of the military leader is "the mission or the men." Theoretically, they are both equally important. But with successful officers a third consideration enters the arena: his career. Many are willing to sacrifice both the mission and the men in order to advance their careers. A careerist has all the right blocks checked. He has recommendations from the important people. In short, he has done all the things a leader consumed with actually leading doesn't have time to do, which is advance his own career.

Fraske had no interest in advancing his military career. Miner was just running out the clock. Smith had expensive software he wanted to sell. Gosling measured success in the number of students he failed. Bovey needed to be liked and couldn't make or stick with decisions. Bayer was at the end of his rope and perhaps acting out of fear of losing control. Where was the pattern? I didn't see one.

If you looked at the Brigade staff, you would see a wide range of competence. Lopez, Bass and Kilmartin were all career bureaucrats who never deployed. They knew and cared little about either Military Intelligence or training. All they wanted was a secure job and steady paycheck. But Colonel Thompson had shown remarkable imagination and initiative. His Command Sergeant Major Alan Anastasiades was an excellent NCO.[97] Why wasn't his influence felt more strongly at the Brigade and the school?

---

97 CSM Anastasiades was not just an excellent NCO but arguably at one time *the best* NCO in the Army. He had participated in the Army-wide Best NCO Competition and not won because he had performed so perfectly the panel assumed he must have cheated. During this period when his influence was badly needed at Brigade and the school, he was doing double duty as the Division Command Sergeant Major

So what accounted for the string of bad performance by the 35M Course Managers? Was there a rubric that selected for bad leaders? I didn't think so. Sometimes we got good leaders and sometimes bad ones. It's just that the bad ones tended to stay and keep doing bad things long after they should have been relieved.

A fundamental problem clearly lay not in the quality of the Course Manager but in the physical absence of the key decision-makers. Nobody at Brigade, let alone Division or the 80th Training Command, was present at Devens. Nobody at USAICS had a clue as to what the day-to-day dynamics were. None of the failures would have happened if a key commander had been physically present on Ft. Devens and saw what was happening. I had enough control over the contractors to manage Raytheon's role in the project, but could only intervene as battalion Sergeant Major when something happened that was actually illegal. Stupid is not illegal. And even when I did intervene, it was usually blunted by the Brigade staff.

Another of the mysteries of the military is the haven it gives to the spiteful. Spite. The motivation to hurt people no matter what the cost while ignoring the fact that it does no one at all any good. It is pure evil. Spite is malice for the sheer pleasure of hurting someone. I've uncovered spite at the foundation of a spectrum of problems that presented superficially as something else. But when good leaders are present, the harm inflicted by the spiteful can be staunched. And the leaders responsible for the school were not present on Ft. Devens.[98]

---

as well. In addition, his background was in Mechanized Infantry and not Military Intelligence. He may have felt somewhat out of his areas of expertise. In any case, Major Sampson was not impressed and thought Anastasiades should be doing more to rein in the chaos that centered on the 35M course managers.

98 The phenomenon of spite has always fascinated me. What makes people do spiteful things? It is as quintessentially human as any defining trait. The Russians are connoisseurs of spite and Dostoevsky's "Notes from the Underground" is well worth the short read. Related to the phenomenon of spite is the "adversarial personality." One of the personality types that has survived the advance of science in psychology is the type that actually prefers making enemies rather than friends. There is enough evidence now to support that it has a genetic component, which leads to the question of how these people manage to pass their DNA on. If no one likes these people,

In the Erwin/Elliott conflict, I wasn't sure whose spite was more dangerous. Erwin wanted to make sure Elliott suffered for snubbing his authority. Elliott wanted Erwin to suffer for his arrogance. The superficial reasons each gave covered the deeper motivation which fueled each person's actions – personal hatred.

Elliott agreed to comply and stay on, but he would not remain quiet. He intended to file an IG complaint and document all the ways Erwin had violated military policy. But IG complaints move slowly.

Sergeant Briere and five other students were transferred to another team in a completely unfamiliar area of operation just one day before the test. She was upset about this, especially when she heard Elliott's version of why this was happening. She was concerned that she was being set up to fail the test, as were the other members of the team. I assured her that this was not the case. No one had it in for her; it all stemmed from a personality conflict between Erwin and Elliott. But she and her classmates had reservations. Reversing my collaborative training method had planted serious doubts about Bayer's commitment to their success. She had been asked as class leader to take the matter higher.

She reported her class's concerns to Bayer and Staff Sergeant Daniel Wilson,[99] the assistant to the Course Manager. I knew Wilson to be a highly professional NCO who would in any case see no advantage to flunking out a half dozen students this far into the course. Bayer said he would take it under advisement, but not change his decision. She wanted to know what to do.

I didn't think the situation was as serious as they feared, but recommended she register her concern with Erwin's superiors just in case the worst happened and she had to appeal. Because the test was the next day, there was no time to talk to anyone from Brigade and in any case, as

---

how do they find mates? The answer is no doubt complex, but the military is a haven for both the adversarial personality and the spiteful.

99 Not his real name.

it happened, all the leadership was in Virginia for a conference, including Colonel Rondeau.

I knew Tim Partin had an open door policy and had demonstrated he was dead serious about welcoming any soldier to talk about any concerns any time. He had done as much for Kirsten when Bovey tried to obstruct her visits. In addition, Mr. Partin was Erwin's rater. In the labyrinth of chains of command, Sergeant Bayer's NCOER would be done by Tim, even though Tim had nothing to do with the administration of the course or management of its personnel. I recommended that she drop in to see Tim and at least get the matter on record. I would be watching from nearby.

Kat and all her classmates passed the test, so the whole matter should have ended happily right there. But spite was about to rear its ugly head and only required my brief absence. I was at home in my rented apartment in the evening later that week when I got a call from Kat.

"I tried to hold out. I'm sorry, but I think I threw you under the bus."

"What are you talking about? What happened?" I asked.

"Can I come over?" she said.

"Yeah, of course. How soon can you be here?" I asked.

"I'm outside your door right now," she said.

I went to my door and there stood a tired and sad-looking NCO. Sergeant Briere dragged herself into my apartment and plopped down on the sofa.

"Want a drink?" I offered.

"No thanks," she said. "I don't drink when I'm depressed. Besides, it's against the rules."

"Why are you depressed?" I asked.

Kat proceeded to relate to me all that had happened in the previous couple of hours. As soon as I had left work, she was called in by Bayer and in the presence of his assistant Staff Sergeant Wilson she was grilled, police style, on who had put her up to visiting Tim Partin. It couldn't have been her decision alone, they accused. Elliott or Dr. Sparks must have advised her to do it. She had no right to visit Mr. Partin without asking permission and being escorted. She tried to hold up and take responsibility as it being her decision alone, but was badgered for a confession. She asked for a battle buddy and was given Bovey, of all people.

I asked why she hadn't just asked for her Sergeant Major to be present. I was five minutes away. Indeed, Bayer should have alerted me without being asked.

"I didn't want to cause you any trouble," she said.

"This is just the kind of trouble that comes with the Sergeant Major's job," I said. "In any case, I'll be having a few words with those two NCOs tomorrow."

"I know. I broke down and told them you told me to visit Mr. Partin," she said. "I tried to hold out, but it was just too much."

"You should have told them right up front," I said.

She was distraught in thinking she had betrayed me. It was nonsense, of course. I was more upset that Bayer had taken this tactic with a student, especially a top-notch student like Briere.

"They fired me as class leader," she said.

"Don't worry. I'll take care of it. Anyway, the class leader position should be rotated. It isn't fair to dump all that responsibility onto one single student. It won't reflect badly on you," I assured her. "And you won't have as much work to do from here on out. You passed Phase 3. All that's left is the Phase 4 field problem and nobody ever flunks that.

The following day I couldn't find Erwin, so I talked with Sergeant Wilson. Why had they grilled my soldier without informing me? He said it wasn't really a "grilling" and there was really no reason to bother me. They just wanted to get clarification on why she had gone to see Mr. Partin without telling them. She was being rotated out as class leader as a routine measure and it would not reflect badly on her.

When I finally found Erwin, he was a little more blunt. He had every right to question a student when a student violates policy, he said. She had no right to see Mr. Partin without informing him. Incredibly, he maintained that if any student wanted to see Mr. Partin, they would have to request it through proper channels, and if approved, be escorted over by a faculty member. This was utter hogwash, but Erwin spoke these words as if he knew the policy verbatim. Moreover, he said, I wasn't her Sergeant Major while she was in school. She could contact her commander but not me.

"How do you do that?" I asked.

"Do what?"

"Say things like that with a straight face," I said.

Apparently Erwin relayed his version of events to Bass and spread it around that I had interfered with the smooth functioning of the schoolhouse in favor of a student who was a known trouble-maker. I got wind of this only indirectly when Major McCabe, our battalion executive officer, was notified of the discontent from above.

Mike Bass was at Ft. Devens the next day for a meeting with the schoolhouse leadership and a planning session. I took him aside him to get his point of view. He looked, as always, worn and frazzled.

"I'm really tired of all the trouble out of the Mike course," he told me. "The other courses don't cause me this many headaches."

`Wanting to ease his burden as much as possible, I asked what I could do to help.

"Are any of my contractors giving you grief?" I asked.

"There are a few names that keep popping up," he said.

"Who are they?" I prodded. "Maybe I can do something about it."

I expected he might name Wilma. She often got flamed by the students as the worst instructor. Or maybe Alice, who was nicknamed the "Dragon Lady" because she supposedly graded so hard. Or maybe Charlie because he seemed to complain so much. But it was none of these. Bass named off three or four of my best instructors and I was shocked.

From that little exchange, it became clear that the source of Bass's headaches was not lack of good instruction. Nor were we failing to deliver on the contract. Being the Contracting Officer's Representative, Mike's problems should be based on not getting what the government was paying for. Instead, he was being called frequently by the Course Manager who complained about certain contractors the Course Manager didn't like and about me for protecting them.

I had stopped Miner, Smith, Gosling, Bovey and Bayer all from abusing Raytheon employees on several occasions. Those who drew the most fire from the Course Managers were the ones quickest to point out the Course Managers' failings. To be sure, I defended the weak performers as well. After all, I was their advocate. But the ones Bass named weren't weak performers.

"I keep asking Raytheon for robots, but they keep sending me people," I said. "We're never going to get perfect employees and we have to accomplish the mission with what we have."

"I just wish this mission would go away," he said.

Later that day in the open session to air problems, Major McCabe brought up the Briere incident. Brigade staff had complained that I had acted improperly by recommending Briere see Mr. Partin.

"How is it that anyone thinks they have the right to prevent the Sergeant Major from seeing his own soldier?" McCabe challenged.

Bass explained the way he saw it, which had been limited. Briere, he said, had not been prevented from seeing Mr. Partin; she had just done it improperly without notifying the Course Manager.

Tim Partin jumped in to remind Bass that no student needs to notify the very person she by whom she feels threatened that she intends to see him. Students fear retaliation and past events had proven these fears justified. Bass was also apparently unaware of the events that had led up to the incident as well as the police-style grilling she had received.

The proper action was never crystal clear in this case. I was both the Site Lead and the battalion Sergeant Major. I worked for Erwin, but outranked him. Briere was both my soldier and Sergeant Bayer's. The convoluted web of authority may have made it difficult to determine who was responsible to whom, but in the end, she had a valid concern and had taken proper steps as an individual and as class leader. Bullying students was inexcusable in any case. Briere felt threatened, as did others in her class.

I was hoping to find a strong leader in Erwin. There was no reason he couldn't be that without being a bully. He had the goodwill of his colleagues before he got the job. A little courtesy and fairness would have cost him nothing. The course was set up to practically run itself when he inherited it. He could have succeeded effortlessly and earned the trust of those he worked with as well as the students. He had destroyed any possibility of that with his own hands by putting Wilma in charge of Phase 3, personally attacking Elliott, and intimidating an outstanding student. He also put himself in a very bad light by reversing General Custer's policy on the new Army Learning Concept 2015.

Even his lack of both physical fitness and recent deployment experience weren't complete obstacles. Most people sympathize with how hard it is to stay in shape and he had, after all, at least deployed even though it was to Iraq prior to 2007 before policy changed. But things had progressed too far. He wouldn't regain any goodwill, let alone build a decent reputation before he was REFRADed for failing the APFT. He expected that Raytheon would give him his old job back, but that position had been filled and even if it hadn't been, none of his former coworkers wanted him back.

One of the truly magnificent instructors we had was Dwight Delorean. Delorean was one of the temps over the summer who stayed on as a permanent contractor. He had spent the previous year and a half in Afghanistan doing source ops. I singled him out as my choice to run Phase 3 after Kirsten left. In addition to being highly qualified, he was tall and charismatic, intelligent and eloquent. He was also working on his PhD in counselling. The students loved him and for good reason.

Dwight had a run-in with Bovey and Gosling during the Staggered Start. He had been in his car in the parking lot studying his role when his absence was noted by Bovey. "Where's Mr. Delorean?" she wanted to know.

It was not unusual for people to retreat to their cars when they needed a little quiet to work. The workspace was noisy and completely lacking in privacy, and the Raytheon rooms were in another building across the parade field. The best and closest space for a little quiet and privacy without leaving the area was the parking lot. I said I would find him. Immediately, both Gosling and Bovey began complaining loudly about contractors being absent without permission. Elliott, who knew where Delorean was, heard it and went to get him.

Delorean came in angry that Bovey and Gosling had slandered his reputation as a professional and asked that he and I talk to them in private at the earliest convenient time.

Behind closed doors, I listened to Dwight politely but firmly tell them that he would not tolerate this kind of behavior. If they had a problem with him, they should tell him directly or Dr. Sparks. He would not be subject to this kind of treatment nor let actions like this slide.

Both Bovey and Gosling were embarrassed. From then on, they availed themselves of every opportunity to slight Mr. Delorean. Nor did the slander stop. Delorean had to remind them, and later Erwin Bayer as well, that he would not stand for personal attacks. They could talk to him in a professional manner or with me, his supervisor, or not at all.

Delorean had been my choice for Phase 3 Lead but been made Wilma's assistant instead. Delorean was understandably offended by this decision. He saw this as yet another personal slight. Even worse, it demonstrated that Raytheon would not stand its ground when contractors were abused. Despite Fred's direct and clear warning, Erwin continued to insist on personally directing the contractors, his wife included. No one from Raytheon was going to call the customer and insist that this practice stop.

Any enthusiasm Delorean still retained for contributing to the course in a meaningful way dissolved at that point. With the humiliation of being made Wilma's assistant, Delorean totally checked out mentally. He still taught a great class whenever asked, but there was no initiative any more. He just passively filled a seat and worked on his studies until tasked to do something related to the job.

The freedom from responsibility at least allowed him to focus on another goal – his PhD. He came to me with a plan.

"I've figured this out," he said. "I can finish up my counselling internship by taking one afternoon and Saturday off every other week in March and April. I have enough PTO and anyway, if you could schedule me around those Friday afternoon and Saturday slots, I can still do a 40-hour week and get my PhD."

I liked this idea. It would be easy to arrange the schedule to accommodate him. In fact, I had done this for others who took classes. There were plenty of hours available outside the normal eight to five workday. The only problem might be if one of his Fridays or Saturdays coincided with a test day in Phase 2, but we could work around that.

I approved the idea on the condition that it not interfere with work.

We filled out the leave requests and sent them to Erwin for approval. He refused to sign.

"We won't know whether we'll need him or not until the class schedule is published," he said.

"Doesn't matter. If the class schedule conflicts, he won't take the time off. He'll reschedule his internship hours," I said.

"We can't give people time off to go to school," he insisted. "That's not authorized."

"It's his PTO. He can do whatever he wants with it," I countered.

"It still doesn't solve the problem of not knowing whether we'll need him until the schedule is complete."

This had been Bovey's major shortcoming and one Erwin and I firmly resolved to fix together. Erwin had the schedule printed for the next class and there were no foreseeable conflicts.

"I think we can do it," I insisted.

Erwin called Fred to get an official statement on using PTO for educational purposes. Fred said absolutely not. That's not what PTO is for.

This surprised me. Delorean wasn't asking for academic leave. He was just asking for time off. Raytheon's policy is quite clear on this point. PTO is available for any purpose the employee chooses and the employee is under no obligation to justify it or even identify it. I suppose it must have been the way Erwin presented it, because the Fred Prince I knew would not have had a problem with a person asking for PTO regardless of the personal reasons. Even more disturbing, Erwin was going to Fred for his support over directly scheduling the contractors. Erwin himself put Delorean's name in on the schedule bypassing me, and Fred – who had firmly stated the Course Manager couldn't do that – let him do it.

So I reluctantly told Delorean his PTO was not approved. He took it hard. I completely sympathized, but the PTO would not be approved because he intended to use it for educational purposes. Vacation was okay. Illness was okay. But taking classes was not okay – even though Raytheon policy says it is.

"What do I have to do?" he asked. "Call in sick every other Friday?"

With that, I understood what Delorean planned to do to finish up his degree. If his PTO had been approved, we could have planned accordingly. He wouldn't have even needed to use much of his PTO if any. I could have scheduled him around the time he needed off just as I did for everyone else. Now I had to anticipate that he would call in sick on the mornings he needed time off. It would make planning more difficult, but this was the course to which we had forced him.

The ensuing events made Delorean something of a pariah not only with the Course Manager but with his colleagues and even Raytheon. His absences for medical reasons were suspicious and wouldn't have been if there had been a more plausible explanation. When he was consistently late or absent, it was easy to forget that everyone enjoyed the flexibility he was shown in scheduling around things like taking children to school or taking a class one night a week. The indignation rose to the point of Raytheon demanding to see his private medical records and Erwin scheduling Delorean in deliberately at times he knew would be inconvenient for him.

Meanwhile, as the end of 2010 approached, Erwin was desperate to preserve his position but realized it might be too late. The holidays were upon him. He and Wilma went so far as to hire a personal trainer, but it was futile. He didn't need advice on how to get fit and lose weight. He had been fit once as had Wilma. He had just let himself go too far.

When word began to circulate that he would soon be forced to take the APFT, the workforce began to take heart that the tyranny might soon be over. Some even took measures to help the process along by bringing in donuts every day and leaving them outside his office.[100] I alerted Fred to the possibility that Erwin may soon be returning to work for Raytheon.

This presented a problem. All good will at the 35M course for Erwin had vanished and the workplace was becoming more and more hostile as time went on. We discussed perhaps moving him over to the 35L course because he was dual qualified, but the Limas didn't want him either. A bigger problem was that Erwin's slot had already been filled and there were no vacancies at the Mike course. Someone would have to leave if Erwin was to come back.

Just when Erwin needed to mend his reputation with his colleagues, he took the opposite path. As we prepared to transition into Phase 4 in December, he decided to add two more exercises and tests to the course. We had a workable Phase 4 based on Huachuca's POI, but he wanted to cram in two more events. That would add two more opportunities to fail and none of us could see any justification for it. He conjured up a mind-blowing training schedule of 14-hour days, seven days a week.

How would we even staff such a schedule, Butch wanted to know at the staff meeting? Butch was the Phase 4 Lead.

---

100 This little plot, humorously referred to as "Operation Turkey Stuffing," was engineered by a couple of instructors skilled in human manipulation. They would bring in donuts every day, pay careful attention to the ones Erwin liked best and buy more of those the next day. Note to self: Never cross a trained huminter.

"What's it to you?" Erwin countered. "None of the instructors have to work 14-hour days. It's just for the students." Erwin was serious about imposing a crushing schedule on the students with no leeway should anything go wrong in snowy December. What was more, this was on the heels of Wilma messing up a Phase 3 that would have run perfectly if we had just left it the way Kirsten had created it.

Jenn Twain, in the politest tone of voice she could muster, asked why we were changing the schedule. The one we had worked perfectly. Why add more to it when the students were already overworked? Huachuca doesn't require this.

"Huachuca has three and a half more weeks to train their students than we do," he said by way of explanation. And he said it with a straight face. We were going to add *more* stuff because we had *less* time to fit it in. It left us speechless. Even Butch couldn't think of anything to say.

We had never failed any students at Phase 4, but this schedule would kill them. I called Donna Ortiz to ask whether she could do something to head off the madness. She couldn't because she lived too far away. I should talk to Bass, she suggested.

Bass only said, "Look, you've all been in the military. You know how this works. Just do what he says."

There was nothing to do but struggle through with it. I told Kat.

Surprisingly, she didn't have a problem with it. It's only seven days, she said. We'll make it. The students had no more energy to protest and could see the light at the end of the tunnel. They'd claw their way through.

Butch Mudslinger, a proud native of the state of Maine, was in charge of Phase 4. Knowing how fierce New England winters can be, he set up a secondary site for the field problem just outside our building. If the weather was too bad, we wouldn't go to the field at all. We'd just pretend we were sleeping in the field and only do the actual exercises outdoors on the lawn in the snow. In addition, he set up a tertiary site in the main assemble hall. We'd be able to do everything including the exercises in-doors if necessary.

When Day One of the field exercise arrived, it was well below freezing with biting winds to boot. Wind chill put the temperature at minus 20. The students were told to wear their cold weather gear.

"What cold weather gear?" asked the new student leader.

"You mean nobody brought any cold weather gear?" asked Mudslinger.

"From Florida? Or California? Three of us are from Hawaii," he countered.

"So what you're saying is you don't have sweaters, parkas, wool caps, etc."

"Some of us do. We could pass them around."

Butch took this discovery to Erwin. "Could we issue them cold weather gear from supply?" he wondered. A quick call to the supply sergeant revealed that we couldn't. There was no winter weather gear available on Ft. Devens for students.

"I guess we'll just have to do the exercise indoors," said Mudslinger. "No problem. We're set up for that."

"We'll do it outdoors as planned," said Erwin.

"You can't put students out in the cold without cold weather gear," said Mudslinger.

"If they get hurt, it's on them," said Erwin. "They were told to bring cold weather gear."

We put the students out in the cold for the first exercise. It was savage. We contractors could dress as warmly as we wanted, but when in uniform, soldiers are not allowed to mix clothing. They had to wear their warm weather headgear which did not protect their ears. Most had only their summer uniforms and many had neglected to bring even their field jackets. There was a clear danger of frostbite and hypothermia so I decided to step in as Sergeant Major. To deliberately expose students to cold weather injury is inexcusable even if it were the students' own fault.

I told Erwin we were moving the exercise indoors. It's too cold. Not only will the students gain nothing from it, it's dangerous.

The conversation had barely started when Jenn Twain stormed into our office. Erwin had not ventured outside himself and was just getting ready to go see whether it was as bad as I said. She ripped him up one side and down the other for deliberately putting the students in the cold while he sat in his office all warm and cozy. Then she left quickly without waiting for a response.

Erwin sat there, his face red with rage and embarrassment. Finally, he told me in as even a voice as he could manage, "I don't want to ever hear one of your contractors talk like that to me again."

"Dude, she was right. You can't put soldiers out in the cold without proper clothing."

"I was about to go check on them," he said.

"I know."

"You think it's going to be warm in Afghanistan? They need realistic training."

"This isn't Afghanistan, it's a school in Massachusetts. We can't let the students get hurt in the name of realistic training. Even if it is their own fault."

We moved the students indoors and completed the training as Mudslinger had planned. All but one student who had made it to Phase 4 graduated. This one exception was a female student who, despite excellent marks up until then, made one careless error and failed a task. She had the option to retest but declined. She was just too exhausted and no longer cared to be a huminter even if she passed. The sleep deprivation and stress had drained all the motivation out of her.

In December of 2010 Kat graduated from the 35M course which now qualified her to apply to the FET in the spring. In addition, as a member of our battalion, she was now eligible for ABIC, the prerequisite course for instructors. I was looking long term for Sergeant Briere. What would she do after a deployment with SF? She would probably have a choice of more deployments or becoming a full-time military instructor. If the FET program succeeded, they would need female instructors with combat experience. She could leverage her experience into work as a contractor. Her future for once was bright and the possibilities were endless.

Kat was more concerned about the short-term. She needed a steady paycheck to see her through until FET Selection in April and now that she had finished school, where would that come from? We signed her up for ABIC right away, which again annoyed staff at the Brigade. Why the hurry? Colonel Rondeau was happy to push the matter, particularly because Brigade had denied him a slot in ABIC. For some reason the commander isn't considered an instructor and therefore not authorized certification as one. (Indeed, I would not have been allowed ABIC as Sergeant Major for the same reason. Anteon had paid for my ABIC course as a civilian contractor.) This made no sense. Officers and sergeants major often give classes. A commander should be as familiar as possible with the common prerequisites his soldiers need. The stupidity of the Brigade only steeled Rondeau's resolve to push for the training his soldiers needed.

Fortunately, Lieutenant Colonel Rondeau had an excellent relationship with Colonel Pearson, the Brigade's caretaker commander. Pearson was a Military Police officer and Rondeau a civilian law enforcement professional. Pearson was not inclined to make any major changes for reasons I've already pointed out, but he was more than happy to see that routine work like getting soldiers trained and certified got done.

Kat got a slot in the next available ABIC over the objections of Bass, Lowman and Lopez.

CHAPTER 16

Replaced as Site Lead

As 2010 TURNED into 2011, the Raytheon project at Devens was running well. We now had almost forty contractors supporting four MI courses with overtime authorized, a 400% growth in revenue in two years. We had demonstrated we could run the courses better than the Army could and whatever expense Raytheon presented was well worth the investment in more, better and cheaper graduates. We had good leaders in place to manage the contractors at each course. We had adequate space dedicated to Raytheon even though we still had no official presence on the post. It looked like Erwin would soon be gone as Course Manager and Raytheon could put him at the 35L course until time healed the wounds his stint as Course Manager had inflicted. The other Lima instructors, including the 35L Course Manager himself, had objected, but it was better than bringing him back to the Mike course.

Despite the overall success of the project, by the end of 2010 the atmosphere at the 35M course was so toxic that everyone dreaded coming in to work. I knew we would lose Delorean and probably Elliott as well. Alice, a struggling single mom, had just about had it with the Bayers' hypocrisy in bringing their infant son to work while insisting others make outside arrangements for their kids. Even our most steadfast employees were quietly looking for jobs elsewhere. Unless I could talk them out of it, both Elliott and Dwight would probably file official complaints against Erwin Bayer and Raytheon.

I was the only one who could talk to Erwin whose mentality by then was in full siege mode. He was beginning to open up a bit to advice on how to soften his leadership style. He wasn't sorry for the bad blood between him and Elliott or Delorean, but alienating others with whom he had been friends bothered him. He honestly did not see himself as intolerant or closed minded and it surprised him that others saw him that way. We had all been in the military. Making the tough calls is what strong leadership is all about and he saw himself as a strong leader.

He began to hint that he'd like to take his old job back as a contractor. Going over to the 35L course wasn't his first choice – he wanted to stay with Wilma as it would be easier on their family life – but there were no open positions at the 35M course.

The big, unspoken issue was the looming APFT. He was heavier than ever and didn't stand a chance of passing it. Ms. Fogelman had become downright hostile to Erwin's refusal to take the test and a showdown was inevitable. It didn't look like his NCOER would be particularly good, either. He had pissed off Tim Partin, his rater, more than once. Putting the students out in the cold had been a huge mistake, one for which he should have been immediately relieved and disciplined. He and Wilma were still bringing in their infant son to work and tap dancing around the responsibility. The other parents who had to arrange daycare for their kids found this particularly irritating.

To compound problems, Erwin was now on Major Sampson's radar since Erwin as Bovey's replacement was responsible for ensuring the course ran better. It was running worse and Gosling was still in charge of the very Phase from which he was supposed to have been removed. Major Sampson had no patience for neglecting physical fitness, which did not raise Erwin's prestige in his eyes.

What really caught Major Sampson's attention was something Erwin did that was so bone-headed, most of us still can't believe he did it. He put his bad NCOER on the share drive for everyone to see. In addition, he included a letter from a soldier he had apparently violated regulations to help. The letter thanked Erwin for intervening, without which he would have failed. In other words, Erwin published a judgement of unethical conduct against himself and included the evidence along with it. Another file he created entitled "Hot Mama" with pictures of Wilma in a swimsuit was a mere trifle by comparison.

Major Sampson took him behind closed doors and ordered Erwin to immediately remove all personal material from the share drive, including the sexy photos of his wife.

For my part, I missed Sergeant Howard who left in December. She left a Kirsten-shaped hole in all of our lives. Her best friend at the course, Jenn Twain, was struggling with depression and missed Kirsten even more acutely. It only took her absence to demonstrate how much fun the job could actually be when approached with a little levity.

I was also disappointed that the Brigade and Division had blocked my transfer to Special Forces for one last combat deployment. There had been no reason to deny my transfer. Indeed, the 80th TTC had nine too many sergeants major and was looking for ways to lean the rolls. A mind-boggling six E-9s drilled at the 5-104th MI Battalion alone. I suspected the intentional foot-dragging had been motivated by nothing more than the fact that I wanted to go. Now I had a pet soldier in the person of Sergeant Briere who wanted to deploy with SF into combat and they resented her as well.

On the whole, the project was doing well and growing beyond what anyone at Raytheon had anticipated. We were poised to duplicate what we had accomplished at Devens elsewhere. Fred Prince, my supervisor, had rated me for a second year in a row as "Far Exceeds Expectations" for managing a 400% increase in revenue with the expansion of the Devens program. The success of the project may not have been universally welcomed in that it loaded even more work onto the Brigade staff, especially Master Sergeant Bass. It should have been the opposite with Raytheon shouldering so much of the burden. Mike was only responsible for ensuring the contract was delivered, not for dealing with personnel problems, all of which I was more than happy to handle if allowed.

So I was caught entirely by surprise when early in the winter of 2011 I received a call from Fred Prince informing me that the customer had requested I be fired.

"Lloyd, the customer has asked me to replace you."

"This is unexpected. What's the reason?" I asked.

"They don't have to give a reason. I'm going to put Sarah Sondheim in the Site Lead position. You'll stay as the Task Lead for the 35M project. You'll get the same pay, of course."

"That's good. I'm sure Sarah will do fine at the job. She would be my choice. Who asked to have me replaced?" I asked.

"Both Mike Bass and Colonel Pearson made the request. Actually, they demanded that you be fired. We got the same request from Colonel Thompson as well, but we defended you based on your record of performance."

This surprised me. I was in weekly contact with Bass. We were on good terms and I thought it extremely unlikely he would initiate such a request. Colonel Pearson, in addition to being a hands-off temporary commander for the 1st Brigade, was also a personal friend. We were both the same age and took no small pride in being among the fittest of the Brigade's members. We had plans to do the "Bataan Death March" together in the spring.[101] Neither of them would have made such a request without talking to me. Colonel Thompson and I were also on excellent terms especially after my rescue of the surge of 2009. Not only had I saved the project, I probably kept him out of jail.

Both Mike Bass and Colonel Pearson firmly denied they had requested my removal and it did not take long to discover from whom the request originated. It had come from Erwin Bayer. I had been replaced in order to, in Bass's words, "crack the whip on the contractors." Raytheon was removing me in order to allow the customer to maintain, and even escalate, a workplace hostile to their employees.

I would be replaced by Sarah Sondheim, who was probably as good as anyone we had, though unqualified. She was an analyst in charge of the 35F course and, like me, a Consulting Training and Development Specialist, which was appropriate for the position. She had a background in Intelligence Analysis, but nothing else. She had a long history with the Brigade as a warrant officer. She was close friends with both Donna Ortiz

101 The Bataan Death March is an annual endurance event held in the New Mexico desert and open to military personnel.

and Tracey Bovey, who Major Sampson had recommended be immediately relieved, and as such did not care much for him.

Getting her into that job would be a little tricky. For the Brigade to request that Raytheon put one of their own officers in the job of civilian Site Lead represented a conflict of interest. The request was particularly suspicious given the longstanding friendship between Sarah and two of the individuals whose relief had been recommended. Putting me in the Site Lead job originally had been perfectly legal because I was a Raytheon employee before I became a member of the hiring unit. I was an outsider. But asking Raytheon to replace me with one of their own staff officers was clearly over the line.

I also worried that her lack of familiarity with the individual contractors might be a bit overwhelming. We now had forty Raytheon contractors working on four different projects and, while I saw them all virtually every day, she only knew the 35F employees. It takes a while to earn an employee's trust and she would have to be their advocate when they were abused. She was coming in as a stranger, known only as the one chosen to "crack the whip."

Colonel Rondeau was shocked when he heard the news. I got a one-word text from him: "WHAT!!!?" He wanted to know what he could do to put me back in the lead position, but I assured him that it was actually a good idea to rotate the Site Lead. I would still be available to advise Chief Sondheim and help her transition into her new job. I was still in a position to manage things directly at the Mike course. I would take no cut in pay and, if anything, have even more time to teach. Problems with the other courses were minor and I was sure Sarah could handle them. Besides, I saw this as an opportunity to free me up to help Fred and Chuck expand the program to other schools.

My fellow instructors at the Mike course had a different read on the situation. They were outraged that Erwin had tried to get me fired just to open a position for himself. He hadn't succeeded, but it was clear that Raytheon was not going to protect them from the continuing abuse. With my removal, three contractors – Roger Cohen, Elliott Warner and Alice Davis – immediately quit. It would be open season on contractors and they had no intention of putting up with a hostile work environment any longer, especially with Raytheon backing down on the issue of protecting them from the abuse. Roger also wanted to get some more field experience in Afghanistan. Elliott quit for obvious reasons. Alice had been particularly angry about Erwin and Wilma's defiance of the no children in the workplace policy while everyone else complied. She took a job with the Forest Service.

This opened up three positions for new contractors, but left no vacancy in the Consultant position Erwin coveted. I was still in charge of the contractors at the Mike course. I encouraged Kat Briere to apply for one of the contractor positions, but she was getting close to FET selection and would only be able to work for a few months. Maybe she could be put on temporary orders as a military instructor.

Despite Rondeau's and my endorsement, she was denied. Not enough experience, explained Mike Bass. I pointed out that we had put soldiers like Wilma on orders with even less experience. Besides, how do you get teaching experience without teaching? We found some temporary duty work for Kat to do at the battalion headquarters, but that was the best we could do.

The dreaded day came when Erwin could no longer avoid the APFT. He failed all three events as well as height and weight. (To be fair, he didn't fail height – only weight.) There was much rejoicing among the staff, both military and civilian. Surely he would be replaced with someone better, and that looked like Staff Sergeant Wilson. Daniel Wilson was competent, professional and had everyone's respect.

Wilson was appointed interim Course Manager but Erwin was allowed to stay as an advisor until he retested, which was required in 30 days. This was not received with enthusiasm. Erwin continued to run the course despite the official change of duties and the toxic atmosphere at the schoolhouse did not abate.

Another month went by and Sergeant Bayer retook and again failed the APFT. But even after failing the retest, he was still allowed to stay. I called Sergeant Major Ortiz to ask how it was he had not been removed like so many others for failing fitness standards. The Army takes fitness very seriously. She told me he was retained "to ensure that the program did not fail."

Nothing could better illustrate the psychotic gulf between the Brigade staff and reality at Devens than a statement like that. There was universal agreement that the biggest problem – the sole problem, actually – at the Mike course was the Course Manager. Yet the Brigade's impression was that he was the only person who could keep things together. So Erwin stayed.

Before long Sarah came over to talk to me, accompanied by Jesse Parker.[102] Jesse was a person of some mystery. No one was sure why he had been hired or what he did. You never saw her without him, and that raised a lot of questions about who he was and why he seemed to wield so much influence. Sarah raved about him, how he was a former Special Forces operator who had done lots of highly classified stuff. SF is a small community and everybody knows everybody, but Jesse wasn't eager to compare notes with me. He didn't know anyone I knew and had never been any of the places I had been. He was a big question mark. He made Major Sampson very uneasy, as well.

Sarah shared with me that she and Jesse were both members of the First Earth Battalion, an organization so outlandish it's almost a joke. The First Earth Battalion was created by Lieutenant Colonel Jim Channon, a US Army officer who wrote an operations manual, envisioning an army of New Age super soldiers. The book and subsequent movie *The Men Who Stare at Goats* is based on Channon and the First Earth Battalion. Creating an unauthorized army within the Army is the very definition of subversion and the organization and its leader would certainly have been stopped were the whole concept not so preposterous.

Soon we began to hear that Jesse was holding classes after hours in clairvoyance and telepathy. Jesse also held a high position within the Freemasons, an organization to which Erwin Bayer also belonged, though I would not allege any connection beyond coincidence. Jesse was also

102 Not his real name.

credited with arranging for contractors to participate during working hours in exercise classes that were being offered to the military in the building where the 35L classes were held. We at the 35M course had no access to that privilege, but billing the customer for time spent in the gym smelled fishy to me. I'm not sure how one would categorize that activity on the timecard.

I'm not sure whether he, like Erwin, had any designs on my job, but he wasn't happy that I was still there. Sarah informed me that I would no longer be the 35M Task Lead and removed me from any duties other than teaching. She said that Jesse would be managing the 35M contractors from now on. Henceforth I would have no responsibilities other than to be available to teach. I was moved to a table in the break room to share my laptop outlet with the coffee pot.

Was Fred aware of this move? He had been informed, she said. I asked the reason for her decision. And why was it her decision and not Fred's? She said that I was the cause of all the problems at the Mike course. Which problems? She couldn't name any. I tried to pin her down on specifics, but she wouldn't yield. Major Sampson had endured the same frustration when he tried to question both her and Master Sergeant Bovey on the nature of the problems at the Mike course. They produced vague insinuations but no facts. No data. Try as he would, he could not get anything concrete out of either Bovey or Sondheim. Now, I couldn't either.

"We all know about the problems that are going on here. You're the one common denominator," she said.

"Not the Course Manager?" I asked.

"Erwin might have some problems, but they all stem from you. You're the main person responsible for the problems here," she insisted.

"Again, Sarah, which problems? You haven't mentioned anything specific," I said.

"I've talked to all the instructors. They all say you're the problem," she insisted.

"I find that hard to believe. I've heard nothing like that from them," I said.

"They don't trust you. They're not going to tell you something like that," she said. "They're afraid of you."

Fear and mistrust would have been the last words any of us would use to describe my relationship with my fellow contractors. We had invested over two years of toil together and most had at one point or another felt safe to share deeply personal problems with me. I had welcomed all into my home on many occasions. I was surprised Sarah would make a statement like that but resisted the urge to call the contractors in and confront her. Perhaps there were problems I was unaware of for which I was to blame. Maybe there were things I had done that needed to be corrected.

"You've got to give me something specific. If I'm to correct something I'm doing wrong, I need to know what it is," I said.

Jesse jumped in. "That's fair. We'll put together a list of the problems as we see them and you'll have something to work with."

"That's all I ask," I said, wondering at his use of the first person plural pronoun.

The problem list never materialized and my fellow instructors were outraged at the suggestion they had implicated me rather than Erwin as the source of any problems at the Mike course. I called the staff together to inform them that I was no longer the Lead and Jesse Parker would be replacing me.

"And Erwin?" asked Norm.

"Still here," I said.

"What reason did Sarah give for replacing you?" asked Philip.

"You all don't trust me," I said.

"She said that?" asked Butch.

"Yep," I said. "Said she talked to you all and you don't trust me. You all want me gone."

"I hope you know nobody said anything like that," Butch reassured me. "I mean, look at all we've been through for what? Two years now?"

"Don't worry. I never believed a word of it even for a second," I said.

"And what exactly are Mr. Parker's qualifications? He's not even a Mike, is he?" asked Charlie.

"Nope," I said. "I think he's just a Foxtrot, but I'm not even sure of that."

"You mean she's putting somebody in charge of the Mike course who isn't even a Mike? Can they do that?" asked Charlie. "Do Fred and Chuck know what's going on?"

"Don't know," I said. "We're not allowed to talk to them anymore. Just to Sarah."

Butch summed it up. "So she thinks all of us want you gone, Erwin to stay, and a stranger to be the new Lead because we don't trust you? You can't make this shit up."

I would have welcomed getting paid as much as I was to do nothing but teach, but the project began to go downhill almost immediately. We never saw Jesse in our building as our newly appointed Task Lead. His official job was in another building. He did not come around to remind people to do their timecards and we started to hear about it from Chuck.[103] The

103 The following is an example of messages we began to get regularly from Raytheon after I was relieved:

Timecard approvers,

We performed poorly on the recent timecard audit. Chuck Atkin's Product Area, which includes all of you and your employees, was only 83% compliant. This was ranked 13 out of 16 business groups in the audit, which is unacceptable. As a reminder, it is a requirement of our contract with the government to report labor costs DAILY. Starting tomorrow, I will check timecards every day (Tue-Fri) around 1300. As per his request, Chuck will be notified daily of task leads with employees whose timecards are not up-to-date. By 1400 on Friday's, (sic) Chuck will be notified of task leads who have not approved their employee's (sic) timecards.

This shouldn't be this hard folks. Let's get everyone in the habit of meeting the most basic requirement for employment with Raytheon.

Regards,
Tonya

Tonya Freeman, PMP
Operations Manager
Raytheon Technical Services Company, LLC

Course Manager and Phase Leads were now scheduling the contractors directly without consulting a Raytheon representative which generated problems we didn't have before. We were also short-handed with the loss of Roger, Elliott and Alice until Raytheon could find replacements. That had to take a sizeable chunk out of Raytheon's profits.

The Phase Leads and Course Manager often failed to ensure that all the instructors were ready for the next day and aware of Plan B. Indeed, there were no Plan B's or C's anymore. I'm not sure what Sarah meant by Jesse being responsible for the Mike course, but it did not involve him doing anything or even being physically present. I just hoped there would be no audits while Sarah was signing timecards without verifying anyone was actually working.

My policy had always been to provide the customer with everything they needed to succeed. I anticipated where problems might arise and had solutions ready. Now, there was no one doing that any more. Sarah intended to limit contractor use to the bare minimum, which of course is in line with the military's intention of weaning themselves off of dependency upon contractors. Whether that is in the interest of Raytheon is another matter, and Raytheon's income from this project underwent a sharp downturn.

Unfortunately, in shooting for the minimum, we often fell below the minimum hours required by the contract. In failing to anticipate problems the customer might face, there were times when there simply were not enough instructors to teach. We had solved the problem of reservist contractors being taken away on drill weekends, but with me out of the process, no one anticipated the drill weekend crunch. Contractors were scheduled to teach when they were away at drill and classes had to be cancelled with no leeway to make them up.

With no one making the rounds every afternoon anymore, timecard compliance dropped off. Contractors got scheduled when they weren't available because no one regularly checked on them anymore. Some started showing up late and unprepared. The number of billable hours dropped to the minimum and below.

Finally, in an attempt to recover something of our lost performance, Sarah designated Charlie Foster the official Task Lead at the Mike course and he finally got what he really felt should have been his all along and I couldn't disagree. It had been Colonel Thompson's decision to choose me over Charlie, but now that belonged to the past. Thompson was gone.

I was glad that Charlie got the job and gladder still that the first thing he did was consult with me. I went over how I managed the contractors and none of the information was new to him. He just needed to make sure everybody did their timecards, was aware of tomorrow's plan and what the backup plan was if something went wrong at the last minute. It was simple NCO business and nothing new to an old hand like Charlie. I let him know about the situation with Delorean. With no one from Raytheon involved in scheduling, there was no one to adjust to Delorean's situation.

Charlie's immediate problem was that the Course Manager and Phase Leads still insisted on directly scheduling the contractors. This frustrated Charlie to no end and heated words were often exchanged. He had no say in how the contractors were scheduled, but whenever something went wrong, he got the blame. He was especially peeved at how the military instructors were far less reliable yet never disciplined when something went wrong. It was alarming and our job security was dissolving before our very eyes.

By the spring of 2011 the project was failing and Raytheon was being blamed.

I had found it best to be flexible with scheduling the contractors. As much as possible, let them schedule themselves in for when they want to work and fill the unwanted time slots equitably from the roster. Now the contractors were scheduled mechanically in roster order and nobody liked it. Sarah backed the policy, insisting that it was the only fair way to distribute the work. Overtime would be allotted the same way.

Although I had filled Charlie in on Delorean's situation, he still found it frustrating to see Delorean scheduled in to a time slot he knew he would have to change at the last minute when Delorean called in sick. Although the situation remained a thorn in Charlie's side, Delorean's situation eventually resolved itself. Not long after receiving his much desired doctorate, he quit to go into private practice in counselling.[104]

Rigid adherence to a roster and schedule sounds reasonable and in large professional organizations it is often the only way to operate. But we were small and had complete control over how we ran things. Both Chuck and General Custer had given us that. Individual situations could always be accommodated. There were many ways to get the job done by being flexible. But for that to happen, a pleasant workplace with coworkers that trust each other is essential. We didn't have that.

Meanwhile, I still had important duties as battalion Director of Instruction Sergeant Major, even if I had no civilian leadership responsibility at the school anymore. The Course Managers still answered directly to the Brigade, not the battalions. But it got me out to Huachuca regularly and in the spring of 2011, I was able to attend a conference in which I had the opportunity to speak with the Sergeants Major of both the 519th and 513th MI battalions, the units deployed to support the Military Intelligence effort in Afghanistan at that time. I asked what we could do at the schoolhouse to better prepare our students for service once they get downrange. I was told that they lose about a third of the new soldiers in the first two weeks to the effects of just carrying a normal combat load around day after day. Sprains, blisters, aches and pains eliminated a third of the fighting force before they even got adjusted to their jobs. Make sure the troops are in shape before they get there.

Just passing the APFT isn't enough. The physical fitness test doesn't assess the ability to do what they will actually have to do. Pushups, situps and a two-mile run in gym shorts and running shoes don't have much relevance in combat (unless they're planning on running away a lot). They need to be able to shoulder a rucksack and carry 43 lbs. of body armor,

104 Dr. Delorean went on to take a leadership position in a non-profit organization that served disabled veterans and, at this writing, is much happier. He left Raytheon without filing a complaint and has no desire to ever work for that company again.

weapons and ammunition. They need to be able to sprint short distances with a weapon and drag a wounded comrade to cover. And they have to do it in extremes of hot and cold at mountainous altitudes.

I smiled to myself. In April Kat had sailed through Special Forces FET Selection. She had made it and would be deploying soon, fulfilling her dream.

Next, the Sergeants Major told me, was to make sure they either spoke the local language or at least knew how to use an interpreter. Working with the local culture, either face to face or with an interpreter, is crucial to success and too many huminters were coming out with no understanding of the Afghans and their society.

Rueful smile. Everyone recognized the importance of language training. Yet our POI included only one block of instruction on how to work with an interpreter and just a few hours of instruction on cultural awareness.

Finally, get them trained on the equipment they will be using before they deploy. There is really no convenient way to train new soldiers in a combat zone.

This was one thing I couldn't do anything about. We had no money, let alone facilities, for whatever equipment they might be using. The best we had been able to do was flush $700,000 down the toilet buying Smith's laptops and software. That argued for the soldiers doing at least some pre-deployment training at a major facility like Huachuca or Belvoir.

I was on a break enjoying the hot Arizona sun when my cell phone rang. It was Kat.

"I'm not going to deploy with Special Forces," she said.

"What?! What happened?" I asked.

"I just got orders from Brigade. They're sending me downrange as a photojournalist," she said with a quaver in her voice.

"How is that possible? They know you just made it through selection and are awaiting orders from Bragg."

"I know. But Lowman just told me I'm going as a photojournalist instead. Said they needed one and I had the MOS," she said.

"That's your *secondary* MOS. Now you're a 35M. Anyway, the directive specifically instructs commanders not to impede soldiers from volunteering for the Female Engagement Teams."

"He said that didn't matter. Sergeant Major, I'll kill myself rather than deploy again as a photographer. Not after coming this far..."

My head was spinning. How could they do this to her? It couldn't be just a random error. I had too much experience with the Brigade and Division staff blocking deployments just to flex their muscle. "It's going to be okay," I assured her. "Let me call you back in an hour or two."

"I swear, I'll kill myself if they do this to me! Right after I kill one or two of them..."

"I'll call back soon. Don't do anything or talk to anybody until then." I hung up.

I knew Brigadier General Heritsch was at Huachuca. I just needed to find out where she was and bend her ear for a minute. It took me less than half an hour to locate her and, as it turned out, she was interviewing Colonel Sandy Raynor, slated to be the next commander of the 1st Brigade. I have never walked in on a general officer unannounced before or since, but this situation demanded it. I knocked on the door, poked my nose in, and told her politely I needed just a few seconds of her time for something really, really important.

"Ma'am, you have a dynamite soldier, Sergeant Kathleen Briere, who has just showered us with glory by qualifying for one of the first Special Forces Female Engagement Teams deploying to Afghanistan. She just informed me that your staff has cut orders for her to deploy as a photojournalist instead. I want to ask you to intervene so Sergeant Briere can continue her deployment with Special Forces next month."

"You're serious, Sergeant Major? They did that? Who did that?"

"I don't know, Ma'am. I only talked to Sergeant Briere a few minutes ago."

"Don't worry. I'll take care of it," she said. Colonel Raynor looked on with a polite smile.

"Thank you, Ma'am. Sorry to disturb you."

"No you're not. Nor should you be. Have a nice day," she said.
"You too, Ma'am," I said, saluted and left.

I called Kat back and told her not to worry. Everything would be fine.

The next day her photojournalist orders were revoked and she was allowed to continue her deployment with Special Forces. I was sure this would cost me. I was no favorite of anyone at the Brigade and now less so for going directly to the Division commander. But that's what being the Sergeant Major requires. If you're not willing to walk in on a general and make demands like this, you shouldn't be wearing the star. And if she had let her staff get away with this, she shouldn't be wearing one, either.

In the spring of 2011, Colonel Raynor took command of the 1st Brigade. Although she was well qualified for the position, she lived in Phoenix and would find it impossible to control the Brigade well from there, let alone the school. I'm sure she was under the impression that the school at Devens would soon be moved back to Arizona, much closer to home. She was able from time to time to visit the school for the ubiquitous military phenomenon known as the "dog and pony show."[105] We saw her from a distance once or twice, but there was no opportunity for her to get to know us, much less understand the conditions under which we worked. Indeed, General Heritsch was in the habit of spending more time face-to-face with us at Devens than Colonel Raynor did. Her staff kept her isolated from what was actually going on at the school and my little walk-in with General Heritsch should have alerted her to their propensity for subterfuge.

With the approval of Lieutenant Colonel Rondeau, I drafted a letter suggesting she designate someone permanently present at Devens as her deputy. The school at Devens was the Brigade's center of gravity, the one big project it was responsible for. She needed eyes on Devens and

105 The term does not refer to an actual canine and equestrian exhibition. It is a pejorative term for a staged event designed to present a unit in its best light to a visiting dignitary and hide any negative information or problems.

no one on her staff, not even Master Sergeant Bass, could do it. She had a battalion right on Devens and it would be easy to appoint Rondeau or some other officer the additional duty of monitoring the school. She thanked me for the suggestion and said she would take it under consideration. She was cordial with me, but apparently less so with Rondeau. In any case, she did nothing and things continued to deteriorate at Devens.

By June, Sarah was in serious trouble. Production had fallen to below the minimum required by the contract. Compliance with Raytheon's requirements had fallen from top of Chuck's projects to the bottom. Timecard compliance was at the bottom as well. Contractors were showing up late and unprepared. After two years of perfect performance, we began to fail to the extent that the customer was regularly writing Memoranda for Record documenting the failures. Hours delivered fell along with student graduation rates. Neither the students, their commanders nor the customer were expressing satisfaction. On top of that, we were transitioning to an Afghanistan-based scenario.

It was a difficult time. I was excluded from any activity other than teaching. The Course Manager and Phase Leads were directly managing the contractors despite Charlie's appointment as Task Lead. Verbal abuse was common and people were worried about just keeping their jobs, let alone being able to plan their vacations. Anyone who dared complain to Sarah about abuse from the military leaders was shut down with, "If you don't like it, quit."

In June, there was a break between classes and most of the contractors took the opportunity to leave on holiday. Personnel requirements were minimal, but we still needed to prepare the new classes for the Afghanistan scenario. Charlie and I were the only contractors around and Gosling asked whether I would be available to help work up the new classes. I said I'd be delighted to do that and took the assignment after clearing it with Charlie.

It required four hours of overtime, but that was easy to document and it had been officially requested by the customer and approved by the

Task Lead, Charlie Foster. When I submitted my timecard, however, Sarah disapproved the overtime. I called to ask why.

"This was not what overtime was to be used for," she explained. "Overtime is only for Phase 2 when we need the extra hours."

"The hours were officially requested and approved," I countered.

"You shouldn't have billed for them," she said. "Common sense should tell you that we don't bill the customer for anything we don't have to."

That's not common sense, I thought to myself. In fact, it's illegal. Raytheon's ethics policy specifically prohibits donating unbilled hours of work to the customer.

"Do Fred and Chuck know about this?" I asked.

"There's no need. It's clear that we don't bill for things like this."

I decided I needed to notify Chuck. Even one incident like this could cost Raytheon the contract if it became known and it sounded like Sarah expected us to deliver overtime work for free as "common sense." Besides, it was to no one's advantage not to use the overtime. The customer was happy, I was happy, and Raytheon stood to make more money. I wrote Chuck a brief description of the incident and cc'd Sarah on the email.

Chuck answered with a generic comment that Raytheon would never seek to profit at the expense of the customer. He apparently wanted to go on record that we were not billing for unnecessary work.

Sarah was livid. With Jesse in tow, she told me I was never to contact Raytheon directly. If I did so again, she would consider it grounds for termination.

"This is the kind of thing Chuck needs to know about. You're not seriously telling me I can't talk to Raytheon about something that could endanger the contract?"

"You can talk to Chuck anytime you want, but not without me present," she said.

Jesse stepped in. "I'm sure you were sincerely concerned about the unpaid overtime, but what you did made us look bad. You shouldn't go higher up without talking to us first."

"I did talk to Sarah first," I said, wondering how Jesse considered himself an equal partner in the Site Lead role. "And I copied her on the email to Chuck."

"Lloyd, you didn't need to put in any overtime to prepare those classes," she said. "You're one of the best instructors we have. You could just wing it."

"I'm one of the best instructors *because* I don't wing it."

The overtime went unpaid. I don't think Charlie was even advised that he shouldn't have approved it. I decided it would be prudent never to accept a request for overtime again unless specifically ordered by Sarah. That caution, however, proved unnecessary. Sarah's policy of minimizing Raytheon's support to the customer made overtime a rare option.

I was puzzled why Raytheon would tolerate this lagging performance. It had been almost six months since I was replaced and everything was going wrong. Hours delivered were down. Timecard compliance was down. Compliance with Raytheon's internal requirements was down. Customer satisfaction was down. When I notified Chuck and Fred of the unpaid overtime along with the policy of reducing hours delivered to the bare minimum, I got generic responses that merely restated policy on overtime and said nothing about the apparent expectation of delivering extra work for free.

It was then I learned that Fred had been replaced. I knew he intended to retire, but had to rethink that when the value of his retirement fund shrank, along with everyone else's in the country. His replacement had already been named and Fred was moved to another job. None of us had been informed that a new person had been put in charge of the project months earlier.

Someone at Raytheon, I was sure, must be looking at the P&Ls (Profit and Loss statements) and forecasts. Raytheon is a top-notch for-profit corporation. I had no insight into who at Raytheon was monitoring our profitability, but Fred's replacement should have been most directly responsible and he was a complete blank.

One day in the summer of 2011, just after we had again been scorched by a flaming email informing us that Chuck was very upset about our lax timecard compliance, we were directed to attend a luncheon sponsored by Raytheon at a restaurant in Ayer. Attendance was obligatory. At this event, two strangers from Raytheon stood up to say a few words about how well we were doing and how our exceptional performance had caught everyone's eye at Raytheon. Our excellent performance was due to one factor – outstanding leadership.

As Sarah and Jesse were publicly congratulated for their brilliant management, the rest of us just looked at one another in disbelief. A mere two hours earlier we had been upbraided for lousy performance by Chuck and now some clueless Raytheon functionary was handing out awards!

That guy turned out to be Brian Keyes, Fred's replacement. He had been in charge for months and either didn't have a clue as to what was going on, or was blowing smoke. Either way, the future didn't look good. He handed out plaques as awards for our years of service.

After his speech, another nameless individual congratulated Jesse for getting everyone through Raytheon's Six Sigma qualification course. The Six Sigma project was another waste of time that had been recently imposed upon everyone who didn't already have the training. I had done Six Sigma two years earlier and understood the concept pretty well. My offer to assist was rejected. I was already qualified and didn't need to be wasting my time. Raytheon had a person specially designated to assign, assist with and grade the projects.

Few of the projects had anything to do with improving efficiency. Some of them were downright laughable. But all passed and none were implemented. Jesse, who had been the point of contact for the Raytheon Six Sigma guy, had high hopes for going on to becoming a Six Sigma instructor himself. Nothing came of it. Six Sigma, like all of the other internal requirements, was treated as a block to check, not as a dynamic tool to improve Raytheon's bottom line. Indeed, the only measurable effect was to increase Raytheon's expenditure for nothing in return.

Ironically, things were becoming progressively more and more inefficient. Along with minimizing contractor support, Sarah also set a policy that the work load be shared equally. This looked fair on the surface, but it eliminated the choice people had previously enjoyed in the hours worked. Contractors were banned from touching the Big Board, which was now the exclusive property of the Course Manager. Simply filling in the hours from the roster without regard to the needs of the individual contractors created a number of unnecessary conflicts, particularly with the contractors who had small children. Contractors who were reservists got scheduled to teach on weekends when they would not be available. Requesting time off was even more cumbersome than before.

Knowing when contractors wanted time off made it easy to create a schedule in such a way that very little time off needed to even be requested. We had a 60-hour week available to get in forty hours. My Big Board served that purpose beautifully. Now we were forced to formally apply for time off, even in increments as small as one hour, by submitting forms in triplicate requiring no fewer than five signatures each.

Applying for time off had always been thorny. It is illegal for the customer to approve or deny time off for any individual contractor. But our application forms had a place for the Course Manager to approve or deny the time off along with the Raytheon supervisor. Now, the Course Manager could not only schedule individual contractors as he wished, he could deny them PTO.

We became more and more worried that someone at Raytheon would notice how badly this project was going and pull the plug. USAICS was talking about moving the whole Devens project back to Huachuca. This made sense from the point of view of cost per man hour and economies of scale. But in 2011, the Army was out of money. The gold rush of the Bush-Cheney years was over. Moving the school would be disruptive and expensive. In addition, there was no place to put the school. Huachuca was full.

Our best hope for keeping our paychecks was to provide value to the project at Devens. As long as we were producing more graduates for less money than Huachuca, the Army would be in no hurry to relocate the school and eliminate our jobs.

I saw Sarah's policy of minimizing Raytheon's support as exactly the opposite of what needed to be done. We had proven we could produce more graduates for less money. We needed to advertise that fact. Use it as a selling tool. We needed to anticipate the customer's problems and have solutions ready. We needed to continue to sell the Army on the value Raytheon provided and standing by passively while the customer failed was not the way to do that.

CHAPTER 17

Director of Instruction

By the summer of 2011, things were desperate. The school was performing badly. Graduation was down to 50% and student satisfaction was nonexistent. Colonel Raynor put my battalion commander, Lieutenant Colonel Rondeau in charge of the Mike course and directed him to get it back on track. She could not have made a wiser decision nor chosen a better man for the job.

Colonel Rondeau was not happy that I had been sidelined. He considered my participation crucial to the success of the project. Now he was able to sidestep Raytheon's decision by putting me in charge on the military side. I would function as Director of Instruction for the 35M course and have full authority to actually do that job. We could choose the next Course Manager as well.

I had several ideas to bring the course into line with the now official Army Learning Method 2015. Colonel Rondeau told me I could fire whoever needed to be fired and perhaps I should have removed Sergeant Gosling. But I felt confident I could get him to comply and actually be productive, so I didn't.

Colonel Rondeau, with my blessing, chose Master Sergeant Ali Hassan[106] for Course Manager. Hassan is an American of Lebanese extraction, a fluent Arabic speaker and former Marine who had interrogated at every level. He was also a critical thinker of high intellect with a distaste for bullshit. He would not be fooled by the "empty shirt" as he called leaders who held rank but were unfit for command.

---

106 Not his real name.

I gave Ali the thumbs up and Rondeau concurred. Ali and I would butt heads once in a while over the coming months – as thoughtful men of conviction often do – but remained good friends through it all with high regard for each other. He was still of the opinion that we had the responsibility to cull out soldiers unfit for the job, but he at least had some basis for making that judgement. Previous Course Managers did not.

Charlie did not get along well with Hassan. Unlike Bayer or Gosling, who hankered for directly managing the contractors, Ali was comfortable with delegating. If he had a problem with a contractor, he went to the Raytheon Task Lead and expected it to be fixed. Ali would meticulously document the infraction and present it to Charlie and Sarah.

This was a first. Where I had begged the Course Managers to let me manage the contractors, Hassan demanded it. Charlie complained about it constantly.

"How can he have a problem with the contractors when his own people are the worst offenders?" he muttered. "The military instructors show up late more than our people do."

Although Charlie wanted the job, it did not come with any extra pay or benefits. He, like me, was still required to teach just as much as everybody else, but he, unlike me, was only paid at his senior level salary. I still received my consultant level salary and now had no other duties than to be available to teach.

Charlie was having a much harder time with the Task Lead job than I had and the friction between him and Hassan finally reached the ignition point.

"Where are the contractors?" Ali asked Charlie one morning when a class had to start late because those giving it were unprepared.

"You manage your people and I'll manage mine," Charlie told him.

Hassan asked Sarah to relieve him of his duties as Task Lead for the 35M course. From then on Ali had to take problems that couldn't be solved on site directly to Sarah, who was never there, and Ali was meticulous about documenting the problems with Memoranda for Record (MFR).

This brought Ali some unnecessary resentment from contractors even though the MFRs had no effect on them directly. Only Raytheon could discipline contractor misbehavior, so they were relatively safe, but the summary firing of contractors for no stated reason was still fresh in everyone's mind and they weren't sure yet that Ali would not stoop to the levels that other Course Managers had. And we all knew that Chuck would not hesitate to fire any employee who jeopardized the project by either not delivering the product or not making the customer happy.

That summer, in addition to transitioning to the Afghanistan scenario, we were also tasked with teaching some newly-required NCO development courses. Only military instructors were allowed to teach these, so they sucked away most of our uniformed staff. To compound the difficulties, several of our military instructors and contractors who were reservists also had to take these courses themselves as well as teach them. It put even more of the 35M course load onto the contractors and magnified the other difficulties.

Somehow Erwin, despite two devastating NCOERs and inability to pass the APFT, applied for the Warrant Officer program and was accepted. I don't know who recommended him from my unit, but the recommendation managed to bypass both me and the commander. He was readying himself for his next job, which would not be at Devens.

He probably could have stayed longer had he just mended his ways, but he got caught illegally helping Wilma while she was taking one of those NCO development courses. He was banned from ever setting foot in our building again.

To his credit, he did manage to pass the Warrant Officer course, which is quite demanding. He must have succeeded in eventually getting himself in shape. He transferred to another unit where no one knew him and he could start over yet again and managed to get orders for service in Afghanistan.

As we prepared for the first class Ali and I would lead, Colonel Rondeau, Major McCabe and Command Sergeant Major Hilton personally visited the 35M instructor cadre to make the commander's intent clear. General Heritsch's stint as commander of the 100th Division came to a close and she was replaced by Brigadier General Mark Arnold who had a Special Forces background. Upon assuming command of the 100th Division, he made it clear that this course would be a success and we'd bend some rules if we had to. Colonel Raynor had not restricted Rondeau's authority in any way and together we purposed to take full charge and implement whatever changes we deemed necessary.

At last I had all the necessary authority to see that the course be run the way I thought it should be.

Introducing collaborative learning techniques would have to be done gradually. Abruptly reversing decades of policy by encouraging the students to work together didn't feel right to those instructors who knew no other way. Using tools like the Internet and open source material, not to mention each other's experience and knowledge, felt like cheating. We had failed students for studying ahead before arriving and bringing material from previous classes. Erwin had even forbidden students from attending study hall unless all students attended together so as not to give anyone an unfair advantage.

But collaborative learning is better and much more effective. It's also more difficult to guide groups of students than to simply read a PowerPoint slideshow to them. The instructors were going to have a tough time adjusting to the new ways if I dumped it on them all at once.

With the start of Phase 1 we reinstated the collaborative, student-centered approach of dividing the students into teams and involving them more actively in their own education. This met with little resistance and we got off to a good start. I personally taught as many of these classes as I could and invited the instructors to watch how I did it. Not many took me up on the invitation so when their turns came to run a collaborative class,

I pretty much wound up either taking over or letting them teach the old way, which at least served to demonstrate to the students the difference between the traditional and modern ways of instruction.

In any case, everyone passed Phase 1 and the new technique got a foothold.

On the first day of Booth Phase, I introduced a new teaching policy to the instructors: Don't let the students get past a single point of performance without doing it correctly. This sparked no objections since that was pretty much the policy for the first few iterations anyway. But I spelled out for them how I wanted it done. If the students miss a point, give them a hint. If they don't get the hint, give them a bigger hint. If they still don't get it, stop the iteration, tell them what they're doing wrong, have them do it right and move on. Don't harass. Don't scold. Don't ridicule. Don't intentionally make it any harder than necessary. Don't mark the point wrong just because they didn't get it on the first try. This is teaching, not testing. At the end during the Critique and Retrain section, review what they had the most trouble with and advise them on how to improve.

I wanted the instructors to simply count the number of points of performance the students did correctly, even if they initially did it wrong and had to try again. Students who made a lot of mistakes would get lower scores because their progress was slower and students who learned fast would get higher scores. We could watch their progress from iteration to iteration and demonstrate learning, something we hadn't been able to do with the old methodology. It also made it easier to identify and address the areas each student was having difficulty with. They naturally spent more time in these areas before getting it right and sped right through the areas they understood well.

I got a little pushback in attempting to revise grading policy, but not much. In the past we took the number of mistakes the student made and subtracted them from the total possible points, which varied widely between scenarios. Each story was different and varied considerably in complexity and number of possible points. One story had less than 200 possible points while another had more than 700, and they weren't presented in any logical order of increasing difficulty. Then we calculated a percentage of the correct answers against the total possible. Sixty percent was the minimum passing score and almost impossible to get in the first few iterations.

I wanted to revise the grading so that the score would be the raw percentage of right answers out of the total available with the number of mistakes playing no role other than to slow the student down. There would still be the basic unfairness of the wide variation in total number of possible answers between scenarios, but at least we could chart actual progress based on the absolute number of right answers which would grow from iteration to iteration as the student became progressively more skillful. After a few classes, we would have enough data to set a reasonable expectation for each iteration.

This method of teaching and grading also provided information crucial to the student as well as the school on how well they were doing. When a student fails over and over again, they don't develop confidence in their learning through positive reinforcement. Ideally, the subject matter should be easy enough for the student to get four out of five attempts right. Eighty percent seems to be the ideal level of difficulty for optimal learning. Any harder and the students don't develop the assurance they are getting it. Any easier and the amount of new learning that can take place drops off.

The insanity of the old method was capped by the fact that none of these grades counted toward the final grade and some questions were considered "must pass" points. If the student failed even one of these, they failed the entire iteration regardless of how well they did otherwise. I once saw an excellent student score an amazing 98% and still fail by missing one "must pass" point.

Until now, all of the schools at Huachuca and elsewhere routinely told the students up front that they are going to flunk most, and maybe all, of the iterations, but not to worry. Most students pass the final test anyway. Now, with a policy in line with modern educational principles, it was likely that most students would pass most of the iterations and 100% was not impossible. In revising the scoring so the instructors checked off all the tasks the students learned correctly rather than marking off mistakes we would actually measure learning rather than failure. We could graphically measure student progress. The students would see progress right from the start and feel more confident.

Having the instructors teach a little differently and score a little differently was easy despite the indignation. What was more difficult was asking the instructors to vary the difficulty of the instruction by tailoring it to each individual student. Go easier on the students having difficulty and ramp up the challenge to students who were doing well. The magic number was 80%. The students should get it right four out of five times they try.

This simple technique alone of not letting the student get past a single point of performance without doing it correctly made a tremendous difference. Students suddenly started learning rapidly. They began passing their booth iterations often even on the first try. Some of the instructors objected. It felt too easy, they said. It felt like we were lowering the standards. They had been taught wrong by instructors who were taught wrong and surrounded by like minds for all their careers. Right looked wrong. But as they began to revise their methodology, the results spoke for themselves. Without changing the standards of the final test one iota, the first class achieved a 95% pass rate, up from the dismal 50% it had been for so long.

The collaborative learning techniques produced much faster and better learning while developing cooperation skills similar to what they would need when they actually deployed. I wanted to introduce the students to techniques that would more closely resemble the environment in which they would eventually work. A student should master all of the basic skills, but they should also learn to work together. I introduced a method that is well-established in the education science literature in which the students would individually write their reports, which would comprise 2/3 of their grade, and then collaborate to produce a group report for the remaining 1/3. In the field, no collector would ever write a report that had not been reviewed by others before being published, so this reflected a necessary skill that had had not been taught until now.

This individual plus collaborative report writing took more time to grade than the old method did, but produced dramatically better reports by allowing the students to learn from each other. What took more instructor time for grading was counterbalanced by the instructor time savings in coaching individual students.

It was not easy to coax the instructors out of the firmly held conviction that part of their job was to cull out soldiers who, in their minds, were unfit for this profession. The concern of many was that the new methodology made the course too easy and would produce huminters who were not emotionally tough enough to handle the stress of interrogation. But deciding who gets to be a huminter is not the prerogative of the instructor; it is the prerogative of the commander who sent them to us. The 35M course is not an ordeal like Ranger school where a major goal is to eliminate those less committed. Our job at the school is to teach everything to everyone. Our goal should be 100% graduation of students mastering 100% of the curriculum.[107] If we fall short of that goal, it should not be for reasons inherent in a poorly designed course taught by incompetent instructors.

The savage failing of half of each class had much wider repercussions than most instructors realized. First of all, we had no tracking system to verify whether what we were teaching actually produced competent intelligence collectors. We had no idea whether the ones we graduated would do their jobs well nor whether the ones we flunked would not. A more

---

107 In my years as a Military Intelligence professional and instructor I came to the conviction that success in this profession depends more on training a few quality people rather than masses of average students. In every class I was able to find a handful of students with exceptional talent and felt my efforts would best be spent mentoring them rather than spreading my attention thinly but evenly around the entire class. The principle also extended to soldiers in my battalion and instructors under my leadership. To this day I maintain contact with a few dozen students and former soldiers and employees, most of whom have not stayed in the profession but have nevertheless gone on to excellence elsewhere.

sensible policy should be, therefore, to graduate as many students as possible and let the rigors of the job determine how well suited they are.

Secondly, failing a military course often results in a bar to reenlistment. When a student fails, they are not allowed to perform this or any other MOS. The Army loses a soldier and the taxpayer's money is flushed down the drain. Occasionally a soldier will be lucky enough to be recycled or return to try again, but that is difficult in the reserve system where money is limited and the time civilian soldiers can take away from their jobs even more so. It also wreaks havoc on the budget which forecasts a certain number of soldiers trained in the MOS for a certain amount of money. When you flunk 50% of the students, the cost per soldier doubles.

No one seemed to make the connection between their job security and the pass rate. If this program turned out to be too expensive – the cost per graduate exceeding the budget forecast – it would be cancelled and our jobs would be gone. That may have been welcomed by Bass and others, but not the contractors. Yet no one seemed to link results to job security. The leap of transitioning from an authoritarian style of instruction to a peer-guided collaborative approach was a huge leap for many instructors who were quite comfortable with the I-talk-you-listen tradition. Seeing the students and their commanders as clients whose satisfaction with the product we delivered mattered was too big a leap for many.

Hassan clung to the idea that we – or at least he – had the responsibility of eliminating students not fit for the profession. He publicly stated, as had Bayer, that he would not graduate a student he would not personally deploy with. Ali at least had firm ground to stand on. He was a real interrogator with years of experience. I wasn't an experienced interrogator, but I had worked in other areas of human intelligence collection where a different skill set was required to be effective. So we agreed to disagree.

One thing we did agree on was that the grading was inconsistent. Erratic, in fact. Scores ranged from 25% to the high nineties and seemed to bear little correlation with either the student or the material. We all believed that some instructors graded harder while others graded easier and we wanted to find out why there were such wide differences in grading between the instructors. Ali wanted the hard graders to ease up and the easy graders to get a little tougher. This turned out to be more difficult than we anticipated.

The instructors with the reputation for grading harder responded with the defense that they were following the grading policy to the letter. Which rules would Hassan want them to break and was USAICS okay with this? Instructors with the reputation for grading easier responded with asking upon what basis we should fail students who had met the requirements to pass? Just asking people to grade easier or harder didn't work. None of the instructors thought they were being particularly hard or easy, just fair.

Hassan and I decided to do a comprehensive analysis of all of the instructors and students and their grade sheets for the entire previous year. It involved hundreds of documents and took us several weeks. The results surprised us. For one thing, it turned out that there was no difference in the range of grading between the easiest and hardest graders. It had been an illusion perpetuated perhaps by the personalities of the instructors, some of whom seemed strict and others amiable. Only one instructor turned out to be far outside the norm and no one had suspected her at all. (I had evaluated her once and found her surprisingly unprepared and clueless about how to teach or grade despite several years of experience. But she had drawn no special attention to herself being neither exceptionally kind nor cruel.)

What did surface was clear evidence that some instructors were measurably better than others. Their students passed more often and with higher scores. They corresponded to the favorites of the students on end of term student evaluations as well. This should have surprised no one, but we had never put much value on good instructors. There was no program to improve the quality of instruction. We made no effort to involve the effective instructors in helping the bad instructors improve. We didn't even have much opportunity to watch each other work, which might have evened out the skills and expectations, particularly in the booth. There was no tradition of equating graduation rates with success. If anything, it was the failure rate that instructors took pride in. If a hard course is a good course, then a hard instructor is a good instructor.

The statistics also revealed subtler but more alarming information. The average score for all iterations was 54%. But the average for the final test was 85%. The difficulty of the final test bore no relationship to what the students had been doing up until then. A score of 54% is little better than random guessing and demonstrated no effect by the instructors. Or at least no positive effect. We didn't even attempt to measure negative effects. Five out of six events – no matter how you sliced it, whether single questions or entire exercises – revealed no effect by the instructors at all.

As mentioned earlier, the optimal level of difficulty to maximize learning is 80%. The difficulty of the material should be such that the student succeeds four out of five tries. Any easier and they won't learn as fast as possible. Any harder, and they will not have the positive feedback to know they are on the right track. Below 70% success, confidence in learning declines precipitously. Below 60% it all but disappears. At 54%, our students were completely confused about how well they were doing and whether they were learning at all.

Our analysis of the data suggested that the students would be capable of learning the material on their own at least as well as with the help of an instructor. When you consider that we weren't even tracking the negative effects of the instructors, it became even more starkly apparent that going to school at all under these conditions was a complete waste of time and taxpayer money. In fact, the data suggested that in many ways, we were doing more harm than good.

Much more.

The waiving of the foreign language requirement for intelligence collectors had always disturbed me. Requiring a translator doubled, even tripled, the cost of deploying a single huminter and opened us up to infiltration by the enemy. Now I had found an even more troubling phenomenon. Sending the students through our school produced no more or better huminters than on-the-job training or self-study. There was also ample evidence that sending students through the 35M course eliminated some of the most talented candidates.

I also applied the 80% rule to validate the questions on the tests. When I performed a metanalysis on the tests and analyzed which questions were being answered correctly and which were missed most often, I found that some of the questions were too easy and didn't measure learning. More importantly, I found that some of the questions were never answered correctly, which suggested there was either something wrong with the question or the subject was not being taught properly. Apparently, once the POI and tests were published, no one checked the validity. No one asked whether the test measured what the test is supposed to measure. We all knew the course was imperfect. It needed improvement. But in the military training environment it was all too easy to blame failure on the students rather than look to the material or the instructors and make improvements.

My new policy began to distinguish competent instructors from incompetent ones. Effective teaching is harder than just presenting material and threatening students. Directing and correcting required more effort than just reading a script and checking off mistakes, but not much. Grading on raw progress was certainly easier than the complex calculations that had been required previously. But adjusting difficulty to an approximate 80% level was hard and harder still to make the difficulty relevant to learning. Only a few instructors even understood this concept and fewer still could implement it effectively. That was probably a major reason why the students learned at least as well from each other as they did from the instructors.

I had always gravitated toward the marginal students. I was required to teach as often as anyone else and being the Site Lead gave me some ability to schedule myself in with the students who were struggling. Even when I was no longer the Site Lead, I could often find a way to spend more time with the marginal students simply because most instructors didn't like the extra effort these students demanded. Sometimes I could trade students. Instructors often disagreed on whether borderline students should pass or not. Often such a student would be failed and recommended to come back again. With active duty schools, it is easy to recycle students into the next class. In the reserves it isn't. It's difficult and expensive. I felt that recycling the marginal students was exactly the opposite of what should be done. If the student has the potential to pass at all, they should pass the first time and it is worth devoting extra time and energy to these students to get them through and keep them from using up another slot that could go to another student later. It was rewarding to hear, "If I could just have you for my teacher all the time, I could really get this."

There was the sad case of Sergeant Lind.[108] He was a police detective in civilian life and had all the skills necessary to pass the course. He just needed to shift his questioning technique from getting a confession to getting information. He had some initial difficulty with this, but toward the end of the course he was getting it and no one thought he shouldn't pass. But on the exam he missed a question that was mandatory to pass the whole test. He had been given wrong information by his instructor and missed the point. I suggested he appeal the decision based on the circumstances. He had a valid case. He had demonstrated he was capable of performing the skill; he simply had not done it on the test because he had been told he didn't have to. He declined to appeal, not wanting to make waves, and felt confident he would pass the retest.

The retest was administered by Hassan, who told me he felt Lind did not belong in the profession. I pointed out to my friend that he was the only instructor who felt that way and that Lind had in fact demonstrated competence repeatedly. Hassan failed him and I advised Lind to appeal, which Ali did not appreciate. I had presented myself to the students as their advocate and Ali didn't think they needed one. He was their advocate. The tyrannies of Erwin were too fresh in my mind but I didn't want

108 Not his real name.

to point out to Ali the obvious. What if the complaint is against you? Are you their advocate then?

Inexplicably, Lind didn't go through with the appeal and by the time I returned the following day, he was gone.

Lind contacted me a few days later from his home in Utah and told me he decided not to go through with the appeal because he felt the hostility of the Course Manager would bias the appeal. He knew when he was unwelcome. It was only two years later I learned that he went through another 35M course put on by the Utah National Guard and passed. I was happy when I heard that but it also reconfirmed my conviction that our posture should be toward helping the marginal students pass rather than flunking them.

Along with improving instruction, I felt it was important to begin preparing students physically for deployment. It takes six months to build the kind of fitness necessary to carry large combat loads day after day in Afghanistan. It's a matter of connective tissue support, which develops more slowly than either aerobic fitness or muscular strength. The program I envisioned would have the students simply walk seven and a half minutes out and the same distance back in their combat boots once a day on break. I was sure this would be well received by the students who were spending most of their time sitting indoors during the course. It would have been better if this had been at Ft. Huachuca, which is desert and almost a mile high above sea level, but it was better than spending the break standing around smoking and drinking coffee.

The Sergeants Major of the 519th and 319th had asked that the students be familiarized with the equipment they would use in Afghanistan. I couldn't do much about that, but we did manage to get some portable biometric identity detection kits.[109] That was something at least. Ken

---

109 Biometric Automated Toolset (BAT) and Handheld Interagency Identity Detection Equipment (HIIDE) are used by tactical units to register and identify locals. In Afghanistan the naming system is quite different from ours, birth records are frequently nonexistent and identity documents unreliable. Biometric identity machines are now widely used to enter biological data including fingerprints and eye

Frickle, one of our newer contractors who had replaced Elliott, was good with that stuff.

I badly wanted to add more practice with using an interpreter to the course. Ali was totally on board with that, but it would require language-qualified instructors and we were fairly rare. Of the instructor cadre, only Hassan, Sergeant Mendez[110] and I had worked in language on actual missions. The most common foreign language we had among the instructors was Korean. Jenn, Philip, Kirsten, Ken, Denny and Alice all spoke it, but few instructors felt confident enough to use their languages for instruction purposes.

By the fall of 2011, the course was back on track. Most of the instructors were beginning to see why the new way was better. Those who didn't like it weren't causing me any problems now that I had the authority I needed. Morale was up and the students loved the new methodology. There was a little friction between me and Ali over a couple of marginal students, but Ali loved to argue just for fun anyway. He was also taking the initiative to remove some of the parts of the POI that didn't make sense, something no Course Manager had ever had the courage to do. His opinion of the student notwithstanding, Ali removed the point of performance that had failed Lind without even asking USAICS for permission.

Ali had his own problems with the Brigade just as I did. He was supposed to be getting a housing allowance for moving to the Devens area, but had been denied for the most preposterous of reasons: now that he was living near Devens, that was his permanent home and no housing allowance would be forthcoming. He had been making quite a lot of money in Boston working in venture capital finance and had given it up to go on orders for a year because we needed him. Now he not only took a substantial cut in pay, Brigade was denying him the housing allowance he

photos with pictures and names of locals the tactical units encounter. They are not simple devices to operate and all Human Intelligence Collectors should be familiar with their use.

110 Not his real name.

was due as well. It seemed he was constantly on the phone arguing with Lopez and Lowman, two of the full-time staff that seemed to always be in the middle of any effort to undercut the Brigade's own soldiers.

I doubted that Master Sergeant Lowman had any personal vendetta against anyone, but Carmen Lopez was another matter. She could be treacherous and had more than once cost us good soldiers who quit rather than work with her. She felt free to address battalion commanders in disrespectful ways, which aroused even more indignation.

One of the things I liked best about working with Ali was that his tongue was as sharp as his intellect. He was smart and liked to debate. He never took arguments personally, something not everyone noticed. He was clearly irritating the staff at Brigade, but felt that was the best way to ensure things got done. I leaned more toward persuasion and compromise.

"See, Lloyd? That's why you never get anything from Brigade. You're too nice. You just let them walk all over you," he said.

"I don't think being agreeable and letting people walk all over you are the same thing," I countered.

"Did you get your language pay?" he asked.

"Eventually," I said.

"All of it?" he asked, knowing the answer.

"No."

"See? I would have been on the phone with Carmen every day until she did the paperwork right. She just walks all over you," he said.

"Did you get your housing allowance?" I asked.

"Not yet. But I will. You'll see."

In addition to revising the teaching, the scoring of tests, the addition of a physical training program and serious language work, I saw a need for hiring instructors who had actually done the job recently and done it well. The whole purpose of a school is to put people with the knowledge and skill together with the students who would soon need it and transfer the knowledge and skills in some efficient fashion. The requirement to have actually done the job well was no longer a consideration for hiring an instructor, if indeed it ever had been. The only firm requirements to be an instructor were the security clearance, ABIC and having at one time graduated from the MOS-producing school. This policy had been in place for so long that virtually all of us had been taught by inexperienced or inept instructors in a long string of instructors at best only marginally capable of actually doing the job they taught. The line stretched back to before 1975.

With Ali Hassan, Sergeant Mendez and myself as the only instructors with actual recent real world experience working in language, the cadre had much room for improvement. Most had never interrogated, or if they had they weren't very good, or if they ever were, it was a long time ago. The interrogation manual had been revised and the military had undergone a major revision of policy in 2007 when Petraeus was given command in Iraq. Qualifications based on experience prior to 2007 was out of date, if not completely obsolete. Additionally, we were now moving to a new Afghanistan-based training scenario and had a revolutionary new training policy, ALM 2015, to implement.

A few quality huminters had come to us as temporary contractors for the Staggered Start of 2010 and I did my best to get them to stay. It would be difficult to emplace new people and displace the lesser qualified instructors. Graham Donaldson, Melinda Holly and Dwight Delorean were among the temps I particularly favored. But the contractor system doesn't hire on the basis of quality and the customer cannot legally (Colonel Thompson notwithstanding) specify which contractors to hire. The best military huminters tend to stay deployed while the worst gravitate to the only jobs open to them – instructing.

Still, I believed that if I were to remain competitive as an instructor, I would need to deploy again before retirement, which loomed in 2012. Even with the institutional restrictions on selectively hiring individuals as contractors, commanders still reached out for quality people when it counted. I had been personally tagged for Information Operations Sergeant Major over dozens of other candidates in 2002 in the ramp-up to the Iraq invasion. Chuck had recruited me specifically to lead the Devens project in 2008 upon my return from a year downrange with DIA, breaking the unwritten rule about not recruiting employees from other companies. If I wanted to stay qualified for the most important Intel jobs in the future, I would have to stay current.

CHAPTER 18

Romania

By September of 2011 we had succeeded in reversing the crash of the Mike course. Graduation was back up to 95% and would have been 100% if we had passed Lind. The students were happy. Instructors were teaching more effectively and progress was being made toward a course that better conformed to the principles of ALM 2015.

To my immense relief, Sergeant Briere returned from her deployment in Afghanistan unharmed, at least physically. There exists a tremendous wall of institutional resistance to the idea of including females on tactical teams. Every female who dropped out, even for reasons that men drop out, served to reinforce the prejudice. Kat, however, had managed to stay the course. She was attached to a Navy SEAL team. No one welcomed her when she arrived and by the time she left, none of the SEALs wanted to see her go.

Sergeant Briere, who should have been on top of the world, returned depressed and despondent. While she was deployed, a finance glitch had ceased making her automatic payments to, among other things, her automobile insurance and the storage of her household goods. Her car was impounded and her son, with no way to get to work, lost his job. The storage facility, though aware that Briere was deployed overseas, sold off her possessions. The action was completely illegal, but the deed was done and Kat was back in the States, divested of most of her worldly goods, with no job and no place to live.

Colonel Rondeau and I immediately lobbied for putting her into a full-time instructor job. This time there would be no waffling about her inexperience. We got her orders and soon she had a job at the Mike course and could begin the long struggle of rebuilding a home for herself and her children.

Soon after Kat came on board as a full-time military instructor, Rondeau announced at drill that Colonel Busher, a mysterious member of our unit no one knew much about, would be accepting a deployment as Commander of the Black Sea Area Support Team and charged with developing two training centers in Romania and Bulgaria. It sounded like a dream job, and I told him so, never thinking the possibility might exist for me to come along as his Command Sergeant Major. But that's what happened. He asked me whether I would be available and I said of course.

Still stinging from having missed the Special Forces deployment, I never thought this would happen either, especially with only a couple of months' lead time. But Colonel Busher put in a request for "by name" orders (which have to be approved by a three-star general) for me. The orders came down and I prepared to go.

But not without a sideshow for a send-off.

I told Ali Hassan I would be leaving in February of 2012 and to plan for that. Ali called Brigade to request a replacement and was laughed at. I listened from the next room while Ali and one of the Brigade staff bet each other a case of beer on the outcome. The Brigade staff was confident this attempt to deploy would be sabotaged as easily as my Special Forces deployment had been. Plus, they still held a grudge for going over their heads to the General in the Briere matter.

At the first sign of delay, I contacted Colonel Busher, who was not at all surprised by the behavior of the Brigade and Division staff. He had seen petty bureaucrats attempt to flex their muscle many times in the past and knew exactly what to do about it. He made a phone call to a two-star general and the orders went through and Ali got his case of beer.

This also opened a win-win situation for me and Kat. I needed someone to look after my home while I was deployed and she needed a home for her family. She moved her family and dogs in just before Thanksgiving.

In December I underwent my yearly evaluation along with all Raytheon employees. Technically, I should have been evaluated by Brian Keyes, who had taken Fred's place. Instead, I was evaluated by Sarah. She rated me as satisfactory in all areas but made no mention of my accomplishments. I asked her to enter the statistics on my performance, i.e. hours delivered, evaluations by the students, evaluations by the customer, accomplishments and qualifications. I had logged more hours teaching than any other instructor and had the work schedule to prove it. My evaluations were at the top from both students and the customer. The Staggered Start had given Raytheon a powerful sales tool to prove value to the current and future customers. I was Six Sigma certified and had a Master's in Education. The customer had adopted my management tools for official use and my changes to the program had raised the graduation rate from 50% to 95%. My metanalysis of instructor performance had also enabled us to focus on weaknesses we hadn't seen before and gave us data against which to plot progress. In addition, I had written an entire, comprehensive Program of Instruction that conformed to the new Army Learning Method 2015 and cut the instructor requirement in half, an immense potential savings to the Army.

"I don't like to manage by statistics," Sarah said.

"Irrelevant. Raytheon requires it. Just read the instructions on how to perform an evaluation," I said. Though I had done dozens of employee evaluations for Raytheon, she had never done any before and didn't understand the procedure. Brian Keyes was apparently new to the process as well.

"I don't think it's necessary," she insisted. "You're getting a satisfactory evaluation. You should be happy with that."

"The data demonstrate superior performance. I've not only exceeded the standard, I'm at the top. That rates 'Far Exceeds Expectations,'" I suggested.

"We're not allowed to rate anyone 'Far Exceeds' anymore," she said. I knew this wasn't true, but was curious about why she was so reluctant to give me the rating I deserved. "Far Exceeds" merits a higher raise than "Exceeds" or "Meets" do.

"Far exceeding expectations is expected of Consultant-level positions. The highest a Consultant can get is 'Meets Expectations,'" she said.

"I was rated 'Far Exceeds' for the last two years by Fred and had data to support it," I pointed out.

"Nevertheless, Raytheon does not allow an evaluation of higher than 'Meets Expectations' for Consultant-level positions," she said. "'Far Exceeds' is the standard for Consultants."

I told her I intended to not concur with her evaluation and would enter the data myself. In business, all management demands measurement and ignoring statistics is not the way real corporations work.

"I don't want to be stubborn, but our raises are based on our evaluations," I said.

"There won't be any raises this year," she said. "Chuck said the program isn't succeeding at the level it should and there won't be any raises."

I wasn't too sure about what to believe. She had said so many things that were completely wrong I no longer trusted her. I wrote a succinct rebuttal to her evaluation, listed my accomplishments and left it at that.

After a year as Site Lead, Sarah had not managed to gain the trust of her contractors. A major reason had been the creation of a culture of secrecy. We were not allowed to communicate with Raytheon except with her permission and only with her present. We still had no idea what Mr. Keyes's role was and how much authority he had actually entrusted to Sarah. In contrast to Fred's active leadership, Brian Keyes was someone we never saw and never talked to. He didn't seem remotely interested in us and we weren't sure how closely he worked with the Site Lead. Sarah had threatened several of us with termination. Did she actually have the power to do that? I didn't when I was Site Lead.

The biggest impediment, greater than all else, was her tolerance for the abuse the customer consistently inflicted. With Bayer gone, Gosling was now the chief perpetrator, but some of the contractors interpreted Hassan's management as abusive as well. There was certainly no love lost between him and Charlie, or for that matter, one or two other contractors whose performance had slipped. Personally, I could not in good conscience call Ali's behavior abusive. He was demanding and occasionally made an attempt at humor that failed to amuse, but I never saw him act maliciously. Even in the Lind case, he acted in good faith and for reasons that to him were appropriate for his position and responsibilities. What was more, he was equally demanding of the military staff, especially the Phase Leads.

Gosling, on the other hand, couldn't resist publicly berating people using the foulest of language. This at the very least should have drawn Sarah to action but went unopposed. Raytheon turned a deaf ear to complaints of a hostile work environment and indeed seemed to support the customer's intent to keep the workplace tense and fear-ridden.

To tell the truth, I wasn't sure anyone at Raytheon even noticed us, much less read our evaluations. They certainly weren't interested in our working conditions. The project took a nosedive when Sarah took charge, yet no one seemed concerned. We had no more direct contact with our project managers. Fred was gone, his replacement was a ghost, and if we heard from Chuck at all it was an indirect scolding about not doing our timecards. Individual contractors were now directly managed by the Army staff with Sarah's blessing, herself a staff officer in the unit that managed the Raytheon contract. A hostile work environment reigned and any complaints were met with some variation of "If you don't like it, quit."

Several contractors did quit. Elliott, Alice and Roger – three of our best – were gone, but willing to return if the climate changed. Those who stayed just tried to keep a low profile.

With regards to my deployment, the Brigade had not managed to do much more than delay my departure and on Saint Patrick's Day of 2012 I arrived at my duty station in Romania. I spent the last six months of my military career in Romania and Bulgaria as Colonel Busher's Command

Sergeant Major. The two of us and fourteen civilian KBR[111] contractors ran that operation overseeing the development of two forward US bases, one in Romania and one in Bulgaria. We had a battalion of Marines to support and regular rotations of Coalition troops going to and from Afghanistan. I functioned as the Security Officer and the Intelligence Officer and the work was exciting. Our bases were strategically important and interesting to foreign intelligence services as well as our host nations.

For me, the opportunity to work in a dozen languages was pure joy. I put in for language pay in my primary language, Bulgarian, and to my astonishment and Colonel Busher's supreme amusement, I was denied. I had been designated the official Swahili linguist for Romania and as such did not qualify for language pay.

"You can't make this shit up," the Colonel observed.

Looking a little deeper, I discovered that the people who had designated me the Swahili linguist were the same ones that had revoked my language pay two years earlier for *not* working in Bulgarian. The stated reason was "needs of the Army." The Army needs Swahili linguists more than it needs Bulgarian linguists.

Colonel Busher handled it in his signature direct way with an added twist of irony to drive home the humiliation. He called a general to explain the situation, who called the language control officer in the Pentagon, and then ordered me to communicate with them only in Swahili until the orders were changed.

Who declared me a Swahili linguist in 2012 with the stroke of a pen? It turned out to be the same office and the same people who had denied me

111 KBR, Inc. (formerly Kellogg Brown & Root) is an American engineering, procurement, and construction company, formerly a subsidiary of Halliburton, which plays an indispensable role in the construction and maintenance of US bases abroad. KBR subbed out much of the work in constructing both the Romanian and Bulgarian bases to a German company, which subbed out to a Turkish company, which hired from, among other places, Iran and Syria. Agents of Hezbollah may have directly participated in the construction of those two bases, but the Colonel and I were even more concerned that much of the hired labor wasn't working at all. Long lunches over pints of beer followed by siestas on the jobsite seemed to constitute the normal workday before he and I arrived.

language pay because I was a Bulgarian linguist, including Ms. Ducklow who told me she had never been able to find this office. As luck would have it, one of the people in the embassy in Bucharest used to work in the Pentagon and knew exactly where the office was and who was in charge.

My conversations with the Army officer in charge confirmed that a soldier's primary language could indeed be changed without any paperwork. She cited "needs of the Army," the Army needing Swahili speakers more than Bulgarian speakers. That I was serving in Bulgaria and not in Africa was not relevant. Nevertheless, she agreed to change my primary language back to Bulgarian if my commander would verify that I was in fact using Bulgarian in Bulgaria.

At this juncture the hope arose of having the revoked $5,400 of FLPP returned that I had earned in other languages. She had just changed my eligibility based on using Bulgarian in the line of duty. The same reasoning applied for my work in 2007 and 2008.

I had been operating under the assumption that the revocation of my language pay had been an honest mistake, an incorrect but sincere misinterpretation of the process. I had never been able to prove that I had been deliberately targeted with a records audit in retaliation for threatening to file an IG complaint. But in forwarding me the denial of language pay in 2012 for Bulgarian, Ms. Ducklow neglected to remove the trail of emails proving I had indeed been deliberately targeted even back in 2009.

The Language Control Officer requested and received a letter from Colonel Busher documenting the need for a Bulgarian-speaker in Bulgaria. I eventually got my language pay along with pay for Swahili. With finally discovering where the decision maker was in the Pentagon who designated primary languages for linguists, I thought I might finally be able to undo the injustice that had been done earlier in penalizing me for working in languages other than Bulgarian.

Unfortunately, my emails went unacknowledged and I had more pressing matters to divert my attention. That small success which should have led to rectifying the language pay mistake went no further and I retired. To the best of my knowledge, the language-qualified soldiers of the 1st Brigade are still not getting their FLPP, and letters from the bureaucrats that deny them are still signed off with hollow phrases about how enthusiastically they support the troops.

I thoroughly enjoyed my assignment in Romania as Colonel Busher's Command Sergeant Major and only staff officer. It was an honor to serve with the Marines. Several of the Coalition Forces soldiers we trained distinguished themselves in Afghanistan and saved lives, including American lives.[112]

It was also an opportunity to get familiar with the rapidly-changing intelligence and counterintelligence environment. It was clear even in 2012 that problems in Syria and Iraq would soon eclipse our Afghanistan adventure and we would no doubt soon be considering yet a new scenario at the school to replace the Afghanistan one we had so recently adopted.

I maintained contact with my friends back at Devens. Sarah asked when I would be returning and when they could schedule me to teach. I would be returning in time to attend the graduation of a class of huminters, so I prepared a brief presentation based on my experience and how that might possibly affect them after graduation.

As my 60th birthday neared, I needed to return home, process my retirement and bid a sad farewell to my life in uniform. If I had my last wish, it would have been to make one last parachute jump on my last assignment, but the magnificent Colonel Busher – who loves jumping even more than I do – was unable to persuade our commanders to put us on permissive jump status. The Colonel and I were just too essential to justify the unnecessary risk.

What I did get, however, was a final screw-up in paperwork. My orders were extended beyond my 60th birthday to make them technically PCS (Permanent Change of Station) and not TDY (Temporary Duty), thus

112 In 2013 there was an incident in which an Afghan contractor guarding a US base turned his weapons on Americans. A Romanian soldier we trained killed the Afghan before he could reach his intended victims, a car full of American officers.

releasing the Army from the obligation of paying per diem. When I returned to Heidelberg to out-process, the whole office which had sent me out was gone. They were being moved to Wiesbaden and were not available to assist. I no longer had a valid ID card and could not even get on post without help.

I was able to find a room at the Patton Barracks a few miles from the post. I bought my own bedding and rented a car. There was no opportunity to get my retirement physical or obtain the benefits available to retired military like medical, dental and life insurance. It was somehow fitting that I kept all my issued equipment rather than turning it in, mirroring how my first enlistment had ended in 1976. I was only able to eventually complete my retirement physical through the VA and get my DD-214 in 2015, almost three years after discharge.

I returned to Devens late in August of 2012 about the same time as Ali, who had also been away. I was no longer the Director of Instruction, which is a military position, but was eager to pick up where we had left off. Hopefully, the instructors would have gotten used to the new teaching and grading policies by now and things would be running much better.

The summer 35M class graduated the week I returned. I was invited to attend and congratulate the students along with the other instructors, though I hadn't actually taught any of them. Neither Ali nor I were asked to present a briefing on what we had done on our deployments. Sergeant Major Ortiz was invited instead as the guest speaker and gave a very entertaining address relevant to those who might one day raise teenage children. Freshly back from the real world of human intelligence collection, I had some difficulty readjusting to an institutional mindset that made no connection between what we were teaching at Devens and what the students would soon be doing with what they learned.

CHAPTER 19

Downsized

UPON RETURNING TO my job at Devens in August, I threw myself back into the work. While I was gone, Ali Hassan had also taken a brief active duty assignment, his skills as a native Arabic speaker being greatly in demand. While we were away, much had been done to undermine our work. Gosling had been left in charge and morale was low. Several contractors had quit and we had temps working in, who were quite confused. No one was shepherding the contract force and problems with absences and unpreparedness were generating a steady stream of MFRs.

The planning meeting for the upcoming class proceeded as if we had never made any changes to the POI at all the year before. They had defaulted back to the old PowerPoint lecture format. The grading system was back to the old rubric of counting up the mistakes and failing anyone who made too many. Not only were collaborative techniques gone, Alice (who had returned after Bayer was truly gone and banned from the site) and Jenn gave a presentation on how we might one day introduce the collaborative learning techniques now required by ALM 2015. Ali emphasized that we would look forward to incorporating such techniques in the future once we work out the details.

I was stunned. I asked as politely as I could what had happened to the collaborative student-centered practices we had implemented just a year earlier. Ali was hazy on the specifics.

"Jenn and Alice just outlined the same techniques we began to adopt last fall," I said. "We already had a good start on it just a year ago. This is all in my thesis."

"Could you send me a copy of it?" Ali asked. Jenn also asked for a copy, which was the blueprint for the new way of teaching 35M in compliance with ALM 2015.

Ali had been quite proactive when we started to implement the new techniques. He was an enthusiastic supporter of implementing collaborative report writing. He had even taken the initiative to change some of the POI without even asking permission from USAICS. Somehow over the previous six months with his absence and his time as Course Manager coming to a close, his mind wasn't in the school game anymore.

It looked like we'd have to start all over, but now I was neither Director of Instruction nor Site Lead and it looked like the next Course Manager would be the single individual least likely to make any changes, the newly promoted Sergeant First Class Gosling.

By August of 2012 the rumors of moving the MI courses at Devens back to Huachuca were strong. The Raytheon contract had been renewed for another year at Devens and no money had been allocated for the move, but it was clear more than ever that the only way we would survive was to reliably produce more huminters per dollar than Huachuca did. I was disappointed that the new learning methodology had not stuck, but by reintroducing them we could get the graduation rates back up and reduce the cost per graduate if the Brigade appointed the right leadership.

Other money-saving options were available to us as well. Phase 3 – Source Operations – was unnecessarily expensive in several ways. We rented 17 vehicles which were necessary to transport the students around to the local towns to practice tradecraft and clandestine meetings. It generally took half a day to do just one meet because of the time involved in transportation. Added to that was the risk of driving and the chance of being reported by a citizen whose suspicions were aroused.[113] A particularly

113 The students and instructors all carried official letters to explain to the police what they were doing, should the need arise, and it often did. The local police were, of course, notified ahead of time that we would be running training of this nature in their area.

difficult problem was contractor use of vehicles. It had to be stated in the SOW to cover the liability of the company should anything go wrong. The students could just drive the cars, but that left contractors vulnerable to unscheduled overtime hours if things ran late. In most cases, the contractors preferred to use their own vehicles, but still felt they should be reimbursed for gas and mileage, which was never in the SOW.

One incident that occurred right before I returned in August illustrated just how much trouble letting a contractor drive a rental vehicle could produce. One of the instructors who must remain nameless (after all, it was a real investigation of a Serious Incident) totaled a rental vehicle in the Rapid Refill parking lot just outside the gate at Devens. She had just finished filling the tank and was beginning to drive away when she struck another vehicle. It was a remarkable feat when you think about it, totaling a car by bumping into another vehicle as she was easing away from the pump. The police report estimated the speed of the collision at an impossible 25 mph. The contractor was to be interviewed by the military investigating officer and I was asked to be present as a witness to the investigator's interview of the driver.

The investigator asked whether she wanted an attorney because she could be tried in a criminal court, be fined thousands of dollars and possibly go to jail. She said no, she was fine. The investigator asked whether she waived her right to remain silent, and she said yes. Neither the investigator nor I could give legal advice to the contractor, though out of pity he cautioned her to think before she spoke. It had no effect.

"Do you concur with the citation issued by the officer?" asked the investigator. The cop was not at the scene when the collision took place, interviewed no witnesses other than the contractor, could not write in correct English, and asserted the clearly impossible, i.e. going from zero to 25 mph in less than 5 feet. She concurred with the police report.

"Do you feel you were being careless?" the investigator asked.

"No. I always drive that way," she answered.

"Have you been in any accidents before?" he asked.

"Not lately," she answered.

"Could the other driver have done something to prevent the accident?" he asked.

"No. He was there before I even saw him."

"Well, describe to me in your own words how the accident happened," he said.

"I was looking around on the floor for something when I spilled my coffee on my leg, which made me hit the accelerator rather than the brake. That's when I plowed into him."

Yep. She actually said "I plowed into him."

If there was ever a person who needed an advocate, it was this contractor in this situation. She was not only in a position to harm herself unintentionally, Raytheon was potentially liable as well. But none was provided by Raytheon nor the Army. She was abandoned to bear the consequences alone.

The greater irony is that there is no need for the vehicles in the first place. Entry-level huminters do not need to be trained in clandestine meets and tradecraft. Most of our students would spend their first assignment inside the wire, in uniform, on some base in Afghanistan or Iraq interviewing local civilians who come in to volunteer information. The chance of a new collector going outside the wire in civilian clothes, driving a private vehicle and making clandestine contacts in Baghdad or Kabul is virtually nil. Yet we had a whole program dedicated to trying to train them to do something like that. (Not that meeting an American playing the role of an Afghan agent in a Dunkin Donuts in any way resembles the real thing.) We rented 17 vehicles every cycle and used them to conduct mock clandestine meetings in towns all around central Massachusetts.

The driving alone involved a few hours for each meet. This meant each team might manage to plan and conduct one meet a day at best. They could have done several meets in a single day by just practicing without leaving Devens as though they were on a US base, which of course is what they would actually be doing if they did source ops at all. Driving to distant towns in rental cars was expensive and time-consuming.

It was also risky. The occasional accidents involving rental cars were always costly. Moreover, lots can go wrong, especially with novices. We all had to carry papers to explain to the police that we were in a military class practicing spying and not actually spying. Suspicious civilians often notified the police and embarrassing situations were common. Even the unforeseen traffic jam could throw the schedule off and we had precious little flexibility as it was.

So getting rid of the rental car requirement could have saved the Army a huge amount of money, lowered risk, and actually yielded more training time on Ft. Devens and right outside the gate.

In the time between out-going and in-coming classes in September of 2012, the Ft. Devens cadre decided to clean up the building. All soldiers were to participate. Sarah ordered us to show solidarity by helping as well. We would have been happy to do so, but as contractors we cannot legally perform any labor outside the Statement of Work. This definitely lay well outside the SOW. In addition, the proper equipment was unavailable. There were no ladders, so cleaning the outsides of the windows would have to be done by dragging picnic tables and chairs to stand on underneath the windows. It was dangerous and one of the most solemn orders I was given by Raytheon when I took the job in 2009 was to avoid exposing employees to danger. Other than Fred, the one Raytheon official we did see regularly was Jason Paris, the regional Safety Manager. Raytheon was serious about safety and we were being compelled to clean windows by standing on stacked furniture.

I told Ali that involving contractors in the GI party would be a violation of the SOW. He didn't think it was. It would fall within the category of normal maintenance of one's work area, but he would check with Bass. As he waited for Bass's answer, I reminded Sarah that we can't demand the contractors do work outside the SOW. Several of the more experienced contractors concurred. Joan Chandler[114] vowed to report the violation to Raytheon if we were forced to participate in the clean-up. Sarah's

114 Not her real name.

response was "Either you come in and work along with the soldiers or stay home without pay."

We all came and did illegal work rather than miss a day's pay. Fortunately, Mike Bass got back to Hassan before too long and gave him the correct information, that contractors cannot be used for work not specified in the SOW. It underscored that, despite almost two years as Site Lead, Sarah still had little grasp of the contractor-client relationship. This wasn't the Army Course Manager insisting on personally ordering the contractors to do work. This was the Raytheon Site Lead herself directing us to do the illegal activity, and with full warning against it by knowledgeable contractors.

It was disturbing that the violations could have gone on for so long – the unpaid overtime, the direct ordering of contractors by military personnel, the ban on anyone contacting Raytheon but her under penalty of termination, the work outside the SOW. Was no one at Raytheon aware of just how perilous the situation was? Or maybe Chuck had just given up on the whole idea, realizing that the Army was pulling all the schools back to Huachuca and, in any case, was determined to eventually meet its mission requirement without contractor support. We were operating way outside the law, the program was failing, and Raytheon was losing money.

To complicate matters, I had to use up my leave time left over from active duty and couldn't just cash it in, so I took a couple of weeks to see my family in San Francisco before the start of the next class, just a month away. While I was there I got a call from Sarah.

"The Army is cutting back on contractor positions and yours has been eliminated," she told me. It was nothing I had done, she assured me. The customer just had to eliminate two positions and mine had been chosen at random.

There were a lot of things wrong with this starting with getting the call while I was far away. I called Raytheon and talked to Patty Dinsmore who verified that the Army had eliminated my position. The fact that I was more highly qualified and experienced than the other Consultant-level employees did not matter. The customer had made that decision. Even more disturbing, the decision had been made the previous spring. They were aware for months that I would be coming back to no job and hid it from me. They knew, yet they continued to communicate with me as though I had a job for another year. It wasn't just Sarah who had kept me in the dark until the last moment. Neither Chuck nor anyone else at Raytheon had said a word, though they all knew. Patty told me that they don't usually inform the employees they will have no job to return to while they are deployed.

"You must have known as early as June, perhaps May or even April, that my position was being eliminated," I said.

"We don't usually tell the returning employees about things like that until after they get back," she said.

"Does that seem right to you? I could have made a smooth transition to another job. Raytheon usually treats its employees very well."

"I suppose they wouldn't want to upset a soldier in a combat zone," she surmised.

"I was led to believe I would have a job. I committed to another year at Devens. I arranged housing, bought a car..."

"That's unfortunate," she said.

"Even though I'm senior? More highly qualified? What happened to first in, last out?"

"It doesn't apply in this case. It was the customer who eliminated your position, not Raytheon."

"The customer would not have done it without consulting Raytheon. When I was Site Lead, every résumé went through me. In fact, I seriously doubt the customer was even informed," I said. "He would have said something."

"Believe me, the customer eliminated the slot," she maintained. "Anyway, you are still eligible to work for Raytheon. We have an office to help place displaced employees." She gave me the number to call.

I made a few quick phone calls in addition to the Raytheon placement office. The first was to Colonel Rondeau who was responsible for the 35M course. He, of course, was very surprised to find that my position had been eliminated. No one had told him, let alone consulted with him on the matter. The decision to eliminate my position would have been made after much deliberation at a much higher level last spring but not without input from the commanders in charge of the various schools. I had participated such planning conferences myself in previous years and sure wish I had been at that one.

Although the decision would have been made much higher up, it was not possible that Sarah would not have been asked for input. The Army decided to cut a Consultant position, but how did they decide on eliminating mine? And why?

Now the fight over my evaluation last winter began to make more sense. Why had there been such resistance to entering data documenting superior performance? Why maintain that Raytheon had a policy that no Consultant could be evaluated as "Far Exceeds Expectations" when I had achieved that the two previous years in a row? She had been put in a position to advise the customer on which Consultant position to eliminate. Could she really be expected to recommend her own position be removed, or that of her close friend Jesse Parker? The Foxtrot course ran smoothly and needed no consultant positions, yet it had two. The Mike course, in contrast, was in deep trouble and badly needed more effective leadership.

With Sarah hiding my impending job loss from both me and Colonel Rondeau, the pieces began to fall into place. Now the reason for my vague and lack-luster evaluation and refusal to enter the statistics that reflected my accomplishments made sense. I asked Ms. Dinsmore about Raytheon's policy of not awarding Consultant-level position ratings higher than "Meets." She assured me this wasn't true. I had been passed over for a raise. Was it true that no one was getting raises this year? No, that wasn't true either. I talked to a few of my fellow workers and discovered that all had received the usual raises. Virtually every word out of Sarah's mouth with respect to my position had been a lie.

As soon as the elimination of my position was announced, nearly every contractor at the Mike course approached me expressing the intention of leaving as well. Working for Sarah was intolerable. It looked like Gosling would be the next Course Manager, which was even worse. Melinda Holly, who had been fed up for some time, walked in, cleaned out her desk and, in a puff of smoke, disappeared without uttering a word.

Ali was unhappy that we would be down two contractors, me and Melinda. We might not be able to meet the 1:2 instructor-student ratio required by the POI. Of course, by using collaborative learning techniques, we could have conducted the course just as effectively with half the instructors, but all of our efforts in that direction had been reversed and both Ali and I would be leaving before the next class began. There would be no one left who knew how to implement the methodology. As angry as I was, I nevertheless felt obligated to share with him and Sarah what I knew about the impending exodus of contractors.

"You're not going to be down just two instructors," I said. "You're going to lose at least six, maybe more."

"Who is leaving?" he asked.

"I promised not to tell. But trust me, you're going to need at least six more contractors in about two weeks and you'd better plan for that," I said.

"I'm confident Raytheon will be able to supply the necessary contractors in time," he said.

"I'm not. But you'd better tell Chuck we're about to need a bunch of new contractors on short notice," I said.

I'm not sure what he or Sarah did to prepare. Ali remained sanguine. He would just roll with whatever situation developed and would be gone in a month anyway. It would be Gosling's problem.

A week before class started, Ken Frickle dropped the equivalent of a literary A-bomb on Raytheon, telling off everyone he disliked, especially Raymond Gosling and Sarah Sondheim. Some people burn bridges; Ken nuked his. I'm including part of it here with his permission for your entertainment. Some of the names have been replaced with initials to protect identities.

Friends, colleagues, and others:

I would like to first thank my friends and colleagues, without whom the 35M HUMINT Collector Course at Fort Devens would not be able to function, nor would I have been able to perform here to my full potential. A.D., J.C., J.C., N.M., P.T., J.K., R.C., S.L., A.A., Noelle Dattilo, and D.G. it has been a pleasure to work with you. Lloyd Sparks and C.F., I have enjoyed working alongside with you, usually enjoyed working for you, and would still follow you anywhere, though preferably under other circumstances than these abysmal conditions.

It has come to my attention that certain individuals within Raytheon leadership and the local military command here at Fort Devens would like to see me leave this contract. Though they cannot quantify the reasons, and likely only wish to display their over-exaggerated power and authority by acting based on their personal and unprofessional opinions of me, they are probably doing me a favor without even realizing it. So allow me to share my sentiments at this point in time.

I no longer wish to support an organization where the mission of training soldiers is overshadowed by the ineptitude, nepotism, ignorance, arrogance, and other personality disorders exhibited amongst the leadership of both Raytheon and the military. Good luck to you all in your efforts to repeat the grave mistakes of the past.

SSG R.G., you will be no different and no more successful than your mentor (W01) E.B. in his style of leadership by fear. Perhaps this is an active effort to bring yourself closer to your peer, E.'s spouse, (SSG) W.G. What you lack in education, technical aptitude and the will to stop playing Zuma and get off of your lazy ass to teach a class, you can continue to compensate for by yelling at people whose job qualifications exceed yours until you get your way. You exemplify the adult daycare system for otherwise-unemployable scumbags that is the Army Reserve of today.

(CW3) S.S., nobody here trusts you, and my colleagues will be awaiting your resignation from your position as soon as you realize that you cannot manage your conflicted interests between your positions with the Army Reserve and with Raytheon. If you stay on the contract at Fort Devens, it will only be a matter of time before my highly skilled peers eat you alive and end your short and fruitless career in the government contracting world. You would do best to return to hiding behind your military rank and continuing to avoid combat deployments.

To the Raytheon leaders who continue to bury their heads in the sand and pretend everything is alright with this contract, you can all go fuck yourselves. I look forward to hearing that you have lost this contract, and hopefully some of you will see legal repercussions for your negligence and fraudulent activities. I myself may myself initiate such action if I see fit to do so between the duties of my new position.

Just remember that there are people who command respect, and those who demand respect, and the difference is usually quite clear in their leadership techniques, or lack thereof.

Sincerely,
Ken Frickle

Ken followed up with a formal complaint to Raytheon and was dismissed with a casual "thanks for the information" from Garth Chandler, the Raytheon leader of Ethics and Compliance. The abrupt resignation of six contractors, all of whom reported activities which should be of concern to his office, rocked no boats.

Both Philip and Jennifer Twain had already found positions, but didn't want to announce their exit until the last minute in case something radically changed. Nothing changed for the better, so they left as well. Both Jim and Joan Chandler,[115] who had been hired when Ron, Elliott and Alice quit, found other jobs at Huachuca and left.

Class started without enough instructors and they immediately had to send six students home. This is bad enough at an Active Duty school, but reservists have to take time off work and the burden on reservists and their families of making time for a two-and-a-half-month military school is immense. To show up ready for a 10 ½-week school only to be turned around and sent home because there are a few instructors missing is a real tragedy.

But theirs was perhaps the easiest lot. They at least would not have to undergo the agony of a botched course and in the end have "failure" on their records and be perhaps barred to reenlistment because of it.

With the best instructors gone and Gosling in charge, the class that started with 24 only graduated six, the lowest number ever. The consternation from the sending units was so great that enough students could not be found to even start the next class, which went non-conduct. The military instructors and contractors found themselves coming to work every day with no one to teach and 17 expensive rental cars to watch over with no one to transport. The program was a dead, black hole that did nothing but suck up taxpayer dollars. And it had all been avoidable.

Positions had opened for the jobs vacated by the Twains, the Chandlers and Ken Frickle. I applied for them through Raytheon but was not selected. Others with lesser qualifications were hired, so it was obvious that someone was blocking my application despite the persistent denials.

---

115 Not their real names.

I was fairly certain that the corporate officers at Raytheon were unaware that an employee had, at the very least, facilitated the removal of an essential member of the team, precipitated a mass exodus of employees at a critical time and then blocked the rehiring of qualified candidates. These actions had catastrophic consequences to the customer who had been deceived by that Raytheon employee. Under the circumstances, I felt justified in filing a complaint with the Raytheon Ethics and Compliance Office and did so in September of 2012. I felt that what had happened was not just bad business, it was fundamentally unethical. Sarah should never have been put in a position to have to choose whether her position or mine would be eliminated. You can't really expect someone to recommend that she herself be fired. All of the lies and deception stemmed from that. I reasoned that if Raytheon took a closer look, the value of my contribution would be brought to light. Several high level military officers representing the customer stood ready to vouch for me.

I supplied Patty Dinsmore with the contact information for those key decision makers who were directly knowledgeable and involved in the process every step of the way: The Ft. Devens Team Chief Tim Partin, his deputy Jennifer Fogelman, Lieutenant Colonel Dean Rondeau, who had responsibility for the 35M course (who was coincidentally both Sarah's and my commander), Major Drake Sampson, the representative of the 80th TTC and the Course Manager, Master Sergeant Hassan. Garth Chandler, the Raytheon Director of Ethics & Compliance assured me the matter would be promptly investigated and Patty would get back to me soon.

Patty took the information but never called any of them. She made four phone calls, speaking only with Sarah Sondheim and unnamed individuals, all of whom had been negligent in the management of the project and ignorant of day-to-day events at Devens. I pestered Patty with a dozen emails and phone calls over the ensuing year. She apologized for the delay, but delayed nonetheless.

Finally, in December of 2013, more than a year later and long after any possibility of saving the project had completely vanished, she informed me that she had found no ethical violations. She had talked to four people who were responsible for the violations and accepted their assurances they had done nothing wrong. She didn't think it necessary to talk to anybody else.

Her letter to me restated that my position was eliminated by "the customer." Had she actually spoken with the customer, whose phone number I provided, she would have discovered the customer knew nothing of the plan to eliminate my position, which he considered essential to the success of the project.

Patty could not have been ignorant of the fact that the request to replace me in 2011 did not originate from the TOR but from the Course Manager who, besides being a Raytheon employee with designs on my job, made the request in order to remove protection from Raytheon employees who suffered daily from his abuse. Her letter parroted the vague "concerns" regarding my role in managing the contractors, which I had hoped she would at least attempt to pin down to something specific. Indeed, I wasn't even in a leadership position in 2011, though she stated that concerns about my leadership affected my evaluation.

One of the central issues from the start had been that Sarah consistently evaded presenting any facts, data or specifics in her decisions to sideline me and ultimately in my evaluation. Indeed, the whole evaluation process had been a travesty of dismissing solid data, presenting instead vague opinions, and smoothing the mess over with assurances that "Meets Expectations" is just fine. The hiring of lesser qualified individuals for positions to which I applied went unmentioned. I found the reassurance that I was still welcome to work for Raytheon while they blocked my applications particularly annoying.

In the end, Patty at least admitted that the raise had been overlooked, but refused to address the misinformation Sarah had presented or that the evaluation had not been done to Raytheon's published standards.[116]

---

116 Mr. Sparks:

This is in response to your ethics complaint regarding your performance rating for 2011 and your selection for layoff September 2012. For the reasons explained below, we have concluded that there has been no ethics violation in connection with these events.

I asked Patty for a copy of the official report on my ethics complaint. She said there would be no written report. I contacted Garth Chandler to report my dissatisfaction with the process. He didn't answer. At least Ken had received a nod. I felt at that point there would be no harm in filing

---

With respect to your concern regarding your performance rating, I determined that you received overall performance ratings of "Far Exceeds Expectations" for 2010 and "Meets Expectations" for 2011. To verify the validity of the 2011 rating, I interviewed the customer Technical Oversight Representative (TOR), Raytheon's operation manager, and the former manager overseeing the Fort Devens Warfighter effort. All of these individuals, and Ms. S.(deletion mine), provided positive feedback regarding your professional knowledge and technical competence as an instructor. However, they also confirmed that there were concerns regarding your performance of your management role, which affected your overall 2011 performance rating and ultimately led to a request from the TOR that you be removed from this position. Although you have expressed a concern that your 2011 performance rating will negatively impact your ability to be hired for another Raytheon job, but as I have previously explained, a "Meets" rating is not negative and should not adversely affect your opportunity for future employment with Raytheon.

With respect to your selection for layoff, I have been informed that, in the third quarter of 2012, the customer directed Raytheon to downgrade or eliminate a number of positions for budgetary reasons. The customer specifically identified positions for elimination by title, including your position of A05 Consulting Principal (sic) Training & Development Specialist. Your 2011 performance rating was not factored into the decision to select you for layoff.

In summary, we have concluded that there has been no ethics violation in connection with your 2011 performance rating or your selection for layoff. The performance rating you received was consistent with management's assessment of you (sic) ability as an instructor but factoring the customer's dissatisfaction with your ability to effectively manage the team. Your layoff was a direct result of the customer's decision to eliminate the A05 consulting position.

During my investigation, however, I determined that the Company did not properly process you for a merit pay increase for 2012. You should have a received a two percent merit increase in pay effective April 28, 2012. We therefore intend to process this pay increase retroactively and send you a check for the difference.

We appreciate your patience as we completed our review of this matter. Please feel free to contact me with any questions you might have.

Regards,
Patty Dinsmore
Human Resources
Warfighter Support Services
Intelligence, Information and Services
Raytheon Company

an ethics complaint against the Office of Ethics and Compliance. They didn't respond.

Ethics and Compliance is a big deal with companies that do business with the government. Millions are invested in educating employees about business ethics and training managers in compliance. Raytheon has one of the best ethics training programs I've ever encountered. They hired the famous actor and comedian Ben Stein to play a lead role which made it entertaining as well as informative.

But the job of Ethics and Compliance isn't so much to ensure ethical behavior and compliance with government contracts as to keep the company out of ethics and compliance-related trouble. The list of ethics issues and failures in compliance with the Warfighter contract at Devens was long and they had every incentive to delay, cover up the violations, and marginalize any potential whistle blowers. Several contractors had reported violations and nothing had been done outside of pretending to investigate.

The contractual relationship between the company and the government – in this case between Raytheon and the Army – presumes that the customer will have an interest in seeing that the company delivers all that it is obligated to deliver. This is the job of the TOR. But what happens when the customer has an interest in violating the contract? What happens when the TOR or the Course Manager violate the terms of the SOW or federal law? The company is then in the difficult position of acquiescing to the violations or reporting the customer to higher authority. Either case jeopardizes continued business with the customer.

Military commanders, staff and course managers had fired contractors and blocked qualified candidates from being hired. The process wasn't restricted to contractors. Several decent military instructors were also denied orders in favor of bringing on soldiers of lesser qualifications and histories of failure. Often the decision was based on pure malice. That was certainly at work in the obstacles the Brigade staff had put up to prevent Briere from getting orders for schools and deployment.

At other times, pity was a major motive. At one point while arguing the relative merits of the various candidates, Sarah pointed out that I wouldn't have any trouble finding a new job, but instructors like Wilma and Laverne would probably never find another job as good as this. Part of her reasoning for eliminating the best instructors was that the best instructors would have no problem finding employment elsewhere. We should keep the worst instructors because they're so bad that no one in their right minds would ever hire them.

Most of the time, though, simple ignorance and stupidity were all that was needed to explain why things went so wrong. With the major decision-makers hundreds, even thousands of miles away, we often watched helplessly while the wrong decision was made and carried out over and over.

With the mass exodus of contractors in the wake of the elimination of my position came a flood of complaints to Raytheon and the Army. Neither the Army nor Raytheon could pretend they didn't know about the contractors being directed by the military, being ordered to do work outside the SOW, being forced to work under unsafe conditions, and delivering unpaid overtime. The evidence of a long-standing support for a hostile work environment ever since Sarah had taken over in order to "crack the whip" on the contractors was overwhelming and contractors were voting with their feet along with their voices.

A Human Resources representative from Raytheon eventually visited to find out why Devens had an attrition rate resembling a combat zone. One would think that if she wanted to find out why people are quitting, she would talk to the people who quit. But she didn't. She only spoke with employees terrified of losing their jobs and the managers who terrified them. I'm not sure what ever came of her visit, but nothing changed at Devens.

Likewise, General Arnold, the commander of the 100th Division reached the limit of his patience with the poor performance of the school and relieved Colonel Raynor, a year before her three-year command term was up. In January of 2013 she was given four months to find a new job. In the wake of sending Colonel Raynor packing, Donna Ortiz and Mike Bass both moved on and Carmen Lopez was given the undesirable job of drilling with the 5-104th in Arizona. Sarah Sondheim quietly transferred out of the 6/98th and the 1st Brigade.

As for Lieutenant Colonel Rondeau who had performed so magnificently after being essentially snubbed by Colonel Raynor, he was promoted to full colonel and served another few years in Civil Affairs before retiring in 2015. We remain good friends. I only wish he had been given the reins of the 1st Brigade in time to prevent the crash of the school at Devens. If anyone could have saved the school, it was Colonel Rondeau.

CHAPTER 20

Counterintelligence Analyst

MEANWHILE I HAD to find a new job. It was clear that Raytheon was not going to place me and probably even less likely now that I had filed an ethics complaint. I was already committed to staying in the Devens area, so Devens was the first place I looked. I had no trouble finding an interesting job in Military Intelligence.

Among the contractors who had refused to continue to work for Sarah were the temps that had been brought on to fill the gaping holes left by the September exodus. I became good friends with Denny Gee, one of Ken Frickle's old buddies from Korea, and he knew of a new project opening up at the ARISC.[117] They needed analysts, but were looking for people with HUMINT experience. I was a seasoned huminter with recent experience in counterintelligence and analysis. Denny and I applied together.

The project was run by one of the Counterintelligence (CI) agents that had worked for me as a temp when I was still the Raytheon Site Lead. He welcomed me with open arms. L-3 Stratis, another of the big league defense contractors, would be providing about forty CI analysts to the project and had to scramble to get enough people before the deadline. They subbed out much of their recruiting effort to smaller companies to fill the roster in time. Their Site Lead, Tim Woodard, was an old friend of mine from the Washington Army National Guard. While in the WANG I had done quite a lot of work as an intelligence analyst in support of the Counterdrug Taskforce. Denny and I were immediately accepted.

117 Army Reserve Intelligence Support Center. Several ARISCs exist throughout the country and provide secure facilities where reservists and contractors perform real-world Intelligence support to global operations.

I had the good fortune of applying to Intecon, a subcontractor based in Colorado. My salary would be a disappointing $75,000 but that was $10k more than L-3 contractors were getting. On our first day, the project leader flew in from L-3 Stratis headquarters in Reston, Virginia, to welcome us and apologize for the low salaries. The heyday of contracting was over and competition between the big companies was keen.

After the customary pep talk about how important our job was, he wrapped up his speech with a reminder that L-3 is a for-profit organization and in the end, if we didn't make money for L-3, nobody would have work.

"The name of the game today is minimal qualifications for the lowest price," he said. "The customer can no longer consider quality in hiring. It's all about quantity, about finding the cheapest labor that meets the minimum specifications for the job."

I nevertheless found myself working with some very good analysts who had recent experience and knew the latest systems inside and out. We would all be trained and certified on all the systems regardless of previous experience, so I wasn't too worried about being left in the dust. And it was real world. We were supporting actual daily missions in Afghanistan, mostly looking for threats to American soldiers coming from our Afghan allies, what we called "Green-On-Blue" attacks.

Obama had already promised that all American troops would be out of Afghanistan within two years and our biggest concern was just getting everybody home safe. There was no longer any talk about winning in Afghanistan and defeating the Taliban or Al Qaeda, who were already fighting amongst themselves for position in the post-American Afghanistan that was emerging.

It was here that I was able to watch the effects that the drop in quality was having on Military Intelligence and our missions downrange. With the dip in graduates from the 35M course, there were fewer human intelligence collectors available to deploy. This deficit either went unfilled or to contractors desperate enough to deploy to a combat zone for less than $100k. Just a few years before, such jobs paid over twice what they paid in 2012.

Our dependence on translators provided the enemy with a bonanza through poorly vetted locals being hired by subs to the larger defense contractors, especially Mission Essential Personnel and SAIC. In more than one instance, enemy agents managed to get hired by companies subbing for MEP and killed Americans in Green-On-Blue attacks. Even the quality of the linguists fell noticeably, forcing us to struggle with translations that were hard to understand and less reliable.

We watched helplessly while the quality and quantity of intelligence reports steadily declined between 2012 and 2014.

While the MI school at Devens languished in preparation for the now certain relocation to Huachuca, we at the ARISC had actual missions and it was exciting. My friends from Raytheon were in constant touch, hoping to score a position similar to mine and I was only too happy to vouch for the better instructors. Unfortunately, I was not able to be of much help. Those who had not deployed in a while had to go to the end of the line. Taking a recent deployment involving counterintelligence and analysis had been a very wise move even if it had cost me my Raytheon job.

Kat Briere returned from Afghanistan a hero and was now working at the 35M course as a military instructor on orders. She had experienced something of the treachery of which the REMF[118] world is capable. My dual knife in the back had been the revocation of my language pay, followed on by the elimination of my job while serving overseas. Hers was the selling of all her stored possessions.

Despite her star status, she found herself relegated to menial tasks. Gosling had been promoted to E-7 and was in full form as Course Manager with no one to rein in his abuse. I was in no position to protect Kat or anyone else anymore, so everyone at the Mike course just kept their heads down and endured.

---

118 REMF stands for "Rear Echelon Motherfucker" and is a derisive term for a military bureaucrat dating at least as far back as the Vietnam era. It is commonly used by combat soldiers to refer to a soldier who has a relatively safe job and is in a position to harm – intentionally or through neglect – the soldiers he is supposed to support.

General Arnold, who was in the process of finding a replacement for Colonel Raynor, sent a committee from Division HQ up to find out just why things were so bad and all fingers pointed to Gosling. At the same time, the principal players at the Brigade came under scrutiny for the roles they had played and old questions about contractor management and hostile work environments were again raised. Ortiz, Bass, Lopez and Sondheim all moved on at this time. Raytheon, as I mentioned, sent someone to investigate as well, and although the investigation was superficial, it demonstrated that at least somebody at the company had finally noticed that something was seriously wrong at Devens.

This should have been a sign to Gosling to tread lightly, but he missed it. His reputation sunk even further – if that were even possible – when he was decorated for an act he had nothing to do with. He was on leave just before a new class was to show up in the winter of 2013 – the first since the non-conduct in 2012. Several of the soldiers showed up without the required DLAT scores.[119] Ray had left instructions that any student that showed up without all the required paperwork should be immediately sent home. Kat took the initiative to go see Mary Hale, the lady who ran the tests at Devens and talked her into coming in on a Sunday without pay just to administer the DLAT. All of the students who were about to be sent home got to stay.

Their commander was elated and sent a very heart-felt thanks to the Course Manager for going the extra mile to keep the students in the course. That letter reached the Brigade and Gosling received an Army Commendation Medal for Kat's work.

Decency would have dictated that he at least mention the role played by now Staff Sergeant Briere, even if he left out the part he had played in trying to achieve the exact opposite outcome. But he didn't. He publicly accepted the decoration and it stunk.

---

119 DLAT is the Defense Language Aptitude Test, a test that supposedly demonstrates a student's capacity to learn a foreign language. Despite the two-decade-long waiver of the language requirement, 35M students were still nevertheless required to have passing scores in order to enter the 35M course and be trained as human intelligence collectors.

A week later, when Gosling again became openly abusive with one of his NCOs, the young sergeant reported it to the Brigade Sergeant Major, who promptly relieved Gosling. From then on until the end of the project, Ray was relegated to the job of mere instructor, forcing him to do the one thing he had always tried his best to avoid, which was teach. He should have been relieved long ago – indeed many times over the previous years – but at least it was some justice at last and maybe some indication that the leadership at Brigade and above might be beginning to show some interest in the welfare of their soldiers.

Kat, meanwhile, again became the target of the ever spiteful Sergeant Major Lopez. Sergeant Briere was "voluntold" to be the battalion's candidate for Best Warrior competition. Nobody likes to be that candidate, but every battalion has to send someone. MI soldiers never win the Best Warrior competition. It's just another chance to put in a lot of effort only to be rewarded with humiliation. Some infantry soldier who served with the Airborne Rangers or Special Forces always wins, so what's the point?

Kat wasn't happy for the extra duty, but she applied herself. Not many were surprised when she won out of all the MI battalions. Eyebrows were raised, however, when she won at the division level. A whole lot of attention came her way when she won Best Warrior for the entire 80th TASS Training Command.

It was a double victory for being both MI and a female. Of course, it was now widely known that she had served with the SEALs in Afghanistan and she was a genuine celebrity. Sergeant Major Lopez's plot to harass and humiliate this magnificent soldier backfired and Kat was sent to Ft. Campbell, Kentucky, for the Army-wide Best Warrior competition.

Lopez had to fly out to represent the Brigade and cheer on her "protégé." On the way there, Lopez became seriously ill with some intestinal ailment and wound up in the hospital with no one but Kat to take care of her.

After that, her attitude toward Briere changed completely and she became her biggest fan. But that wasn't enough to deflect the negative attention Lopez received from everywhere else. She had accumulated too many enemies over the years.

Lopez was reassigned to duties as Sergeant Major at one of the battalions and made a strategic error. She had been double dipping as the Brigade's unit tech and drilling as sergeant major without portfolio. Taking her reassignment as a demotion, she put in for retirement and in doing so, lost her job which required that she also serve as a reservist in the unit she worked for. Her passing was not mourned.

My new work environment at the ARISC was pleasant and stimulating. I had great people to work with and enjoyed coming to work every day. We had some flexibility to our schedule. The ARISC was open ten or eleven hours a day, but we could only work forty hours a week. You could come in late and work late, or come in early and leave early. You could work weekends instead of Monday through Friday. But it was clear that, as elsewhere in Military Intelligence, there was a great difference in quality of individuals doing the work.

It is very difficult to measure the effectiveness of intelligence analysts. Simply counting reports processed or targets located doesn't reflect the quality of reports or the availability of targets. And of course there is no way to know how much an analyst misses. But even lacking objective measures of effectiveness, there was very little disagreement about who the best and worst analysts were. You could take a vote and find out who to keep and who to fire.

That unfortunate task fell to Denny one day.

After I had been there about six months, our Site Lead, my old friend Tim Woodard, had to leave. I applied for the newly opened the Site Lead position and had a good résumé. There was another individual by the name of Jessica who wanted the job as well and she was well qualified except that she had never been in the military. But the nod went to Mark Sandborn[120] for no other reason any of us could discern than he had been a career First Sergeant. He had no experience as a contractor or managing

120 Not his real name.

civilians, but he got the job. Jessica thought it was a clear case of discrimination. She had a superior résumé, but had been passed over because she was female and had no military experience. I was disappointed as well.

Sandborn stepped into the position like a First Sergeant. He began to station himself at the door and record the exact time each employee arrived with the intention of ensuring all forty of us did our forty hours. It was annoying and completely unnecessary as the security system logged us in and out automatically every time we went through the door. He appeared to play favorites as well and made himself the target of ridicule.

One of our best analysts hands down was Colin Kenny.[121] He also had a biting wit and was soon on Sandborn's black list. Half way through the contract, the company announced that it would have to let a few people go. Colin was one of the first to be cut and it appeared that Sandborn may have played a pivotal role in Colin's selection. A small conspiracy of Colin's friends coalesced to complain to the company and have Sandborn removed as Site Lead, but one act really steeled the conspirators' resolve.

Our team would have to nominate one member for elimination and Sandborn wanted the team lead, Shawn Noble[122] to name who should go. Shawn, fortunately for him, was gone for the week and left Denny in charge in his place. Sandborn had suggested letting Glenn go. Glenn was a quiet guy who didn't record everything he did, so to those who didn't know him, he looked like a weak performer. But he was actually one of the better analysts. Another member of our team, Bill Durer,[123] who spent most of his time chatting with people about football, had not really produced much. Denny was loath to name anyone for the axe, but after securing a promise from Sandborn that his recommendation would be entirely secret, named Durer.

Sandborn assured Denny that, as Site Lead, he would be the one to give Bill the bad news. He did, and when he presented his decision, he told Bill that Denny had recommended he be fired.

---

121 Not his real name.

122 Not his real name.

123 Not his real name.

You can imagine the storm of vitriol that followed. Denny was furious that he had been set up. No apologies to Bill could undo that act. From then on Bill, who was not in the habit of sitting quietly at his desk for eight hours anyway, did his best to not only not do a bit of work for the remainder of his time, but to intentionally make himself a distraction as well as a hugely vocal critic of both Denny Gee and Mark Sandborn.

Then fortune intervened. Another contractor had to quit for medical reasons and the decision to cut Bill loose was reversed. Bill stayed and started to work in more earnest, but never reconciled with Denny.[124]

The conspiracy to remove Sandborn never came to fruition either. Sandborn found himself a better job elsewhere and quit. Such is the tumultuous world of defense contracting. People come and go so regularly and for unpredictable reasons that it is almost never useful to either try to better one's position or to make enemies.

The Site Lead position was again open when an event typical of the now cut-throat world of defense contracting intervened. Mission Essential Personnel – another of the defense contractor giants that specialized in hiring translators – sued L-3 over the contract and won. In less than a week, L-3 was out and MEP was in. MEP abruptly offered all of us the option of staying with a $10k cut in pay or leaving and we had only 24 hours to decide.

I stayed, of course, along with everyone else. MEP brought in an outsider for the Site Lead position, Devon Parkhurst, who was a competent, fair and compassionate leader and things cooled down. It was probably the best thing to do. Unlike Woodard, Sandborn or the rest of us, Devon

124 Both Bill and Denny were examples of talent that cannot be quantified. Bill had a virtually photographic memory which he applied passionately to sports. He knew every player, coach and event in football and baseball for the previous century and the statistics that went with them. Had he been able to arouse in himself the same passion for intelligence analysis, he would have been worth forty good analysts. Likewise, Denny had a creative genius that he applied to music, his passion. Giving Denny a musical instrument – any musical instrument – was like giving Michelangelo a rock. Denny could be relied upon to find creative approaches to analytical problems when the rest of us ran out of ideas and conventional approaches produced no results.

had no duties as analyst to divide his attention and he completely understood the contractor game. It was a pleasure to work for him.

In the fall of 2013, we received a visitor from Afghanistan. He was the project director and liaison between MEP and the military customer in the field. I was expecting that he would be making a pitch to reinforce in us just how important our work was to the soldiers in the field, but the thing that stood out most for me was his apology. He apologized for the drop in quality of intelligence reports over the previous two years. The collectors were just not of the same quality they had been up until 2011. They rarely went outside the wire to collect information. They were clueless about the culture and language. The useable intelligence in their reports was getting progressively weaker and weaker.

That was the most solid independent confirmation yet that the downward trend at the MI schoolhouse had a tangible result in the field. In my early days on the analyst job, it warmed my heart whenever I came across an intelligence report produced by one of my students. I was particularly proud of Pyotr Lyshenko, whom the Course Manager had tried so hard to fail because of his difficulties with English. This collector, despite his appalling written English, produced hundreds of reports, all in perfect English. There was a handful of former students out there doing good work, but they trickled off as they left the field to be replaced by more recent and inexperienced – and of course cheaper – graduates. Lyshenko eventually left as well.

The 35M course had not only failed way too many students, it was ineffective in training the ones that did graduate. But then, by the end of 2012, most of the instructors with recent deployment experience had been fired or chased away. There were no more instructors at the Mike course who had ever done the job the way it needed to be done in Afghanistan. The only exception was Kat Briere and she was marginalized by Gosling when she should have been given prominence. Melinda, Ali and I were gone. Sergeant Mendez's orders ran out and he moved on. None of the really great temps like Delorean and Donaldson were welcome to return.

By mid-2013 the school at Devens was virtually shut down. It was supposed to move back to Huachuca, but there was no room for it and no money to finance the move. In addition, a new policy came into effect that all 35Ms should have a Top Secret clearance. That narrowed the field considerably and put a delay on deploying 35Ms who were waiting for their clearances. To make matters worse, at a time when Military Intelligence was experiencing a surge in requirements for security clearance investigations, the Army cut back on investigators as well. The US Army produced virtually no 35Ms in 2013 and there was no money for hiring quality people from the contractor force. Salaries for deployments to a combat zone had dropped to under $100,000 and policy focused on finding personnel with minimal qualifications desperate enough to work for the lowest pay.

The market truly was for the least qualified and cheapest labor available, as the L-3 manager had informed us. In this climate Erwin Bayer, despite his weight problem and lifetime ban from ever setting foot on Ft. Devens again, transferred out of the 6/98th into yet another unit that did not know him or his record and managed to get orders to deploy to Afghanistan. I heard that he survived that deployment and somehow found work at Huachuca.

I have lost track of him and Wilma since, though I still get mail for them at my place, reminding me of happier times. They had been my guests, after all, and had a child in my home. The spare bedroom, which had been Chris's nursery, is still known as the "Winnie the Pooh room" after the decoration scheme his mother Wilma had chosen and lovingly created.

Drifting around from contract to contract and from unit to unit between the reserves and the National Guard like a vagabond is a difficult life, but the sheer complexity of the contractor/reservist world makes it possible for people to find temporary work, fail, and move on with minimal consequences to being hired again. The military-industrial complex is huge and there are many places to hide.

Neither is it going away just because the defense budget is shrinking. Many of the important jobs are merely being moved from Department of Defense to the State Department and other agencies in a giant shell game all funded by the American taxpayer. Eisenhower worried about the "the acquisition of unwarranted influence" and "the potential for the disastrous rise of misplaced power." I worry more about entrusting the security of America to the minimally qualified lowest bidder in a system where accountability is virtually non-existent.

Postscript

In December of 2013 during a routine medical examination I discovered my PSA (Prostate Specific Antigen, a marker of prostate activity) had more than doubled in six months. I had no symptoms and my physical examination was normal, but this one lab test was ominous. It signaled the likelihood that I may have an active cancer in my body.

The biopsy in February of 2014 revealed that my prostate indeed contained cancer cells, which is not unusual for men over sixty. Neither is prostate cancer a particularly aggressive disease as cancers go. But genetic analysis revealed that this one was different. It was aggressive and near to breaking out of the organ, after which the probability of surviving even two years drops dramatically. I needed to get treatment and get it right away.

Although I retired from the military in September of 2012, I was still waiting to complete my discharge physical at the VA. I was also insured through each company I worked for, but Raytheon, Intecon and MEP all had different insurance programs. Each time we switched, we had to change programs and find new doctors. Some benefits were not immediately available, either. As a result, an aggressive cancer that should have been detected and cured by August 2013 was not treated until almost a year later.

Despite being fully insured, it didn't take long for my medical expenses to exceed my income and assets. Navigating my way through the healthcare maze and fighting with insurance companies began to take more and more of my time. Being a cancer patient is a full-time job.

Despite having no symptoms, just complying with the requirements of diagnosis and treatment quickly ate up all my leave time.

My company MEP put me on unpaid medical leave. It allowed me to keep my job should I survive and recover completely, but it also made me ineligible for unemployment compensation. As my medical expenses in 2014 rose, my savings vanished along with most of my income. When my anniversary with the company arrived in August of 2014, which would have made me eligible for paid medical leave, my contract was cancelled along with my insurance. For most working Americans, this would be illegal, but not for "at will" employees.

While working for MEP, I underwent my Periodic Investigation (PI) to renew my security clearance, but because I was on medical leave, completing the PI was not a priority for the company. The investigating officer, who was a contractor for CACI, told me that budget cutbacks had left them with fewer investigators. That, along with the surge in Background Investigations now required for the 35M MOS created a huge backlog. My case was not a priority.

After completing my treatment, I attempted to return to my old job with MEP. I left the company with an open PI. In order to close the PI and renew my TS, I needed to be working for the company, but in order to be hired back in my old job, I needed to have an active TS. In a classic Catch-22, they refused to hire me back. They could have hired me back, closed out the PI, and then either put me in my old job or let me move on. They stood firm. Without an active TS, my career as a contractor in the intelligence field was over.

After my experience with Raytheon's Ethics office, I thought it unlikely that MEP's attitude would be any different. Contractors are commodities, not employees. It was time to move on anyway. Time to get out of the contractor industry and go back into medicine.

And I had a book to write...

Acronyms and Abbreviations

THE MILITARY'S PENCHANT for acronyms is legendary. Applying an acronym to an idea lends an illusion of legitimacy and that illusion is especially comforting to people who struggle with complexity and have a greater need for order and simplicity. I have attempted to resist the use of acronyms, knowing that many of my readers may have no background in the military, but it's impossible to do a decent job of relaying the feel of this culture without using them. Here are a few of the common ones I've used in this book.

ABIC	Army Basic Instructor Course – A two-week course that qualifies a soldier to teach as an instructor.
AGR	Active Guard or Reserve – The full-time soldiers that staff National Guard and Army Reserve units.
ALC 2015	Army Learning Concept 2015. The blueprint for revising the way the Army teaches, trains and supports ongoing learning. When finally approved and accepted as doctrine in 2012, ALC 2015 became the ALM, the Army Learning Method.
Analyst	A person who processes information to turn it into intelligence
APFT	Army Physical Fitness Test
ARISC	Army Reserve Intelligence Support Center
ASA	Army Security Agency, discontinued in 1976
BI	Background Investigation – Performed by a badged and credentialed officer, the BI is an extensive interview to

	determine the safety of allowing an individual access to classified information. To obtain a Top Secret clearance, the officer will need to account for every month of the candidate's life since high school and will be interested in where he or she lived, what they did, how they earned a living and who they knew, especially with respect to foreign nationals.
BFRR	Battle-Focused Readiness Review – The statistics that measure a unit's readiness for deployment
CI	Counterintelligence – The profession of preventing enemies, adversaries and even friendly nations from collecting intelligence on US forces
CIAC	Counterintelligence Agent Course
CO	Commanding Officer
COR	Contracting Officer's Representative, also referred to as the TOR, Technical Oversight Representative
CONUS	Continental United States
DD-214	The official document verifying service and discharge from the Army
DIA	Defense Intelligence Agency
DLI	Defense Language Institute, the Army language school
DLPT	Defense Language Proficiency Test, the officially approved test for establishing a person's skill in a foreign language
FET	Female Engagement Team. These are teams of female service members tasked with engaging in the female populations of Iraq and Afghanistan pioneered by the Marine Corps. The concept was adopted by the Army and evolved into Cultural Support Teams, or CSTs.
FLPP	Foreign Language Proficiency Pay (pronounced "flip") is pay for maintaining proficiency in a foreign language. The amounts have varied widely over the years depending upon the language and time period. FLPP was changed to

	FLPB, foreign language proficiency *bonus*, which is taxed at a higher rate than pay, but the old term is still in common use.
GED	General Equivalency Diploma
GI party	A military cleaning project. To clean something as in "to GI the barracks."
GS	General Schedule – The job and pay scale for government employees.
HUMINT	Human Intelligence – HUMINT is intelligence derived from human sources. A "huminter" is a specialist in the collection of intel from human sources, which may be prisoners, refugees, detainees, spies, and others.
INSCOM	Intelligence and Security Command, located at Ft. Belvoir, Maryland.
IO	Information Operations – A concept of warfare that attacks adversary information and information processing while guarding our own. IO focuses on decision-makers, their decision-making processes, and the means of transmitting information. It encompasses the staff functions of Public Affairs, Civil Affairs, Psychological Operations, Computer Network Operations, Electronic Warfare, Military Deception and Operational Security. Paradoxically, Military Intelligence is not an integral part of IO.
IRR	Individual Ready Reserve
ISIS	The Islamic State of Iraq and Syria or Islamic State of Iraq and al-Sham, also known as the ISIL, the Islamic State of Iraq and the Levant. ISIS is an Islamic fundamentalist jihadist group.
IT	Information Technology, the office and personnel who maintain the computers and communications systems
MI	Military Intelligence
MFR	Memorandum for Record

NCO	Noncommissioned Officer. In the Army, Air Force and Marine Corps these are sergeants; in the Navy, petty officers.
NCOER	NCO Evaluation Report
NCOIC	NCO in charge
OCONUS	Outside the Continental United States
OPSCO	Operations Coordinator
PCS	Permanent Change of Station
PIFWC	Person Indicted for War Crimes
POI	Program of Instruction – The schedule of courses, content and hours of every class in a course.
PW or POW	Prisoner of War
REFRAD	Return From Active Duty – To be taken off active duty orders and sent home, usually for a reason that does not reflect positively on the soldier.
RSC	Regional Support Command
SF	Special Forces
SMA	Sergeants Major Academy, located at Ft. Bliss, near El Paso, Texas.
SOW	Statement of Work
TASS	Total Army School System
TDY	Temporary Duty
TOR	Technical Oversight Representative - Also known as the COR, Contracting Officer's Representative, this is the military officer or NCO responsible for ensuring that the contract with the contracting company be delivered in accordance with the written agreement.
TS	Top Secret
TTC	TASS Training Center
TRADOC	Training and Doctrine Command – The major Army command tasked with regulating training and doctrine.
USAICS	US Army Intelligence Center and School – The Army command tasked with training all specialties within Military

Intelligence. USAICS is located at Ft. Huachuca, Arizona, adjacent to Sierra Vista about 90 miles southeast of Tucson.

WANG	Washington Army National Guard. Also WAANG.
XO	Executive Officer

Selected Bibliography and Recommended Reading

Alexander, M. (2008). *How to Break a Terrorist.* New York: Free Press.

Berman, L. (2007). *Perfect Spy: The Incredible Double Life of Pham Xuan An, Time Magazine Reporter and Vietnamese Communist Agent.* New York: HarperCollins

Hagedorn, A. (2014). *The Invisible Soldiers: How America Outsourced Our Security.* New York: Simon & Schuster.

Lemmon, G. T. (2015). *Ashley's War: The Untold Story of a Team of Women Soldiers on the Special Ops Battlefield.* New York: HarperCollins.

Plaster, J. (1997). *SOG: The Secret Wars of America's Commandos in Vietnam.* New York: Onyx.

Prince, E. (2013). *Civilian Warriors: The Inside Story of Blackwater and the Unsung Heroes of the War on Terror.* New York: Penguin Group.

Singer, P. W. (2008). *Corporate Warriors: The Rise of the Privatized Military Industry.* Ithaca: Cornell University Press.

Wagner, T. (2008). *The Global Achievement Gap.* New York: Basic Books.

Made in the USA
Columbia, SC
19 November 2021